D0828623

TRACING YOUR ENGLISH ANCESTORS
A Manual for Analysing and Solving Geneological Problems
in England and Wales, 1538 to the Present Day

Colin D. Rogers

This text, a guidebook for amateur geneologists
whose ancestors came from England and Wales, is
designed to provide useful alternative strategies
for investigating leads when traditional sources
do not yield results. Rogers specifically concentrates on solutions and suggestions for simple
problems that arise in the course of geneological
research.

Colin D. Rogers is Lecturer at Manchester
Polytechnic and an Associate of the Institute
of Population Registration.

181 pages   ISBN 0-7190-3172-9   LC 89-8132 $19.95

Tracing your English ancestors

A manual for analysing and solving genealogical problems, 1538 to the present

COLIN D. ROGERS

MANCHESTER UNIVERSITY PRESS
Manchester and New York

distributed in the USA and Canada
by ST. MARTIN'S PRESS

To my parents;
to Maureen (despite her cats), Mark, Sue,
Keith, Angela, Christopher John and Jennifer Mary;
Geoffrey, John, and all their descendants

Christopher John 17 Sept 1983 – 15 March 1989,
struck down by disease we should have eradicated years ago,
cannot now know the joy of having children as beautiful as he was

First USA edition 1989
First published in Great Britain as The family tree detective, 1985
Published by Manchester University Press
Oxford Road, Manchester M13 9PL, UK
and Room 400, 175 Fifth Avenue,
New York, NY 10010, USA

Distributed exclusively in the USA and Canada
by St. Martin's Press, Inc.,
175 Fifth Avenue, New York, NY 10010, USA

Library of Congress cataloging in publication data applied for

ISBN 0–7190–3172–9 *(hardback)*

Typeset by Northern Phototypesetting Co, Bolton

Printed and bound in Great Britain
by Biddles Ltd, Guildford and King's Lynn

Contents

Abbreviations   vii
Acknowledgments   vii
A note on presentation   viii
Preface   ix

I—Preamble   1

II—Looking for parents

Introduction   12

Birth Certificates, 1837 to the present day   12
Failure to find a birth entry in the indexes: 18
   Registration in another district   18
   Birth not registered   18
   Birth incorrectly indexed   19
   Birth not in England and Wales   20
   Index entry missed by searcher   21
   Base information incorrect   22
   Child was adopted   23
   Change of name after registration   25
Finding more than one possible birth   27
Indexes or certificates not accessible – alternative sources: 28
   Marriage and death certificates   29
   Military records   30
   Education records   31
   Health records   36
   Pension and insurance records   37
   Affiliation orders   38
   Trade union and friendly society records   39
   Miscellaneous records   40

The Census, 1801 to the present day   40
Censuses less than 100 years old   41
Censuses 1841–1881:   45
   Failure to find individual addresses in the census   46
   Failure to find individuals in the census   48

Censuses 1801–1831   51

Church baptism, 1538 to the present day   52
Failure to find an Anglican baptism: 57
    Baptism in another parish   58
    Baptism not recorded   69
    Entry missed by searcher   72
    Base information incorrect   72
    Change of name after baptism   75
    Late baptism   75
Finding more than one possible baptism   76
Non-Anglican baptism   78
Registers not accessible – alternative sources: 81
    Bishop's transcripts   82
    Other copies of parish registers   84
    Military records and school registers   85
    The poll tax   86
    Records of the College of Heralds   86
    Inquisitions post mortem   87
    Freemen rolls   88
    Apprenticeship records   88
    Manorial records   89

III—Looking for marriages

Introduction   91
Marriage certificates, 1837 to the present day   91
Failure to find a marriage entry in the indexes: 95
    Registration in another district   95
    Marriage not registered   96
    Marriage incorrectly indexed   97
    Marriage not in England and Wales   97
    Index entry missed by searcher   97
    Base information incorrect   97
    Change of name before marriage   98
Finding more than one possible marriage   99
Indexes or certificates not accessible – alternative sources   99

Marriage in church, 1538 to the present day   101
Failure to find an Anglican marriage: 106
    Marriage in another parish   106

Marriage not recorded 112
Entry missed by searcher 113
Marriage not in England and Wales 113
Base information incorrect 113
Finding more than one possible marriage 115
Non-Anglican marriage 118
Registers not accessible – alternative sources 118

IV—Looking for deaths

Introduction 119
Death certificates, 1837 to the present day 120
Failure to find a death entry in the indexes: 122
  Death in another district 122
  Death not registered 122
  Death incorrectly indexed 123
  Death not in England and Wales 123
  Index entry missed by searcher 123
  Base information incorrect 123
Finding more than one possible death 124
Indexes or certificates not accessible – alternative sources: 124
  Local Authority burial records, 1827 to the present day 124
  Cremation records, 1884 to the present day 126
  Undertakers' records 127
  Gravestones, and failure to find them 127
  Monumental masons' records 130
  Obituaries 131
  Hospital records 131
  Trade union and friendly society records 131
  Coroners' records 132
  Professional body records 133

Church burial, 1538 to the present day 133
Failure to find an Anglican burial: 135
  Burial in another parish 136
  Burial not recorded 137
  Burial not in England and Wales – evidence of emigration 139
  Entry missed by searcher 141
  Base information incorrect 141
Finding more than one possible burial 142

Non-Anglican burial   142
Registers not accessible – alternative sources   143

Probate records   144
Wills proved since 11 January 1858   144
Wills proved before 11 January 1858, and failure to find
    them: 147
    Wills proved by another jurisdiction 149
    Wills not proved   151
    Wills poorly indexed   151
    Wills proved late   151
    Lost wills   152
Letters of Administration   153
Miscellaneous probate records   153

V—Epilogue   155

Select bibliography   156
Appendix 1 The Federation of Family History Societies   160
Appendix 2 The Guild of One-Name Studies   162
Appendix 3 Registration districts in England and Wales   164
Appendix 4 Principal record offices in England and Wales   171
Appendix 5 Employing professional help   175
Index   178

Endpapers – A common situation for the genealogist; suspicion without proof that an ancestor is related to another family in the same parish – see pp. 57–76 (*courtesy of John Vernon Lord*)

Abbreviations

BT   Bishop's Transcript(s)
CRO   County Record Office (see Appendix 4)
DRO   Diocesan Record Office
FFHS Federation of Family History Societies (see Appendix 1)
GRO   General Register Office
IGI   International Genealogical Index
MI   Monumental Inscription(s)
PCC   Prerogative Court of Canterbury
PCY   Prerogative Court of York
PRO   Public Record Office

Acknowledgments

I owe a sincere debt of gratitude to so many people that singling out any seemed at first invidious. However, over the years Miss Eileen Simpson, formerly Senior Assistant Archivist in the Cheshire Record Office, and Mr Jeffrey Adams, Registrar of Births and Deaths in the Manchester Register Office, have been particularly helpful to me, and eliminated some of the grosser mistakes from an early draft of this book; Mr Philip Simpson, professing to know nothing of genealogy, once said this sort of approach should be possible when I, thinking to know a lot, did not believe him; and I owe much to my tutor, the late W. E. Tate, from whom I first caught the infection called local history.

A note on presentation

The book is organised around the need to solve problems rather than around records, the three basic problems in genealogy concerning a search for parents, for marriage, and for death. For example, the section on marriages discusses the reasons why you may be failing to find a marriage entry in the indexes, and what you can do about it.

I have with an easy conscience omitted some things which are commonly found in many other books on genealogy (illustrations, for example) and detailed accounts of certain specialist areas such as military records and non-parochial registers which have been admirably described by others; nevertheless, I have tried to show how and when these records should be used. On the other hand, education records are treated at length, as they are largely ignored in other books.

References in the text are to the authors and books listed in the bibliography. A year is included in each reference to distinguish between different editions or different books by the same author, except for the prolific J. S. W. Gibson, whose works are given a number.

Throughout I have used the word 'genealogist' to describe anyone who is tracing a family tree, only occasionally distinguishing amateur from professional. 'Family historian' is normally avoided, having wider concerns than the genealogist; I believe that the intellectual demands and demographic needs of genealogy should give it an academic respectability in its own right.

For American readers, I have left in certain sections of the British edition which assumes that researchers can gain access to records in person, in the hope that all will one day enjoy the excitement of handling the documents written about, or even by, their ancestors. See Appendix 5 for advice on employing professional help.

Preface

This book is for beginners and for those who have already been tracing their ancestors for some time.

Its publication requires some sort of explanation, for you could already half fill a bookshelf with recent works on genealogy, a sure reflection of the enormous growth in its popularity over the last decade. Some books centre around an individual family tree; others give a chronological account of documentary sources; some assume that all their readers have easy access to London repositories, especially the magnificent collections of the Public Record Office (PRO), described by Cox and Padfield, 1981, a work to which this book is in some ways complementary, and the Society of Genealogists; others that the reader has a working knowledge of English social, legal and political history.

Having taught several hundred people how to trace family trees over the last sixteen years, having broadcast on the subject, and run an advisory service, I was convinced that most amateur genealogists require more guidance than is currently available in print: in particular, they need a set of alternative strategies to employ when the normal sources of information do not produce results. They want to know not only, 'How do I find out?' but also, 'What can I try next when it doesn't work?'

This book, therefore, is written for those who have no formal qualifications in history (or in anything else, for that matter), who do not normally have access to London (especially now that many PRO records are transferred to Kew), who do not have the money to pay for professional help (or prefer not to) when things go wrong and who are therefore lost when the genealogical source they are using appears to let them down. For, be in no doubt that all genealogists reach an impasse sooner or later, no matter how expert they may be, and that there are many reasons why this happens. A problem may be impossible to solve because the necessary evidence has not survived, or was never recorded in the first place. On the other hand, many amateurs never know whether the information has survived or not, but give up far too easily when it is not where they expect it to be.

What follows shows not only the normal ways to discover genealogical information, but also other routes which might be needed, either because the normal one fails, or because the alternatives are quicker or cheaper to use. It concentrates on the last four hundred years and largely omits areas which the beginner will probably not encounter – mediaeval records and heraldry, for example. Most of my examples are from the North West, but I have used only those which are generally applicable. I have deliberately resisted relying on London-based documents, knowing how difficult it is for most genealogists to spend long periods of time there. It should be added, therefore, that for the fortunate minority the Guide to the PRO and the facilities available to members of the Society of Genealogists can open out new dimensions to discovering and studying ancestry.

Ebenezer Chapel, Tintwistle
November 1982

Note to the second edition

This edition updates some of the information from the first, and incorporates new or expanded sections on abandoned children, adoption, professional body records and stillbirths. Particularly for overseas readers, there is an introduction to the sources of evidence, still to be found in Britain, for the emigration of individuals from these shores.

I continue to be very grateful to the many correspondents, friends and officials who have provided constructive advice.

January 1985

Note to the American edition

Welcome to the fascinating exercise of establishing your genetic connections with individuals who were centuries, and thousands of miles, away from present-day North America. These connections are surely the main basis of our 'special relationship', proving as they do our common heritage.

The UK government has issued a consultative document proposing significant changes to the current rules governing access to entries in civil registers of birth, marriage and death. As legislation will be required to effect such changes as a result of this consultation, they have not been included in this edition.

February 1989

I—Preamble

One of the great attractions of genealogy is that, no matter how clever you may be at exploiting surviving documents, you can never be certain of discovering the next generation further back. Taking an optimistic view, if a normal English surname is being traced, the mid-seventeenth century seems a reasonable target. Beyond this point life begins to get markedly more difficult; but there are some who will fail to find their great-grandparents, and a few for whom even this would be impossible anyway.

There are no strict rules governing the way ancestors must be traced, and there is nothing illegal about inventing a whole family tree, unless there is an intention to defraud. Success comes from a combination of knowing which records exist, how to get access to them at a price you can afford, being able to select from alternative solutions and knowing how to use several documents in combination with each other. However, there is a normal way to proceed and often a set of options if the normal way proves fruitless.

A student in my first evening class illustrates one approach which cannot be recommended. She had been attracted to genealogy having been told of a belief that her family was descended from the second Duke of Buckingham. Blissfully unaware of the possibility that this was the name of a pub rather than a person, she had spent a large part of her life tracing the second Duke's descendants, the first generation of whom were illegitimate. Needless to say, although she had acquired a lot of information, it was probably the most inefficient and expensive way to establish a family connection because the descendants of all the children of each generation would have had to be traced – and even then the rumour might have been incorrect in the first place.

If your tree is not to be a figment of your imagination, you may adopt the opposite extreme and feel you should accept as family connections only those which are nothing less than certain. However, genealogists adhering to this approach had better choose another pastime, for they will not be very successful at this one. Paternity can never be proved, even when no-one has expressed any doubt about it. Often a connection will have to be accepted because there is no apparent alternative; and sooner or later all genealogists must consciously accept what is only the most probable solution to a problem they are trying to solve.

How then can the genealogist build up a family tree which is based neither on absolute truth nor on the imagination? In my greener days, I tried to find the baptism of one Thomas Rogers in or about 1790 in the parish in north Cheshire where he married. It could not be found in either this or the surrounding parishes; but there was only one local Rogers family which could have given birth to him and, on the assumption that my unbaptised Thomas was one of their offspring, I happily traced their ancestors back to the 1630s. The bombshell which hit me when I subsequently discovered that Thomas had been born in Lancaster brought mixed emotions – all that work down the drain; but now I had something closer to 'the truth'. What I should have done origi-nally was to make sure that all the available evidence had been consulted before deciding what to do and what to believe. I am still poor at taking my own advice when tracing my own family tree and, as we shall see, it is sometimes very difficult, psychologically, to take steps to try to disprove something which you are half convinced is the truth.

The beginner should not be surprised if progress comes in fits and starts. Reactions of my students over the years have varied from ecstasy and almost disbelief when an entry they had long been seeking comes to light, to terrible frustration when nothing seems to work, or people take months to reply to letters – if they reply at all. Threatening to give up genealogy, however, is no remedy; once you have the bug, you have it for life, and it is a bug which thrives on frustration. You may discover three or four generations in a single day, or you may take several years to discover one, but, however far back you are, it will always be a source of annoyance that you have not found that next one further back still.

Where to start

One of the many questions asked by the beginner is, 'Which line shall I trace?' The simple answer is, whichever you want. There is no obligation to trace any one line except, perhaps, for members of the Church of Jesus Christ of Latter Day Saints (the Mormons). They believe in baptism after eight years old, either in life or after death, so that even previous generations can be given the retrospective benefit of choosing the Mormon religion if they wish. If you try to trace all your ancestors, it will be a lifetime's commitment because of the very large numbers involved. From the late middle ages, when most English surnames began to be inherited, we might each have one million ancestors, though this number will decrease whenever relations marry each other. (Three of my mother's great-great-grandparents can be traced to a common predecessor some generations earlier.)

If all your ancestors are being traced, your problems, costs and the time you need to put in will all double with every generation discovered. Most people start more sensibly, probably with the surname they were born with – married women usually prefer to trace their maiden name. If you know your four grandparents already, my advice would be to choose first the family which used to live closest to where you are living now; or, if that line is of no interest to you, the rarest of the four surnames. There is no doubt that it is easier, quicker and cheaper to learn about ancestors who lived in a county which has a record office or substantial public library within comfortable travelling distance of your own home. Similarly, a rare name is usually easier to trace than a common one (though I am trying to find a Cheshire family called Greenaker which seems to disappear altogether in the mid-seventeenth century). A surname which is also the name of a township, village or parish is also to be recommended because there is then a greater chance of reaching back to the early Middle Ages – say to seven hundred years ago – than if you have any other kind of surname, few of which became hereditary before the middle of the fourteenth century. However, there is still a snag in that where a name originated, it is quite normal for families of that surname to have been more numerous than Smith, Jones or Taylor; and one of the commonest problems in genealogy, as we shall see, is to decide between various possible couples who might have given birth to an ancestor you have already traced, so the fewer the candidates the better. Despite popular belief, place names tended to give rise to surnames near their actual location rather than far away from it – so, sooner or later, a family called Ashton will be traced to one of the eleven places called Ashton in this country;

with Hemmingway, Wolstencroft or Dearnaley, however, there is only one possible place of origin.

However, the surname is only one of many factors which will affect the time and cost of tracing your family tree. Others are: how far away the records are; how quickly you learn to manipulate them to best advantage; whether there are serious gaps in the main series of records, especially the church registers, in 'your' parish; how mobile your ancestors were; and what was their social status or profession. On the whole, because they leave more records, the rich are easier to trace than the poor and those who had a profession for which they had been trained than those who did not; criminals who are caught are easier to find than the honest. It should not be assumed that the most successful genealogists are those who have had rich, professional criminals in their families – but it certainly helps!

The quickest way to acquire a long family tree through your own efforts is to trace one of the easier lines first until you get stuck; then, instead of waiting weeks or years for the mud to clear, you should transfer to the female line of the earliest marriage you have already traced, and follow that one. If you can exploit some-one else's efforts, it may be even quicker. Another student in my first class was told by an uncle to look in the back of the case of an old grandfather clock in his attic – inside was a list of his ancestors since 1740. More recently, an elderly student who had very little time to trace her family tree made little or no progress during the twenty-week course. On the final evening, a keen young beaver who had obviously done a lot of work long before the class started brought in the fruits of her researches. It was one of those magnifi-cent wall-paper charts (the reverse side of wallpaper is commonly used by those who acquire vast acreages of information and feel the urge to display it on a single sheet of paper). The first lady looked at this in awe, then admiration, then disbelief, for there at the foot of the chart, was one of her own relations!

Getting organised

Setting out the information can indeed be quite a problem – or rather, it is two problems. Firstly, most books advise the beginner to write notes in a logical order so that the information is both presentable and easily accessible. This advice ignores the fact that most readers will have already accumulated large files full of undifferentiated data before they realise that they need to seek advice on how to organise it properly – by which time it is often too late, for the genealogist is already buried under tons of paper. Correspondence, scraps of notes on old envelopes scribbled during a quick half hour in the library, the odd birth certificate, all become boxed in a great jumble and the whole lot has to be searched every time you need to see who married great-great-great-grandfather. Secondly, there really has to be a better answer than wallpaper for the presentation of the final product, even though it never will be final. (Alexander Sandison (1972) compared genealogy to a jigsaw puzzle which has no boundary edges.)

Several writers have offered solutions to these problems, but in the end the answer must be whatever suits the individual best, so long as it is methodical and consistent. The method which I use, a combination of various others, is as follows. A loose-leaf folder for pedigree charts, arranged in reverse chronological order and with each chart having a connecting reference to earlier or later ones, allows me to search very rapidly through all the direct male and female lines over as many generations as have already been traced. Uncertain or unproved connections are entered in pencil until confirmed, and no further research goes into those lines until they are firmly established. These blank charts are obtainable from a variety of sources, and many societies affiliated to the Federation of Family History Societies produce their own for a few pence each. (See Appendix 1.)

Associated with the chart folder, I use a loose leaf file in which there are sheets for each individual ancestor, in alphabetical order, recording birth, marriage, children, occupation, wealth, death and miscellaneous matters. If the data on any one person become too numerous, I put these on separate sheets immediately following, together with any copy of certificates, wills and other documentary remains of this mortal existence.

Finally, but by no means of least importance, I include a sheet devoted to each of those ancestors whose birth, baptismal record or marriage has not yet been discovered and is presenting difficulties. After a statement of the problem, I write a list of the direct and circumstantial evidence and a list of possible ways by which the birth or marriage might be discovered. It is most important not to treat this as a once-and-for-all compilation made in a few minutes; rather, it is the result of thinking about the problem over a long time, and I note down possible ways to solve it as they occur to me – on the train, in the bath or wherever. (I once thought of a quite beautiful way of getting round one problem while cleaning out my poultry house, but did not make a note of it right away and then could never remember what it was.) Finally, it is useful to note down on this sheet all the searches which have already been done without success – otherwise it is quite possible to find myself going over the same ground twice, wasting valuable time, effort and perhaps money.

I keep this dual filing system up-to-date on a regular basis and consult it whenever it becomes possible to visit a library, record office or other likely repository of the information I am seeking. A glance through the pedigree charts quickly shows which are the next problems to be solved; the alphabetical file will then show what I have already done to solve them and what ideas I have had for where to look next.

My system did not evolve slowly; it was a radical response to a situation which was rapidly getting out of hand, with my old notes in a chaotic state as more and more information came in. Although it took a little time to go through them all to make the rearrangement, it has repaid the effort many times since, saving on time, frustration and loss of data.

Asking questions

Frustration is experienced not only by those who are in danger of being overwhelmed by a mountain of miscellaneous pieces of paper. It is also common among beginners who also have to cope with the fear that they are going to be one of the unlucky ones whose grandfather, for example, had no birth certificate or whose father was a foundling or adopted. My student who was (or was not) descended from the Duke of Buckingham had at least done the correct thing to start with – she had gone to her most elderly relatives and asked a series of questions. Responses are usually helpful and valuable information may be gleaned in this way. 'Well, I remember my mother telling me . . .' spoken by a lady in her eighties will even now be carrying the budding genealogist back into the nineteenth century. However, a not uncommon response is, 'What do you want to know that for? Nothing interesting has ever happened in our family'. Roughly translated into English, this normally means, 'There are skeletons in our cupboard, and I'm not going to help you youngsters to uncover them'.

It should perhaps be said that in all families there will be found, sooner or later, criminality, insanity, and/or illegitimacy. For illegitimacy see, for example, pages 16, 38 and 56. About one in four hundred was a certified lunatic a hundred years ago, but an instance of criminality probably creates more hostility among surviving relatives and places more barriers in the way of innocent questions from those trying to trace the family tree than anything else. If a crime has been committed in the recent past, there is no doubt that its subsequent discovery would be very embarrassing to all concerned, not least to the genealogist who uncovered it. However, crimes which were committed over about fifty years ago are slowly becoming transmuted into a prime cause for historical, or perhaps antiquarian, interest. Once crimes are over a century old, the criminal becomes an object of pity or occasionally mirth and even admiration. For instance, my wife actually boasts because she has an outlaw in her family tree in 1372.

Another sensitive area is illustrated in the reaction, 'There's no money left, you know'. Those of us who trace family trees quickly become so fascinated by what we are doing that we forget that normal people have no interest in it themselves and, because they cannot understand what the interest is for others, that they may simply put a base interpretation on our motives – and there is no doubt that, as we shall see, the rules governing access to records are so illogical that we are encouraged to ask nosey questions. You can, for example, see a dead neighbour's recently proved will, or learn your living neighbours' christian names, but you cannot see your own birth entry because of the Registrar-General's directive that the public shall have no right of access to any register book except those currently in use, or those required during litigation.

Please ignore all attempts to deter you from tracing your family tree. The greater the difficulties, the more that is hidden from you, the greater the pleasure in making the discoveries. I do not wish to be offered my family tree, complete, back to the middle ages – I want the interest and excitement of finding it for myself.

There is a useful and methodical way to proceed when older relatives are being questioned, without which much information might be lost. I can illustrate this by describing what happened when my wife once tried to find a gravestone. She was puzzled to find that although two uncles described the spot where their father had been buried she still could not find the stone after visiting the cemetery twice. Eventually an aunt let slip the fact that the family could not afford a stone. When our looks elicited a defence from the uncles, they simply said, 'You did not ask us if there was a stone'.

'You did not ask us'. Remember those words and that other people are not normally reticent and secretive because of malice or forgetfulness, but because they do not realise which pieces of information are important to you. Ideally, you should seek the date and place of birth of the parent of the oldest living relative along the line you wish to trace. For example, if your father is alive but your grandfather is dead, you require the information about the latter. Date and place of birth, however, are not discovered easily, so you normally need to ask a variety of other questions which will help with the search for your grandfather. These should cover:

full names and nicknames;

date and place of marriage;

wife's maiden name;

birthday – women often remember days in the year when people celebrated their birthday;

religion;

date and place of death and burial and whether there is a gravestone;

addresses and house names;

any family heirlooms – bible, notebooks, diaries, certificates, records of military service, including medals and newspaper cuttings. (Some assessment of the credibility of entries on the fly leaf of a bible may be made by noting the date of publication relative to the date of the entries concerned); for the interpretation of old photographs, see Steel & Taylor, 1984;

any family rumours – but beware of exaggeration;

occupation;

brothers and sisters and whether he was the youngest, eldest and so on;

other living relatives who might remember more about him;

connections with other parts of the country.

At the same time, ask about other branches of the family – one day, you will want to trace them so you might as well have the information while it is still available. Using such a questionnaire ensures that most of the important pieces of evidence are sought, and creates a purposeful impression. It cannot be over-emphasised, however, that replies from elderly people (i.e., anyone over the age of about twenty) should not be completely trusted, especially when you are expecting them to remember events which happened generations ago. A useful device is to make a second or even a third visit and ask some of the same questions, but feeding in information you have acquired since the last one. My father, then about seventy, could not remember the name of his own grandfather, so I had to buy the birth certificate of one of his children, which gave the name I wanted. Next time I saw my father, I told him that his grandfather had been called William. 'Oh yes, now I remember; he married Alice Millington'. Now, it is quite probable that no one had mentioned Alice Millington for half a century (she died in 1920) but it was hearing the extra information which triggered off the name in my father's memory.

Putting these questions to relatives who may remember events and places years ago saves time and money. It is also a way of collecting all those trivia which make our more recent ancestors more colourful than those in remoter times, most of whom will be little more than a name and a note of baptism, marriage, work, children and death. The fortunate beginner will be blessed with an aged relative who, even though their recall of the intervening years may be clouded, still retains a clarity about childhood and the events of a couple of generations ago.

My wife's grandmother was born a Washington, which seemed an admirable line to follow, having a famous bearer of the name and a place name to boot. She could remember her own grandfather, Joshua Washington, a farmer in North Wales, selling his produce at Corwen market, living at a place beginning with the letter G between Bala and Corwen and talking Welsh. So, to save time and money, we decided to miss out her own father, John Webb Washington, and try to discover more about Joshua.

Using a holiday in Barmouth as an excuse for the journey, we tramped round both graveyards at Glan yr Afon (the only place beginning with G between Bala and Corwen) without success; we searched the local directories for a farmer called Washington, and found none. We left an enquiry at the local County Record Office (CRO) which elicited the response that the only Washington in the area had been an Irish navvy who lived in a shed at Bettwys Gwerfil Goch. This unpromising situation was clarified by another relative who thought that Joshua might have lived in the next valley, which was in the next county, and that the place began with Ll, which would sound like G to an English child. Off to Llangollen, and more unproductive graveyards (there are always at least two in Welsh villages and for anyone with Welsh ancestry there is Hamilton-Edwards, 1985). So eventually we did what we should have done in the first place – followed the standard procedure and sent for John Webb Washington's birth certificate. Back it came after several frustrating weeks, showing that John Webb was not the son of Joshua but of George Washington, a plumber in Chester!

Moral – never believe what older relatives tell you. Note it down; check it; but do not be surprised if it is wrong. In the above case, the old lady had clearly confused one branch of the family with another; a relative said of her, 'She doesn't tell lies, but she does romance a bit'. Others will fail to remember dates or occupations and will prefer to give any answer rather than admit loss of memory or appear to be unhelpful. This type of confusion casts some doubt, incidently, on the genre of historical writing which has become popular in the last few years, based on old people's reminiscences. (See Taylor, 1984). In the end the genealogist must rely on documentary evidence, though even this is not necessarily reliable. The most important guideline is to seek all the available evidence, and only then judge what to believe and decide what your next course of action should be.

This is not to say, of course, that you should ignore other people's efforts, though you should always check their results whenever feasible. Genealogy has been a popular hobby for over a century, and it is surprising how many beginners are told that 'old uncle so-and-so tried to do that once'. Some family tree records have been kept by individual families; many others have been deposited in libraries and record offices and a very large number have been published. Lists of family histories can be obtained in Barrow (1977), Marshall (1967), Thomson (1976), and Whitmore (1953). Contact with others tracing the same surname can sometimes be made via the National Genealogical Directory; see

Burchall, (1984 and annually).

You may find that, in investigating the more recent history of your family, there are residents in the area where your ancestors lived who have information about them. Writing a letter to a local newspaper has been known to produce marvellous results, though some now make a charge because they are inundated with such letters. In the case of a rare surname, you could even write to many with the same name, obtaining their addresses from telephone directories. A student of one of my classes wrote to one such entry, chosen at random with a pin, and received in return several sheets on which her family tree was written, back to 1728 and with herself included at the foot!

II—Looking for parents

Introduction

It has been said that the history of population is all about sex and death; genealogy is all about parents and how to find them. It is true, of course, that sooner or later anyone tracing a family tree will be interested in marriages, gravestones, tax returns and a host of documents which supply evidence about named individuals; but in the end, when human beings have learnt how to avoid death and have outgrown marriage as a social institution, the genealogist's basic task will remain the same – to discover parents. It is a genetic quest – few people would prefer to trace foster or adoptive parents rather than their real ones. Thus, early registers which record baptism without naming the parents of the children will probably mark an end to the search for that particular branch of the family. Until those registers are reached, possibly four hundred years back, there are several basic sources of information about parents, and it is quite possible to trace a family tree by using only the main ones – the state birth certificates, the census and church baptismal registers.

A great deal has been written about these sources. The following discussion therefore goes into their history only where doing so will help the genealogist to exploit the documents fully, at the least cost and trouble, and where it can help users to overcome the problems which can sometimes occur with sources of this kind.

Birth Certificates, 1837 to the present day

Everyone born in England or Wales on or since 1 July, 1837 should have had their birth registered by the state, which keeps a record of the event in the form of a registration entry. This shows information which an informant, normally the mother or her legal husband, provides to the registrar within six weeks of the birth. The registrar sends to the Registrar-General a copy of each entry at the end of each quarter year; as soon as the registrar's current record book is full, it is handed over to the Supertendent Registrar, who keeps it permanently. There is normally one Superintendent Registrar in each major city and several in each county, the number having fallen from 615 in 1837 to 418 in 1983. There were some boundary changes between districts in 1853 and again in April 1974 (at the same time as local government reorganisation). The office of each Superintendent Registrar has lists and addresses for all the other offices in England and Wales, together with a register of the whereabouts of the records for those districts which were reorganised in 1974. Appendix 3 gives the full addresses of the Register Offices, with some advice on how best to approach them. If you are in the UK and wish to telephone a Superintendent Registrar, these offices are listed under 'Registration of Births, Deaths and Marriages' in phone books which are available in most large libraries for the whole country. Maps showing registration districts and parish boundaries can be obtained from the Institute of Heraldic and Genealogical Studies, Northgate, Canterbury.

Thus, there should be in existence two birth entries for each ancestor back to 1 July, 1837 – the original with the Superintendent Registrar of the district where the birth took place, and a copy with the Registrar-General at St Catherine's House, 10 Kingsway, London, in registers which occupy a mile of shelving. Both sets are indexed, those of the Superintendent by district and by year, arranged alphabetically. The general public has the right to search the district indexes for a specified, dated event. The search is free of charge so long as it does not cover more than a five-year period, or slightly longer if the Superintendent deems it justifiable. Should you wish to search more than five years' indexes for one entry or more, you are allowed six continuous hours for which a fee of £12.00 may be charged (which includes up to eight verifications).

Searches in these local indexes can be in person or by post, provided you give the approximate year of birth, allow the Superintendent a week or two to reply, and supply the reference number from the index if you have already found it yourself. Postal application to a Superintendent Registrar should include the fee, (made payable to "The Superintendent Registrar", though it actually goes into the coffers of the local authority, towards the cost of the service) and he can refuse to undertake the search if he deems your information to be insufficient. Do not go into long, rambling details about your family history – just send the basic question, with as much relevant detail about the event as possible.

The cost of a certificate, by post or personal application, is £5.00, a figure which has not increased since 1 April 1985. (Overseas applications should be in sterling money orders, with two International Reply Coupons.) Only by claiming that it is needed for a 'statutory purpose' can a certificate be obtained more cheaply. When civil registration started in 1837, the cost was 2/6; it rose next in 1952 – to 3/9; now, the Registrar-General is more than keeping pace with inflation and seems determined to make this aspect of the service pay for itself, as the Treasury directs.

Genealogists tend to forget that civil registration is not run for their benefit; indeed, only one type of record referred to in this book was written basically for a genealogical purpose. Nor is the registration service adequately staffed to cater for all our needs, and there is no statutory requirement to provide a postal service. Paying the price, therefore, seems inevitable until it is recognised that these records should be classed as public documents under the 1958 Public Records Act and made available to the public after, say, a hundred years. Unfortunately, the cost of opening them to the public in this way would be substantial.

Certain anomalies in the present system could, however, be removed without such a radical change. For example, we have seen that a general search in the Superintendent Registrar's office costs £12.00, but you can search the indexes of the Registrar-General, which contain more information than the local indexes, free of charge, and without a time limit. The indexes in St Catherine's House cover the whole of England and Wales, and are arranged in alphabetical order within each quarter-year. The mother's maiden name (which is sometimes the only information you actually need from the certificate in the first place) appears in the national indexes from 1911, but in the local indexes only 1969, unless you are lucky. The GRO is not as assiduous in ensuring that minor variations in spelling should not prevent the correct identification of an entry, an all too frequent cause of complaint by genealogists. (See the advice on the back of the application form.) Also, although a copy of each certificate costs the same £5.00 from St Catherine's House, it will cost £13.00 by post (£11.00 if you supply the reference number). £8.00 is retained if the entry requested proves to be the wrong one (£3.00 if it was an application in person). St Catherine's House will supply a certificate by post for the basic £5.00 only in cases where the Superintendent Registrar's copy has been damaged. Certificates from the GRO are copies from microfilm, often partly illegible – you should ask for a legible copy from the manuscript entry in that case.

The Superintendent Registrar and Registrar-General have their own separate indexing systems, and reference numbers are not interchangeable.

Thus the majority of genealogists, who live beyond easy reach of London, are doubly penalised compared with those in the capital. They must pay dearly for their local general searches, and pay extra for their postal requests to St Catherine's House. This advantage enjoyed by those in the home counties explains the concerted effort a few years ago to prevent the Registrar-General moving the national indexes to the provinces (*Local Population Studies*, vol. 14). A more likely development in the forseeable future is that the entries will be transferred onto computer; the cost of the exercise would be covered by continuing to charge a fee for access – but the fee would be smaller than at present and access would be much quicker (*Genealogist' Magazine*, vol. 20, no. 5). Entries in the GRO registers have already been microfilmed; Birmingham has reindexed its birth registers back to 1837 and microfiched the new index, an admirable lead which is being copied by some other districts.

So far so good. We know that there are two ways to obtain a copy of a birth certificate. Which method you use will depend on how much information you already have about the birth. If you know where the person was born, and the approximate date, it is quicker and normally cheaper to apply to the relevant Superintendent Registrar; if the place of birth is not known, you will need to use the national indexes. You are advised to order the certificate while you are at St Catherine's House, but there is a two-day wait for personal collection and often over two weeks if it is sent to you by post.

The certificate itself will tell you the forename of the child, its sex, the name and occupation of the father, the name and maiden name of the mother (which leads you to the parents' marriage), the place of birth, the informant's signature, name, address, and the dates of birth and registration. Until modern times, when some of the larger offices send photocopies of the original entries quarterly, the informant's signature can be seen only on the Superintendent Registrar's copy. Column 10 of the certificate, normally blank, records any change of forename up to twelve months after the original registration based on information on a baptismal or naming certificate; (see page 25). Such an addition can be entered at any time afterwards – over a century later in at least one case! Informants can be minors, so long as they appear to be 'of credible age'. If time of birth is given in the entry, a multiple birth can be inferred except in the first year or so of civil registration. However, if one of a pair of twins was stillborn, the time should not have been included on the other, a rule which must be borne in mind by anyone searching for evidence of twinning in the family. The sex of the child may seem superfluous, though in a few case it is not obvious from the forename, and it establishes which sex you are allowed to marry, despite any subsequent sex change! Incidentally, I have never understood why most names are associated with one sex rather than the other, but it is a good thing for the genealogist that the practice exists!

The surname of the child (which can be any name the parents choose) has been entered only since 1 April 1969. Before that date it has to be inferred from the parents' name. In the case of an illegitimate child, only the mother's name is normally given; if the father's name does appear, the mother of an illegitimate child will probably be called, for example, 'Elizabeth Smith' instead of 'Elizabeth Jones, formerly Smith', although, of course, a married woman can have an illegitimate child and still provide her maiden and married names in this way. Until 1969, the surnames of both mother and father were indexed if they appear on the entry. Elizabeth Jones 'otherwise' Smith implies an alias. Before 1875, the mother was allowed to name any man as the father; he was not required to acknowledge paternity. (The name of the father of an illegitimate child might also appear on the child's later marriage entry.) An illegitimate child can now be issued with a birth certificate which gives him or her the surname of either the father or the mother, but the father's name can appear on the entry only if an affiliation order has been issued, or if he signs the entry, or if he has acknowledged paternity through a statutory declaration. The 'short' birth certificate was introduced in December 1947 for those who did not wish for their parents to be entered. It is much cheaper to buy than a full certificate, but (with one exception) it is of no genealogical value, and shows, incidentally, only the name in column 10 (space 17 since 1969) if that has been completed.

If the father of the child was already dead when the birth was registered, the word 'deceased' should appear after his name or in his occupation column, but does not always do so. Occasionally, the registrar would omit the father's name altogether if he was dead, or provide both his name and occupation while he had been alive.

Until 1977, foundlings were registered by Boards of Guardians or Social Services departments, and are indexed in the usual way under the name given by those agencies, and the age assessed by medical examination. Following the Children Act of 1975, foundlings now form the bulk of entries in the GROs Register of Abandoned Children, and should no longer be registered by district registrars. Astonishingly few – about half a dozen a year – have been entered so far, perhaps because the requirement is not well enough known. In the same register are older, abandoned children who might already have had their birth registered in the normal way. Entries in this register contain no more information than that found on a short certificate, and all are included in the main series of birth indexes, distinguished by an unusual reference number. Since 1 April, 1969, the format of the birth certificate has changed, so that the child's surname, and the place of birth of each parent and their usual address all now appear. Registrars now also collect information about the number of children already in the family, the dates of birth of each parent, whether the mother had been married before, how many live and stillbirths she has had before and how many of her children have died, but unfortunately for the genealogist this information is sent to the Registrar-General for statistical purposes only and is then destroyed. The occupation of the mother was introduced in 1986. However, after 1978 it may be found on Anglican baptism entries and it is also in Health Authority records – see below, page 36.

Once a birth certificate has been obtained, the next step is to seek the marriage certificate of the parents (see page 91). For the majority of families, this will be straightforward. The only problems so far will have been the practical ones of access to the indexes. For a large number, however, one of a series of difficulties will have already occurred. The following sections explain why they arise, and what you can do about them. In my experience, these difficulties will occur in up to one third of all attempts to locate an entry in the indexes.

Failure to find a birth entry in the indexes

This often happens and there are many reasons why. The solution depends on the cause, which you might not recognise until you have tried several solutions.

Registration in another district

Births are registered in the district in which they happen. This district need not necessarily cover the home address of the parents. I once tried to illustrate to some students how a registrar finds a particular entry among the thousands (or even millions) in his or her keeping by trying to discover the record of my wife's birth. Much to their amusement, it could not be found. The entry was eventually discovered in a nearby district, recording the birth in a hospital a few miles from her parents' home. The indexes to several or all sub-districts in the Superintendent Registrar's area should therefore be consulted if necessary; after that, those at St Catherine's House. Registration districts are so separate that it was only in 1911 that each was given statistical information about its residents' children born in other districts. Until 1929, registrars were paid on commission, encouraging registration in the wrong district.

Birth not registered

In some parts of the country as many as 15 per cent of all births were not registered during the first decades after 1837. There was no penalty on parents for failing to register a birth until 1875, when a £2 fine was introduced, and parents often wanted to hide the true age of a child in order to send it out to work as early as possible. From 1833 a series of Acts of Parliament made it illegal to employ children under certain ages in industrial occupations. The 7/6d penalty for late registration after the permitted six week interval following a birth did not encourage the stragglers to come forward, and registration was not permitted after six months anyway. Until 1875, the onus was on the registrar rather than on the parents, a fact which helped to determine the original size of the districts. Parents were bound by law to answer the registrar's questions, but not to report the birth in the first place.

Many believed that registration was not necessary if the child was baptised. In 1844, the Registrar-General complained that thousands were escaping the net. Modern research suggests that the problem was worst in Surrey, Sussex, Middlesex, Essex, Shropshire and Wales, and in the period before 1860; it fell to almost nothing by the 1870s.

The easiest way to overcome this problem in the nineteenth century is to use registers of baptism (pages 52–80), the census (pages 40–52) and wills (pages 144–54). It might also be possible to trace the parents from a known brother or sister (gleaned from the census) whose birth *was* registered. Failure to find siblings registered would be another indication that the parents had omitted to have your ancestor recorded. Other alternative sources are discussed below, pages 28–40.

Birth incorrectly indexed

Early in November 1977, I stood in a Superintendent Registrar's office next to a very upset and worried lady named Edith Williamson, who had searched through all the nearby districts for her own birth certificate. She knew that it was there, because she had once had a copy; yet it had not, apparently, been indexed. Eventually, almost by accident, she found it – indexed under Wilkinson.

The causes of poor indexing are not far to seek. Until modern times, certificates were handwritten and subsequently indexed by a different registrar, so that simple misreading of the original writing is quite possible. Confusion over capital letters T, F, J and I is common, as is the adding or dropping of a capital H or silent W. H, W and M can easily be mistaken for each other. Every time the records are copied, errors can creep in, so that the indexes of St. Catherine's House contain more mistakes than the local ones. The original entry was copied by hand; the copy was indexed by hand; and in many cases, the original indexes are now so worn through use that they have been recopied, again by hand. Microfilmed copies of GRO indexes 1837–1980 have been bought by various institutions, mostly libraries and CRO's, though some have acquired the years to 1912 because of the higher cost of those more recent. See Gibson (9) for a list of which institutions world-wide hold which years.

An index entry can also be wrong if the original certificate was incorrectly completed (see page 22). Normally nowadays, every effort is made to make sure that the informant can check what is written on the certificate. We do not know how thoroughly this was done in the last century, but illiteracy was widespread, so that such checking was in many cases impossible. If the informant was not the brightest of sparks, the problem might be compounded. One mother of an illegitimate child, asked by the registrar to name the father, looked puzzled, and asked 'Will the Social Services know?' Names were written either as common sense suggested, or pronunciation dictated. Some of these errors will cause few problems. Most people with my own surname have to suffer the indignity of it spelled Rodgers, and will look under both spellings almost automatically. Hibberts, however, might not look under Ibbert; and the most difficult cases are those where the registrar has misheard the name or had no idea how to spell it. The birth of Elizabeth Hallett on 5 January, 1878, was registered by a neighbour and recorded as 'Allot'. Again, the name might well have been misheard if the informant had a bad cold at the time.

You can get round the problem of poor indexing in exactly the same way as you can overcome the problem of an unregistered birth, but at first it is worth using a bit of imagination and ingenuity to consider various possible spellings under which the name might be indexed. Remember, too, that the spelling of forenames can vary – Elizabeth might be indexed as Elisabeth.

Birth not in England and Wales
However 'English' the surname might be, a surprising number of our ancestors were not born in England. The surname itself might be a clue to foreign origin, and a good dictionary of surnames should be consulted. The most obvious areas where immigration might have occurred in the nineteenth century are near the Scottish border and in the industrial north and midlands, which drew large number of immigrants from Ireland, especially after the 1830s. A register of immigrants from Scotland is being compiled by the Anglo-Scottish Family History Society. Scotland, Ireland (north and south) the Isle of Man and Channel

Islands (both Jersey and Guernsey) have their own registration systems, and it has always been optional for British citizens (males only until 1983) to register the birth of their children born abroad with a British consul or, from 1950, some High Commissions. Registration in the host country may, of course, be compulsory. Those births which are registered with a consul are recorded in the Consular Returns and/or the Chaplains' Returns (from 1849). These are now in the PRO, which also houses Miscellaneous Registers of births abroad. St Catherine's House has separate registers and indexes for births and deaths at sea (from 1837), in the air (from 1948), and (believe it or not) on hovercraft (from 1972). The GRO will supply certified copies of the entries in these and in Consular or High Commission Returns for the same fee as normal certificates. See Yeo, 1984.

The Department of Trade is responsible for the General Register of Shipping and Seamen, Cardiff; their records of births and deaths prior to 1890 have been transferred to the PRO, and the more modern records are not open to the public. The Registrar-General will, however, search his records for the appropriate fee.

The normal way to discover the birthplace of those living in Britain but not born there is by consulting the census (pages 40–52) or military records (Hamilton-Edwards, 1977) for the ancestor or his brothers. The PRO also has details of the naturalisation of aliens from 1789. Their names were published by HMSO (1844–1900 in one volume) until 1961, when the job was taken over by the *London Gazette* (see PRO leaflet no. 6). Jews naturalised between 1609 and 1799 are in the *Jewish Historical Society of England*, vol. 22 (1970) and the oaths taken by foreign protestants upon naturalisation, 1708–1712, have been printed by the Huguenot Society. (See Colwell, 1984, chapter 5).

Index entry missed by searcher

This is the sort of problem that happens only to other people, until it happens to you. It is unnervingly easy to miss the entry you are seeking, especially if you are not used to searching indexes, or if you have been at it for an hour or so continuously already, or if the handwriting is not the easiest to read, or if the surnames are collected together under initial capital letters but not arranged alphabetically. (See also page 72.)

Make a note of which quarter years you have already searched.

It is quite common in the GRO to find that someone else is using some of the indexes you want, and a few minutes later you can easily forget which ones you have omitted to search unless you have kept a record. Some index volumes will be missing altogether, taken away for rebinding. Ask the advice of the staff at the enquiry desk in this case; they will normally do the search for you if the volume is to be off the shelves for some time.

The indexes are arranged by date of registration, not by date of the event, and births can be registered up to six weeks after the event. Thus, a birth at the end of one year can be indexed in the first quarter of the next. If the child was unnamed at the time of registration, it will be indexed under the surname only, as 'male' or 'female'; if an entry is subsequently made in column 10 (space 17), it is reindexed under the correct name.

Base information incorrect

Officials at St Catherine's House will tell you that this is the commonest reason why you might fail to find the entry you are looking for. Hearsay from relatives is notorious for providing incorrect information. Any wrong element – surname, forename, date, place – can be leading you into a blind alley, and each should be rechecked if possible. For example, at South Shields in 1868 Edward Arthur married Jane Benton, then aged 18. There is, however, no birth certificate for Jane Benton because she was actually called Jane Bentham, born 13 May, 1849 in South Shields. Both birth and marriage certificates are correctly indexed as the names appear on the respective certificates. An incorrect name might appear for several reasons; perhaps the person was registered under one name but was called, and even baptised, another. In the above case, Jane was illiterate, and could not check what had been written on the marriage certificate. My own mother was known as 'Pat' throughout her life, but was registered as 'Martha'. Variants of Christian names are quite common, of course, and if you are in any doubt about them, consult the *Oxford Dictionary of English Christian Names* for details.

There are many other reasons why you might be looking in the wrong part of the index. If you fail to find the birth entry of a woman whose name you have obtained from the marriage indexes only (see pages 91–5) bear in mind that she might have been a widow or divorced at the time of marriage. Perhaps the person you are looking for had two or more forenames of which you are aware of only one; go through all the Christian names in the indexes in order to find a possible double Christian name entry. A special difficulty for 1866 and from 1 July, 1910, is that any forename other than the first is indexed in the GRO by the initial letter only. Some illegitimate brides and grooms have been known to invent a father's name to put on their marriage certificate, giving a totally misleading clue for identifying the birth certificate.

Normally you will know if the date which you have tried is based on guesswork: for example, 'His eldest child was born in 1865, so let's start in 1850 and work backwards to find his birth'. Sometimes, however, a marriage or census record can suggest a misleading year of birth, though they should not be too far out; ages on death certificates are more prone to error. When elderly widows or widowers die, sometimes leaving the informant to guess the age at death, gross errors may easily creep in – though National Health Service records since the second world war now help to minimise this problem. Gravestones can also give the wrong age, because many are erected or inscribed years after the death. It is also easy to mis-read figures on the gravestone, confusing 1 and 4, 3 and 5, and 6, 9 and 0. '21' on a marriage entry can mean 'over 21'.

Illegitimate children will normally be indexed only under the surname of the mother unless the father's name appears on the entry, so that if the child subsequently grew up using the father's surname, finding the entry will not be easy. The name on the marriage entry of an adopted child will be that of the *adoptive* father, and the fact of adoption will not be indicated. The remedies for all the above problems are obvious, though in some cases it may take a long time to find the correct entry. Try applying for a birth certificate of a known brother or sister; be less willing to believe everything that is written down; seek further evidence to help confirm a doubtful case – for example, find the name of the father and mother first from a census entry before you apply for the child's birth certificate.

Child was adopted

Before 1927 there was no such thing as legal adoption, though the word itself was often used for guardianship or foster-parenthood. This status was not automatically recorded and, in theory, there should have been no change of surname from the original birth certificate; but some children were undoubtedly brought up with the surname of their foster parents. For the period before 1927, see the Census (pages 40–52) and miscellaneous probate records (page 153). See also Currer-Briggs (1979) and health records (pages 36–7).

Since 1 January 1927, over three quarters of a million children have been adopted, and for them (or now, in turn, their own children) there are two main problems – how can anyone tell if they are adopted, and if so, how can they discover their natural parents? Most parents have the good sense to bring up these children in the knowledge that they are adopted, and the full adoptive certificate, issued by the Registrar-General after the court proceedings, shows the date and court of the order, the new name and surname (legal from the date of the order), the child's sex, the name, surname, address and occupation of the new parents, and the date and district of birth.

In the absence of this full, adoptive certificate, the only sure way to distinguish an adoption is by interpreting the short birth certificate. This will have been issued by the Registrar-General, not a Superintendent Registrar, and will have an Adopted Children Register reference number, instead of the normal volume and page or, after 1939, NHS number.

If the adopted person is unaware of the details of his original birth entry, he can request the Registrar General to arrange a counselling interview at which this information will be given, as laid down in the Children Act, 1975. (See Terry, 1979.) A social worker who provides this counselling will not only give advice about the personal problems involved but can also describe the circumstance of the adoption, and whether the natural parent has expressed to the Registrar-General or Social Services department a willingness that she be approached by you. (All the administrative barriers are against the natural parent making first contact with the adopted child.)

The original birth entry (both at GRO and Superintendent Registrar's office) will have been marked "Adopted" in the margin, and this will be put on any copy of a full (not short) certificate issued. Only the Registrar-General has the complete national index which will connect the adoption certificate with the original birth entry, though the information will be held by an adoption society, the NHS, a Social Services department, and of course by the court of adoption for a minimum period of time (some local authority files were reportedly lost during reorganisation). Few GRO staff have access to the connecting index.

Making contact with a natural parent can then be quite difficult, even when you know who she is, because of the long period of time which has elapsed since and the probable subsequent marriage of the mother (75% of adopted children being originally illegitimate). It is especially difficult if the adoption took place before the substantial Social Security systems developed after the second world war.

Access to an original birth entry, described above, applies only to an adopted child over the age of eighteen. If any other person (e.g. a grandchild) wishes to gain access, application should be *not* to the Registrar-General but to the original court issuing the adoption order, the High Court, or the Westminster Court (the last because St Catherine's House falls within its jurisdiction), for a direction under s. 20(5) of the Adoption Act, 1958.

Change of name after registration

One of the commonest refuges of the bad amateur is to jump too quickly to the conclusion that an ancestor whose birth entry cannot be found must have changed his or her name during their lifetime. Unless you have some direct evidence that this happened, try some of the other explanations first.

There are several ways of changing a surname. The most famous, and probably the commonest, is by deed poll which may be enrolled in the Supreme Court as a permanent record. Deeds poll were entered in the Close Rolls until 1903, and after that in the Supreme Court Enrolment Books (see also Phillimore and Fry, 1908). Only British citizens living the UK can change their name by deed poll. Access to the records is in person at the Filing Department of the Central Office of the Supreme Court. Names have also been changed by Act of Parliament and by Royal Licence. All these methods record only *intent*; what really matters is usage, and legally a change of name requires nothing else. If you simply start using a new name, with no intention to defraud, then you have legally changed your name; (see PRO leaflet no. 5, and Josling, 1985).

People who want to change their names have commonly

announced their intentions in local newspapers, or in the *London Gazette*. However, documentary evidence of the change is required for certain official purposes and it may be that this is the easiest way to discover the fact – for example, through passport or bank records. Many people will have obtained their evidence by swearing out a declaration before a JP or Commissioner for Oaths.

Some lawyers believe that a Christian name given in baptism cannot be changed, only added to in the way that Churchill added "Spencer" to 'Winston Leonard'. In the debate leading to Civil Registration in 1837 the Church claimed that a child should be named only through baptism, and that therefore the state registration service should not do so. However, all this has not prevented people from changing forenames. The Church of England gives the right to change the baptised name at the time of confirmation, and the Roman Catholic Church allows additional names to be given to the original baptismal name. (See Burn, 1824). (Records of confirmation, by the way, tend to be modern – i.e., twentieth century.) We have also seen that it is possible to change the forename on a birth certificate up to twelve months after the birth has been registered by using column 10 of the old certificate (space 17 since 1 April, 1969). The certificate is then reindexed. However, as few people know about this procedure it is not often used, and the surname, indicated in the entry only since 1969, cannot be changed anyway.

The only restriction on changing a forename through column 10 of the birth certificate is where the child has been baptised with the name with which it was originally registered. In this respect, the Births and Deaths Registration Act of 1953, Section 13 (1), provides an unusual incursion of religious ritual into a civil process. It is therefore not in the interest of parents who might wish to change the registered name of their child either to baptise it or to admit to having done so. In the same way, children known to have been baptised before adoption should not be rebaptised later.

If the child was given a name after the initial registration, and the registrar was not informed, the indexes at St Catherine's House will include the child simply as 'male' or 'female' at the end of the list of the relevant surname. (See also p. 75.)

Another means of confirming a change of name is by using the notices of marriage which often have the phrase "formerly known as . . .", though this should have appeared on the marriage entry. (See pages 95–6.)

Finding more than one possible birth

I once applied for the birth certificate of Sarah Hargreaves, my grandmother, born in 1858. The Superintendent Registrar replied that she could not help because two girls with the same name had been born in the same district within a couple of days of each other. If I had not known the registration district in advance, this problem could have been magnified several times in the indexes at St Catherine's House; and as for applying for a John Smith. . . .

In such cases, and they are very common indeed, it is essential to have more information than the name, year and place of birth. If the child's birthday can be discovered (for example, from an education record or gravestone), this will usually solve the problem, but not always. In many cases the real date of birth does not correspond with the date on the certificate. This is either because the informant, especially if it was the father, could not remember the date, or more likely because the birth was registered late, outside the six weeks' time-limit allowed, in which case there is a strong temptation to falsify the date of birth. This can cause some distress when, years later, the child reaches pensionable age!

Identification might be facilitated if you can supply to the Superintendent Registrar the signature of the probable informant from, e.g., a will or marriage entry.

If the child's father or mother can be named in advance (for example, from the census or a marriage certificate), this will also help the registrar to identify the correct one – though it is often just to obtain that information that you are asking for the certificate in the first place! Knowing the child's later occupation can occasionally help, especially in those trades, such as blacksmith, which tended to be passed from father to son – but this can never be conclusive in itself. An exact address also helps. Although it is impossible to get for many country areas in the last century, it is perfectly possible for towns (see the census, pages 41–5).

The GRO and Superintendent Registrars will verify a correct entry if you supply enough information to make an identification possible from among several index entries; the fee is £2.50 per entry.

Always remember that negative evidence may be very useful in eliminating one of the possible births, and that it is sometimes easier to obtain than positive evidence in favour of the correct one. For example, infant mortality remained high throughout the nineteenth century; perhaps you can show that one of the two possible entries died young.

It should also be added that, until 1929, registrars were paid by the number of entries made, and in the early years of the system there were a number of scandals – at South Shields and Marylebone, for example – in which the same entries appeared, and were presumably indexed, more than once.

If your problems cannot be solved by any of these methods, you will need to use the alternative strategies described in the next section.

Indexes or certificates not accessible – alternative sources

In some ways, registrars can be a law unto themselves because, since 1837, they have had no legal employer (though they are paid by Local Authorities). In practice, however, their actions are controlled rigorously by the Registrar-General's office, and (since 1843) supervised by an inspectorate. On the whole they carry out their duties in a most conscientious and professional manner. However, Superintendent Registrars have been known to refuse access to their indexes, saying simply that the public has no right to use them. If this happens to you, ask him to consult his Handbook for Registration Officers, section XV. In the unlikely event that you have further trouble, you should complain to the Registrar-General.

It is worth mentioning at this point that genealogists can help to make life easier for themselves, as well as for the registration service, by taking certain precautions. Some of the smaller register offices are staffed on a part-time basis – by solicitors, for example – and are not open during the whole of normal working hours. (Nowadays, however, these part-time solicitors are not being replaced as registrars when they retire, and their districts are being merged with other registration districts.) It is also worth remembering that even Birmingham, the largest of the register offices, will not welcome genealogical searchers on a Saturday, because so many staff are busy conducting marriages on that day (more people now marry in register offices than churches), or on a Monday, when a large number of weekend births and deaths have to be registered. Try to avoid lunchtimes if possible when a reduced staff have to deal with more than the normal number of clients. Ideally, confirm the hours of opening and let the office know in advance which indexes you wish to search.

Most of the current trends in genealogy are making the hobby easier and cheaper, as more records are now open to the public, and more entries are being computerised. Historians are increasingly interested in demography and more and more people from all walks of life are becoming anxious to trace their ancestors. However, the rising charges of the Registrar-General are running counter to these other trends, and the cost of certificates will soon make the period from 1837 the most expensive to research out of the last four centuries. Some genealogists are already finding it hard to raise the cost of several certificates and have to find cheaper ways of obtaining the same information. While the current Registrar-General's fee policy lasts, postal requests to St Catherine's House must be minimised – but that means many unnecessary letters to Superintendent Registrars, letters which are frequently unprofitable to both parties. Sources which cut costs are church registers, the census, gravestones and wills. All of these are dealt with later in this volume, but many other sources make identification of age and place of birth easier, and can even replace the birth certificates altogether. These sources are discussed below. See above, pp. 19–20. It should also be noted that the Mormon branch libraries are buying microfilmed copies of the Victorian birth indexes in St Catherine's House, 1837–1980.

Marriage and Death Certificates

Marriage certificates give the age at marriage and the name of the father for both bride and groom. Death certificates give the approximate age at death (until 1 April, 1969, since when exact date and place of birth should be entered, together with the maiden surname of a married woman.) Both types of certificate therefore provide a basis for calculating the year of birth. This calculation should be repeated from the burial record and should not necessarily be taken at face value. (A marriage entry in a local newspaper might also provide parents' names and addresses. So will an entry announcing a birth.) For further discussion of marriage and death certificates, see pages 91–9 and 120–4.

Military records

It is not proposed in this book to go into army records in detail, as a first-class acount of them has already been written (Hamilton-Edwards, 1977); for a detailed look at the records of the First World War, see Holding, 1982, 1985 and 1987.

Regimental registers in the GRO record births, marriages and deaths of soldiers *in the UK* from 1761 to 1924; marriage entries have a space for the names, births and baptisms of the subsequent children. The Army Register Book (1881–1959) contains births, marriages and deaths *outside the UK*, and there are similar books for the Royal Navy (1837–1959) and the RAF (1918–1959). Since 1959, all three are in the same books, with a common index since 1964. All are in the GRO, and certificated copies may be obtained at the same cost as normal certificates. Baptismal certificates of officers have survived from 1755 and are now in the PRO. Leaflet 9, issued by the PRO, lists the records which provide birthplaces of all soldiers, but once again it is important to know the regiment. Swinson (1972) gives the history of regiments, including amalgamations.

Place of birth can be obtained for any ancestor who died in the first world war from the War Office publication, *Soldiers Died in the Great War*. However, it is not easy to find this work as it is available only the largest libraries. Using it involves a long search, unless the regiment and battalion are known in advance; within these categories, names are in alphabetical order. The National Roll of the Great War gives details of military careers, medals and addresses of supposedly all who fought in the first world war; but this was published for only Bedford, Birmingham, Bradford, Leeds, London, Luton, Manchester, Northampton, Portsmouth, Salford, and Southampton, and is not complete even for these areas.

Parentage of officers in the Royal Navy may be obtained from a series of books listed in Gardner and Smith (vol. 2, 1959, p. 167). Ages and birthplaces of other ranks are available in Ships' Musters, which go back to the late seventeenth century, and

Bounty Papers (1675–1822). Both sets of records are in the PRO.

Merchant Navy records and Muster Rolls supply the date and place of birth or baptism, but most from before the nineteenth century have been lost. Those which do survive are once again in the PRO, which issues a very useful series of leaflets on military and naval records, including the Mercantile Marine.

Education records

Most of our ancestors in the last hundred years attended elementary schools, the pre-1944 forerunners of primary schools. These go back for well over four hundred years, but it is very rare to find any records surviving from before the nineteenth century. One set which is now in the Cheshire CRO is for a charity school called Seamon's Moss near Altrincham. It illustrates the type of information which such records may contain. In addition to the normal trustees' minute books, which rarely name children or parents, there is a detailed school register which gives the names of children and parents, ages, dates of admission, periods of absence and even reasons for absence. My favourite entry is for ten year old George, son of George Podmore of Dunham Massey, who in 1788 'informed me that his mother had leave . . . for him to absent from school 3 weeks to take care of the family while his mother assisted Mr Carter to make hay. But they took 10 days more. NB This Account being false'. Poor little George then disappears from the register.

From 1833, the state gave church schools substantial financial aid, and voices were raised in Parliament in the 1850s calling for increased accountability to go with such grants. From 1862, therefore, schools receiving state aid were made subject to a 'payment by results' system, which was designed to make education either cheaper or more efficient. This system is now anathema to the teaching profession, but it opened up an Aladdin's cave for the genealogist. Because it became far more important than before to keep accurate records – after all, the teacher's salary now partly depended on them – registers began to include the names and addresses of children and parents and the children's dates of birth.

Since 1880, local authorities have had a duty to ensure that children in their area are being suitably educated. (Some have done so since 1870.) The 1876 Act allowed authorities to establish a data base for this task by requesting information for all births in the area from the registrar. Stockport Public Library has a good run of these lists from 1880 to 1948 (with gaps), containing for every child born in Stockport name, date of birth, address and parental names and occupations. See the *Genealogists' Magazine*, Vol. 21, No. 6 (June, 1984).

Unfortunately, local education authorities (LEAs) no longer seem to acquire this information, with the result that none whom I have consulted is able to say with certainty which children in its area are of school age, or pre-school age; unless neighbours inform the LEA that children are not attending school, there seems to be no way of ensuring that all children are being educated.

Even if the school register has not survived, you should ask to see the school log book which was (and still is) kept by the head teacher to record the curriculum and any unusual day-to-day events. A very large proportion of a school's population can sometimes be found in these log books. I have looked through those for where my mother went to school at the turn of the century, and found her brothers and sisters winning prizes, being naughty, being late, ill with smallpox, off school for the potato picking and many of those other activities which will take you back to your own childhood. In the log book, or sometimes in a separate register, you may also find punishments, which will give the name of the offender, the nature of the offence and the punishment inflicted.

Very few, if indeed any, of these documents have ever been published, so finding the originals is essential if you wish to consult them. The first problem to overcome is that very few records, outside the educational institutions themselves, will tell you which schools your ancestors attended. Contemporary town or county directories (see page 42) will tell you which schools existed close to where they lived. If this was in a rural area, it is probable that there was only one school within reach – almost certainly Anglican. The real problem comes in the towns and cities where there might be several schools within walking distance of the child's home. He or she might have attended the nearest, the nearest of one particular denomination or the cheapest – the established church complained that protestants were sending their children to catholic schools because their fees were the lowest. Perhaps the child containued to attend a more distant school in an area from which the family had moved; perhaps he or she did not attend school at all.

On the question of school attendance, I have doubts about relying on the word 'scholar' when used for a child in the census. Since 1851 the censuses have recorded at least minimum information about schooling. Enumerators were asked to record which children were educated daily at school. (In the 1851 census this was limited to children over five; and those being tutored at home were designated separately.) However, I believe that you should not automatically assume that 'scholar' meant that a child was certainly on a school register, or even formally educated at home; correspondingly, I am sure that some of those who were not described as scholars were actually at school. The 1851 urban census returns for scholars are higher than the contemporary, and separate, school census of 1851 would suggest, though I must confess that the census officials themselves thought that the number of real scholars was under-represented.

Perhaps part of the explanation lies in Sunday schools. Between 1780 and 1880, the only form of education for many children was in a Sunday school, which at that time taught the fundamentals of reading and writing as well as religion. This was particularly true for those young children who were at work during the rest of the week. Some of the Sunday schools in urban areas were remarkably large. For instance, the one in Stockport catered for over three thousand children. Its registers, running from 1780 to 1920, provide names, ages, dates of admission, class, educational attainment and date of leaving. Other Sunday school registers such as those of Tintwistle, now in Derbyshire, also provide parents' names.

Records of all types of elementary school, of whatever denomination, have sometimes found their way into CROs. Many schools, as well as those of the Church of England, could survive the nineteenth century only with such substantial state aid that they had to be taken over by the local education authorities, and their records, together with those of the Councils' own schools, are now normally kept in the LEA archives. These, in turn, are often to be found in the local library or archive office. Many other schools have never centralised their records, especially the log books. In this situation an approach should be made directly to the head teacher (or, if it is a church school, the local clergyman).

There is no charge for consulting school records, but nor does the public have any right to do so. In my experience, head teachers are only too pleased that someone is taking an interest in their old records, and will deny access only to the most recent of them – certainly to those compiled within the last generation. Record offices, however, may operate up to a fifty-year restriction on access to deposited school records.

Thus, there is no easy way to locate the records of individual schools, and advice should be obtained from the County Archivist, the local education offices or the schools section of the religious denomination concerned. The search is well worth the effort, as the log books in particular provide the most fascinating insights into social and educational attitudes of the time, as well as putting some flesh onto the bones of your family tree.

Until the twentieth century, separate institutions for older children consisted almost entirely of grammar and public schools, though it should be remembered that, even until 1944, most children spent their entire school career in elementary schools. Grammar schools existed in surprisingly large numbers as early as the seventeenth century, when most market towns possessed one. Strangely enough, their records are not as illuminating as those of the post-1862 elementary schools. However, the grammar schools run by LEAs since 1902 have log books and there are usually trustees' or governors' minute books, and often the register. Only the last need normally be consulted by the genealogist.

A number of grammar and public school registers have been published. Relatively up-to-date county lists are available in articles in the *British Journal of Educational Studies* (Wallis, 1965, 1966); see also Jacobs (1964). These list only the published registers; others are to be found either in the schools themselves, in education offices or the CRO. The published versions often have the double advantage of having editorial annotations about the child's family or subsequent career, as well as an alphabetical index; but published so-called 'registers' from before the eighteenth century are sometimes misleading because they include only those pupils who went to university; you should check in the introduction whether this is the case.

Over the centuries, grammar schools tended to generate many other records which can be used by the genealogist. For example, petitions to trustees or to those who had the right to appoint the teachers sometimes provide long lists of local residents. Eighty inhabitants of Farnworth near Widnes complained in 1631 that the teachers 'old Weaknes', Francis Hawarden the headmaster, and 'yong Idlenes', Robert Williams his assistant, had turned the spring time of their school into an autumn – 'the little plants wee send there are no sooner budded but blasted'; see pages 58–69 for the genealogical use of such records.

University records are the easiest of all education records to use, but it is only in very modern times that even 10 per cent of the population has attended. When, in addition, you remember that the only universities in England and Wales before the 1820s were Oxford and Cambridge, your reaction may well be that none of your forebears will be found there. However, for a number of social and religious reasons, these two universities expanded the number of undergraduates dramatically in Elizabethan times so that, by the early seventeenth century, a greater proportion of children was attending university than at any time before the 1950s. (There was a marked decline after the middle of the seventeenth century.) A very large number of families will therefore find at least one of their ancestors in the Oxbridge records, and the search is so easy that it is well worth the effort.

Foster (1891ff.) and Venn (1922–1927) contain the known students at Oxford and Cambridge, arranged in alphabetical order. Foster is not as full, nor as accurate, as Venn, but using these two works, you can hope to obtain the names of the students, their parents, home town, age, where they had been to school and even the names of their schoolteachers – as well as editorial information about their subsequent careers. These registers should be found in large municipal libraries. Starting with London in 1828, and Durham in 1836, other cities in Britain later developed universities, often based on earlier technical colleges; their registers have been published until relatively modern times (see Jacobs, 1964). You can contact the registrar of the university concerned with a specific enquiry. Some of the directories referred to on pages 43–4 provide clues concerning which university your ancestor attended.

Many institutions other than universities have catered for post-school education or training. Catholic children, for example, were often sent to colleges on the continent, and their 'Responsa', or replies to the admissions questionnaire, have been published by the Catholic Record Society. Puritans and dissenters sometimes sent their children to Scottish, Irish or even Dutch universities, which also have published their registers, or, after 1662, to the growing number of dissenting academies. The students of the earliest, Rathmell in Yorkshire, are listed in Oliver Heywood's diary (see Turner, 1881/5), but few other registers have survived. Records of eighteenth and nineteenth-century colleges, such as Owen's in Manchester and Manchester College, York, are kept by the universities of which they later became a part. Military and naval colleges have similar records, but these must normally be consulted in the PRO or in the colleges themselves.

Health records

From 1871, duplicates of birth certificates (though normally excluding the mother's maiden name) had to be made under the Vaccination Act. Where these have survived, they have found their way into the CRO, which may also hold other duplicates of birth and death certificates among the Medical Officer of Health records. Some surviving in Cheshire are as recent as 1935, and the series in Cambridgeshire lasts until 1948. Each vaccination certificate is dated a few months after the birth itself. After 1898, however, parents could refuse vaccination for their children on grounds of conscience.

In modern times, vaccination comes under the District Health Authority (Area Health Authority before 1 April, 1982) as part of the child health programme. Records of birth in each area are collated from general practice, hospital, clinic and midwives' reports, births notified to the District Medical Officer within three days and the lists of births sent to the relevant Superintendent Registrar of births. Both the Registrar and the Health Authority are then in a position to chase up events which appear in only one list – discrepancies can lead to those failing to register a birth being discovered and, occasionally, to baby snatchers and abandoners being identified.

Meanwhile, the health visitors maintain a file on each individual, starting with their copy of the notification of birth. The most thorough Health Authorities record parental occupations, previous confinements of the mother, the social conditions under which the children are being raised, the subsequent medical record of the children at the formal stages of vaccination and pre-school examination, the schools attended and all the addresses at which that individual lives until the age of twenty-five. At that point, however, the file ends and will be destroyed, which is a great pity from the point of view of our historically-minded descendants. The public has no right of access to these files except via a court order. As this record will also state whether a child has been adopted (though probably the original name will have been erased) it might be possible for an individual to discover the fact of his or her own adoption on personal application to the District Health Authority concerned.

Incidentally, general practitioner NHS patient records are the property of the DHSS and are centralised and destroyed as soon as the patient dies.

If the child you are tracing was born in hospital, there will be yet another record of the event in the hospital's own archives. Hospitals usually keep their own records, but an increasing number are now being persuaded to deposit them in a Local Authority archives office. Even when this is done, the records are not open to public inspection until they are 100 years old.

We are all aware of the existence of the NHS records above, because they are the tip of the iceberg visible to patients. The heart of the NHS record system is its Central Register which contains a manual card on each individual from birth to death, distinguishing each by a reference number which will be found on their medical card. The NHS number started as a security identification number allocated as a result of the enumeration of the UK on 29 September, 1939; since then, all registered births, and all immigrants registering with an NHS doctor, have been issued with such a number. Access to this system is strictly limited for a few legitimate purposes within the NHS, and for the most dire emergencies – of which genealogy is not one, however obsessive about it you may have become.

Pension and insurance records
Place and date of birth should be obtainable from pension records, both public and private, because every individual claiming a pension would, at some stage, have had to prove his or her age with their own birth certificate. Indeed, in the early days of the state's old age pension scheme, which started in 1908, some applicants had been born before birth began to be recorded in

1837 and were therefore required to produce a certificate of baptism. Years ago, one of my students learned when and where her great-grandfather had been born by this method, but only a small minority of early pension records have survived. However, the DHSS will pass on to any living person in the UK (whose address at a certain date since 1946 can be provided) a letter of enquiry about the family. For further details, see Rogers (1986).

Some text books recommend consulting insurance records, which are still largely in the hands of the insurance companies themselves. However, unless you already know with which firm your ancestor was insured such a search is probably not worth the effort needed to locate the records. There is some guidance in articles in the *Journal of the Chartered Insurance Institute*.

Affiliation orders

One of the most annoying situations for a genealogist is to see your friends galloping back to the eighteenth century while you have been saddled with a modern bastard – often a genealogical non-starter. If the father of an illegitimate child is not named on the birth entry, his name and changes of address can sometimes be obtained from bastardy files resulting from the Poor Law Amendment Act of 1844 which introduced the concept of maintenance into statute law. There was further legislation in 1872 and 1914, when the term 'affiliation order' was adopted. Magistrates' courts could grant such an order at the request of the mother, the legal guardian of the Poor Law Guardians if the child had become chargeable. (Guardians' records should be consulted, therefore, if the court affiliation orders are not available.) Application had to be made within a specified time after the birth (one year at first, later increased to three years), and maintenance could be awarded while the child was of school age. The father's changes of address during the period of maintenance should have been recorded, which is very important from the point of view of finding him in the census.

Affiliation order files are not open to the general public, but that should not prevent you from enquiring. They are kept in the archives of the Magistrates' Courts, normally in the area where the mother lived at the time, and you should make a formal approach to the Clerk to the Justices to have them inspected. What you might be asking for, however, is a long search through dirty piles of documents in a remote part of the court buildings by hard-pressed staff who have no statutory duty to oblige you!

Trade union and friendly society records

Documents about individual members of trade unions rarely survive from before the mid-nineteenth century. The most useful are apprenticeship and membership registers. The former provide the boys' signed declarations and their addresses; the latter are more useful as they provide names, addresses, ages and marital status. More rarely, you might find names, addresses and numbers of dependent children in the records of benefit paid during strikes or short-time working; you might also pick up the names of many of the more active members from the minute books.

Locating trade union records is not straightforward, however. Many of the smaller unions have been aggregated into larger organisations, some of which are not necessarily familiar with their separate individual histories. A list of these smaller unions, together with the names and addresses (head and district offices) of the larger ones into which they have been amalgamated, has been published in Eaton and Gill (1981). The local CRO will advise whether the records of individual union branches have been deposited with them; this is most likely to have happened in areas where there are active local projects which encourage such a transfer, for example in the Calder Valley, Coventry, Manchester and Newcastle, where calendars of deposited records are being compiled. A pamphlet, *Trade Union and Related Records* (1981), published by the University of Warwick, and an index to material about trade union records in the *Bulletin of the Society for the Study of Labour History* are also useful. It is unlikely that there will be more than a thirty-year restriction rule on access to deposited trade union records, and probably no restriction at all.

If the records have not been deposited, you should apply to the district secretary of the union for permission to approach the branch which you think your ancestor might have joined. It is probably worth going to the branch even if the district office thinks that the records you seek do not survive, though you may find it hard to discover the secretary's name and address.

Few friendly society records of individual members survive from before the twentieth century, and not all of those provide genealogical information. Occasionally, however, you can find in them a real goldmine. The admissions book of St Michael's Friendly Society, 1845–1941, in the Lancashire Record Office, gives each member's name, trade, place of birth, current address, date of joining the Society and his age at that time.

Surviving friendly society records are either in the possession of the Society itself (or its modern counterpart), or are deposited in county or city record offices. See *The Local Historian*, Vol. 16, No. 3 (Aug. 1984).

Miscellaneous records

It is possible to work out when a voter reached the age of 21 from a study of electoral registers (pages 41–2); notices of birth have appeared in newspapers for over two centuries, but only in relatively modern times have these been on a large scale; similar notices of marriage can provide parents' names, and even obituaries (page 131) can be useful in pinpointing date and place of birth. (It is worth asking if there are indexes available.)

Post 1834 workhouse admission books, usually in the CRO, give name, year of birth, parish of settlement, marital status, cause for seeking relief, religion and a physical description. Prison records, available for much of the nineteenth century in the PRO and CRO's, sometimes include place and date of birth.

The Census, 1801 to the present day

Most recent books on genealogy give directions about using the census to find ancestors. It is enough to say here that the national census in England and Wales was first taken in 1801. Earlier attempts failed in Parliament because of religious and libertarian opposition; some enumerators still felt the need for police protection in 1841. Since 1801, a census has been taken once every ten years, excluding 1941 (though there was a full enumeration on 29 September, 1939), and a 10% sample in 1966. There is always a firm undertaking that the returns naming individual people will be regarded as confidential for 100 years, though a statistic analysis of the material is published as soon as possible. (For the first four censuses the returns themselves were destroyed after the analyses were completed.) Once the enumerators' returns are 100 years old, they are transferred by the Registrar-General to the PRO, Portugal Street, London WC1, where they may be seen on microfilm free of charge. So we are back to London again, normally out of the reach of most genealogists except on rare occasions.

Census material divides into three distinct periods, each of which presents different problems.

Censuses less than 100 years old

Strictly speaking, it should not be possible to obtain information from these records, but during the 1960s the Registrar-General was prepared to release information about named individuals from the 1901 census or earlier. Because of the furore surrounding the census of 1971 this facility was withdrawn for a time, but it is again possible to obtain details from 1891 and 1901. The Registrar-General has decided not to bring the 1911 or subsequent censuses into the same category because the undertakings of confidentiality given at that time. In consolation, it should be said here that it was disrupted as part of the suffragette campaign; *Punch* had a cartoon showing a lady hiding from the enumerator behind her lace curtains. The caption read, 'The women of England have taken leave of their census'. The census of 1891 was taken on 5 April, that of 1901 on 31 March, and that of 1911 on 2 April.

The way to obtain information from these censuses is to write to the Registrar-General, enclosing the following: the fee, currently £19.26 including VAT; your reason for wanting the information – genealogy is acceptable; a statement saying either that the person about whom you are enquiring is dead and that you are his/her descendant, or that the person is still alive and gives written permission for the enquiry to be made and that the information will not be used in litigation; the name and exact address of the person at the time the census was taken (though the entry for the whole household can be requested).

It is the last which will cause you most trouble. If you do not know the exact address already, it can be obtained from a registrar's certificate, (place of event or address of informant), baptismal and burial records, or from a number of other sources. Electoral registers, which are now held in town halls or CROs and can be consulted free of charge, should survive from 1832. (There are just a handful of earlier ones.) Until 1939, they contain both home and qualifying addresses, where these are different. Relatively few people are found in them until 1867, when there was a large increase in the urban voters – still men only, however; from 1884 almost all men over twenty-one appear in them, and from 1918 women over thirty. Women over twenty-one were given the right to vote in 1928, though they can be found in the local government election Burgess Rolls after 1869 if they had the necessary property qualification. Normally, electoral registers are now in street order; but some authorities maintain name indexes (available for some London boroughs before the Second World War, for example), and many nineteenth century registers are in alphabetical order of surname ward by ward. However, there were many reasons why eligible electors were excluded from the registers; see Seymour, 1970.

Early telephone directories are rare. They date from 1880 and contain relatively few individuals before the second world war; my copy of the local 1935 telephone directory covers, in one volume which is smaller than two of the present London directories, the whole of Lancashire, the Isle of Man, Cumberland, Westmorland, Durham, Northumberland, Yorkshire and much of Cheshire; only one household in twenty was then on the 'phone. British Telecom itself has a full set of these directories, but it is in London at 135, Queen Victoria St, EC4V 4AT. They welcome postal enquiries.

Of greater use for obtaining addresses are the town or county trade directories, of which Kelly's is the most famous. These directories do not normally pretend to list all householders, let alone all inhabitants, though the town ones are fuller than the county. They were first developed in the seventeenth century in order to give commercial salesmen an idea of where potential customers lived. By the 1770s, they were being issued for large towns such as Liverpool and Manchester, where the notorious Mrs Raffald combined her interests in running a boarding house for commercial travellers with producing the town's first directory. By the nineteenth century, most towns and counties had directories issued at regular intervals. Acquiring them is now an expensive undertaking for the antiquarian book collector. Lists of known directories have been compiled (Goss, 1932; Norton, 1950) and most public libraries and record offices possess at least a few nineteenth century editions for their own area.

There are also more specialised directories which are useful to those who have ancestors in certain trades, occupations or professions. The earliest are those for law and the armed services, but in the nineteenth century other professions followed suit. They often have the added advantage of including academic qualifications and where they were obtained; reference to the educational records (see pages 31–6) can then lead to more information, including parents. The list which follows is not comprehensive, but it includes series which were being published regularly before the second world war. (The year given for each entry is the earliest date of publication.)

Annual Register of Pharmaceutical Chemists, 1842
Army List, 1642, annual from 1702
Catholic Directory, 1837
Chemical Industry Directory & Who's Who, 1923
Congregational Yearbook, 1847
Crockford's Clerical Directory, 1858
Dentists' Register, 1879
Directory of Directors, 1880
Directory of Insurance Brokers, 1922
Directory of Shipowners, Shipbuilders & Marine Engineers, 1903
Dod's Parliamentary Companion, 1832
Electrical Contractors' Association Yearbook, 1918
General Assembly of Unitarian & Free Christian Churches Yearbook, 1890
Incorporated Brewers' Guild Directory, 1924
Incorporated Society of Musicians – Handbook and Register of Members, 1900
Institute of Actuaries Yearbook, 1928
Jewish Year Book, 1896
Law List, 1775
Lloyd's Register of Shipping: Register Book, 1764
Lloyd's Register of Shipping: Register of Yachts, 1878
Masonic Year Book, 1775
Medical Directory, 1845
Medical Register, 1859
Methodist Church, 1847
Navy List, 1772
Register of Architects, 1932
Religious Society of Friends: Book of Meetings, 1801
Royal College of Veterinary Surgeons: Register & Directory, 1844

Royal Society of London: Yearbook and List of Fellows, 1898
Royal Society of Tropical Medicine & Hygiene, 1908
Salvation Army Yearbook, 1906
Schoolmasters' Yearbook & Directory, 1903
Solicitors' Diary, 1844
Wisden, 1864

We put addresses on a wide variety of documents during our lifetime of course, but a large number, such as most income tax returns and DHSS records are destroyed. Among those which do survive, however, are rate books of many kinds which may exist from the last three centuries. Rates have been known under other names – assessment, ley, and mize for example – and are usually thought of as a local tax; but a rate is a collection for a specific undertaking whose cost is calculated in advance and divided between those rateable; so a rate could be national and a tax could be local. The oldest rate books were those of the parish officers, and are to be found in the parish chest. They are well described by Tate (1983) and Darlington (1962) and include the poor rates, collected by the overseers of the poor, the church rates, collected by the churchwardens, and the highways rates, collected by the constables or highway officials. These rate books will normally provide details of who paid, or was due to pay the rates concerned, and will perhaps also describe the properties which formed the basis of their assessment.

By the nineteenth century however, when the question of addresses becomes more acute for the genealogist, the county or borough rates are of much more use. Local authority rate books can provide exact addresses sometimes decades before they become available in directories or electoral rolls. They are normally to be found in the archives of the rating authority concerned, whether it be county or borough. The archivist can advise you about which books exist and how to locate any one person within them from information you already possess.

Addresses are also given in the published National Roll of the Great War, on jurors' lists (among Quarter Sessions papers in the CROs), on dog licence applications (see Dowell, 1965), in trade union records (see pages 39–40), in school registers (see pages 31–6), and in Boards of Guardians' outdoor relief papers; (see *Local Historian*, Vol. 16, No. 1, Feb. 1984).

If you suspect that your ancestor was a member of any form of society, trade union, association or profession, you should always contact its modern headquarters in order to find out whether there is any information (accessible on request to the general public) about individual members (see for example, pages 30, 88). The police and Post Office, for instance, can be very helpful with information about former employees.

Censuses 1841–1881

It is no longer necessary to travel to the PRO in order to see the census returns for these years. For some time now, local libraries have been buying microfilm copies of returns for their own areas and it is normal for a CRO to have film for all five censuses taken between 1841 and 1881. These usually cover the whole county. Exceptions include Lancashire, whose enormous nineteenth century population makes this procedure very costly. It would also mean duplicating holdings already in the large towns and cities within the county. Regrettably, census copies are one of an increasing number of records for which some CRO's are now having to make an access charge.

An excellent source for all local historians is Gibson (4), who lists the holdings (years and areas) of copy census material in local reference institutions. He has also produced a companion pamphlet (6) which lists the areas which have produced surname indexes to censuses, a development which has been encouraged by various family history societies. There is now a name index for the whole of Nottinghamshire in 1851, for example. In addition, Mormon libraries (at cost of postage) will make available to any visiting member of the public a specified census reel, not just from England and Wales but from anywhere in the world where census microfilming is permissible. Requests should be sent to the librarian in advance of a visit, as he might have to order the film from stock or have it copied in Salt Lake City. It should be added that genealogists owe a considerable debt of gratitude to the Mormons for opening their facilities to the general public in this way.

The information available for England and Wales for each person in the 1841 census is as follows: township or street; names of all living persons in household; age, normally rounded down to the nearest five years, except for those under fifteen, for whom exact ages should be given; occupation; and whether or not the individuals were living in their county of birth, or were born in

Scotland ('S'), Ireland ('I') or foreign parts ('F'). The answer to the last question is quite unhelpful; a 'Yes' might mean that he or she had been born in the same house or at the other end of the county; a 'No' might mean a hundred yards away across the county boundary, or at the other end of the country. 'S' can mean anywhere north of the border, sometimes referred to as 'North Britain'. An improvement made in 1851 and in subsequent censuses until 1951, was to ask for place of birth. The naturalised foreign-born were distinguished from 1861. In 1961 and subsequently, however, the question again asked for country instead of place of birth. Another improvement in the 1851 returns is that everyone had to give their exact age and state their relationship to the head of the household.

When using the census, you should try to copy the names of all the people in the same house, and, if possible, in the adjoining houses, if the occupants have the same surnames. It was common for relatives to live quite close to each other, but the relationship between households will not be clear from the census itself. The information might fall into place only after subsequent research. Thus, almost at the very point (1837) before which there are no birth certificates, the census will tell you where everyone was born and how old they were, as well as the identity of parents of children who were living at home at the time. Needless to say, all this sounds too good to be true, and once again there are many reasons why this source of information can fail to give you the answers you want.

Failure to find individual addresses in the census

Alternative sources for discovering people's addresses have already been described in my discussion of censuses which are less than a hundred years old (pages 41–5); but knowing the address you are looking for is one thing, finding it is quite another. In rural areas, where addresses were often not used in the nineteenth century, the fact that no address is known will create few difficulties because it takes relatively little time – under an hour – to search the census returns for whole parishes with up to 4,000 inhabitants; for urban areas, the census abstract might help to locate the registration district of a particular township. For towns of over 40,000 inhabitants, in some cases occupying up to thirty thousand census sheets, street indexes are available. These are listed by

Gibson (4). In addition, individual libraries have often prepared their own street indexes. These will tell you which enumeration district, hence which reel of microfilm, contains the address you want. Such indexes are not infallible guides, however, and you sometimes need to use other methods in order to locate 'missing' streets. These methods are described below.

The main problem, clearly, is in those towns with large populations but, because they are somewhat under 40,000, have no street indexes. If you have plenty of time to spare, of course, you will simply require patience and reasonable eyesight. A short cut is to apply for a detailed map which marks the boundaries between enumeration districts, and to locate the address where your ancestors lived, on a contemporary map if possible; once the enumeration district has been identified by using the two maps in conjunction, the address can be found relatively quickly from the reel list which the librarian will have. However, such maps do not exist for all urban areas. At the start of each enumeration district in the census, you will find a description of its geographical boundaries.

The address occasionally cannot be found by this method because some small streets are unnamed on maps; in this case, consult a contemporary town directory. This should have a full street index, normally in its first few pages. Small streets can then be found, next to the larger streets off which they run; you can then find the larger street first in the census.

There is a slight possibility that the enumerator himself missed the household or even the street altogether, as apparently happened to Grosvenor Square in 1851, or that the PRO has missed a section during microfilming (which is happening to perhaps one page in a thousand); or once again that you have missed the address through tiredness, eyestrain, or illegibility of the microfilm copy. The latter is a particular problem with the 1861 census. You should also remember that when the PRO makes a microfilm copy, it is of the returns based on geographical boundaries as they existed at the time of the census concerned. Subsequent boundary changes must be taken into account, and your librarian or archivist will advise you how to find out what these changes have been.

Even when you have found the street, you may be unable to find the number of the house. There are three basic reasons why this happens. Firstly, the census enumerator sometimes failed to enter the house numbers, and indeed in 1841 it was not normal for them to be included at all. Marks in the edge of the columns containing people's names are the only indication where family groups and households end. Do not be confused by the number in the extreme left-hand column; this is an enumeration number, not a house number. Secondly, it was normal for the enumerator to start another street before he had completed the previous one. A main road would be covered down one side only until a side road was reached; the side road might then be completed, at which point the main road would be resumed. Searching for an inhabitant of the main road therefore might mean having to pass over the returns from several side streets before your number is reached. One long street might be in more than one enumeration district, and you may have to consult several reels in order to cover it from end to end.

Thirdly, it is worth remembering that Victorian cities grew very rapidly, that streets changed their names, and that sometimes they had more than one house sporting the same number. Arthur Harry Pole was born at 4, Mycock Street, Manchester in May, 1862; at the time of the 1861 census the street had not yet been built and by 1871 it had changed its name. Finding his family in the census would be impossible unless the change is recognised.

British ships in port or in navigable rivers on census night should be found in 1851 and later censuses, but not in 1841.

Failure to find individuals in the census
Even if you find the street, and find the house, you still might not find the person you are looking for. The usual reason is that the family was not living there, for the chances are only one in over 3,650 that the source of the address – a marriage certificate, for example – has the same date as the census. If the whole family has moved, you might consider buying another certificate, that of the birth of an ancestor's sibling, for example, closer to a census date. There was an astonishing amount of movement in Victorian towns, before the days of mass home-ownership and council housing. (Even today, the average family moves once every ten years, with high mobility in London and the south, lowest in Wales and Yorkshire. Residential mobility is particularly high at

times of marriage, childbearing, widowhood, and nowadays divorce.) If the address has been obtained for a directory or electoral register, it is worth remembering that these documents were compiled months before the date which appears on the title page. Find a directory for 1872 or even 1873 if your ancestor was not living at the address shown in an 1871 directory at the time of the 1871 census.

The census is taken on a particular date (which changes from decade to decade) in the spring. In 1841, this was 6 June (see *Family History News and Digest* vol. 1, no. 2, p. 38); in 1851, the evening of 30/31 March; 1861, 7/8 April; 1871, 2/3 April; and 1881, 3/4 April. The enumerator's schedule should show those who were actually at the address on the date in question, not those who normally lived there. Occasionally, the same individual was entered at two addresses – but a genealogist's usual problem is not to find the entry at all. If he had died the night before; if she was visiting relatives; if he was in jail; if she was working as a domestic servant living in the house of her employer; in short, if anything had taken your ancestor away from home that evening, the entry will not be found with the rest of the family. The statistician John Rickman, who had a major hand in designing and analysing the first censuses, objected to holding it on a Sunday because so many Londoners were 'out of town', and the first four were held on a Monday. In and since 1841, it has been taken on a Sunday evening, but the late date in 1841 meant that many were away on holiday. A few families even moved before the enumerators could collect the schedules which had been distributed to them; at Hollingworth, Cheshire, for example, an unnamed family in the 1861 census had 'removed and taken the schedule with them', and one of my students discovered an ancestor recorded simply as 'occupant found dead'.

There were other causes of omission. There was a widespread belief that very young infants, particularly those not yet baptised, should not be included in the returns, and it has been estimated that up to 4 per cent of children under five years old are missing from the 1841 census and perhaps 3 per cent from the three later ones. From all censuses until 1911, up to 6 per cent of all children under the age of 1 year were omitted. Very few individuals actually refused to complete the schedule, but sometimes the number of children returned is smaller than the actual number in the family in order to avoid accusations of overcrowding. If the whole family is 'missing', they were simply living elsewhere at the time; if individual members were missing, it should not be assumed that they had died, or that you have found the wrong family – though of course this is possible. It was very common for teenage girls to be living away from home in the mid-nineteenth century, and for boys to have left home altogether by the time they were eighteen. Also, enumerators simply missed people.

Children of remarried widows should be entered with their original surname, but are sometimes to be found with their stepfather's surname (see page 98).

If the address you have is from a marriage certificate, you should realise that a large number of brides and grooms married from their future partner's home address, or from an address of convenience, in order to fulfil residence requirements; if it is from a death certificate, remember that the deceased might not have died at home – and in one instance I know of, the place of death was incorrectly stated anyway. A funeral director of my acquaintance once helped to carry a corpse from a public house (where the deceased's wife had forbidden him to go) to the house of a friend, whose address then appeared on the death certificate.

Other mistakes arise from the fact that, from 1851, the enumerators had to rely on a schedule which was completed by the head of each household or, in the case of institutions such as prisons, by the head of the institution, who often recorded individuals by initials instead of full names. Unfortunately for the genealogist, these schedules were destroyed many years later by the GRO, so we are left with the enumerators' interpretation of what the householder had written, or what he was told by those too illiterate to complete the form. Enumerators were actually instructed to alter what they thought was 'manifestly false'; the supervising district registrars often made 'corrective' changes, and so did the clerks at the census office who did the final counting. The last, by the way, are responsible for those marginal ticks which sometimes mislead you into thinking that your ancestor recorded the fact that he or she was deaf and dumb in the final column. It was not unknown for Victorian enumerators themselves to be accused of being poorly educated (they were supposed to be between eighteen and sixty-five, to be literate and to have some knowledge of the area of between 25 and 200 houses which they each covered); they certainly varied markedly in their ability to apply the instructions, though these variations are more serious for the historical sociologist than for the genealogist. One recent survey shows that a quarter of forms in Manchester had to be filled in by the enumerators because the respondents were illiterate, and that in one sub-division the figure was as high as two-thirds.

Finally, if there was more than one street of the same name, they might be indexed together, giving the impression that only one of them appears in the census, whereas both should be found if all the references are followed through. Thus, in 1861, there are two addresses for 27, Chapel Street, Salford in two separate streets – but the two are merged in the index. If you did not know that there were two such addresses, you would probably miss the second one, having found the first.

Censuses 1801–1831

I have already mentioned that the 1801 to 1831 returns containing the names of individuals were destroyed as soon as the statistical information had been extracted. However, over the last few years, various local copies of the original returns have been coming to light, together with additional data collected at the time. Those which have been housed in record repositories or written into parish registers are listed by Gibson (4). Compared with later censuses, however, these early returns contain less information, as from 1811 only the head of the household was named. The census dates were 10 March, 1801, 27 May, 1811, 28 May, 1821 and 30 May, 1831. The armed forces, registered seamen and convicts were not to be enumerated.

Because the surviving documents are not those officially returned, and are not always in the form requested, they vary in content. At the least you should find the names of all householders in 1811, 1821 and 1831 (arranged in order of named streets), the number of families living in each house and information about occupations. In 1821, the ages of all males and females are given separately in groups of five years. This question was voluntary for enumerators to ask and respondents to answer, but it seems to have elicited a 90 per cent completion rate. Some large towns in the north and midlands and many parts of London did not make this return, however. The 1831 census is less complete, providing simply the number of males aged twenty or over.

It is clear that the enumerators – the Overseers of the Poor – went to the trouble in some areas of finding out the names and ages of all the inhabitants (as at Winwick in Lancashire), even though in 1801 they were not asked even to name anyone in their official returns.

Church baptism, 1538 to the present day

The most important documents which can be used to trace parents prior to 1837 are records of baptism. (Quakers, and sometimes Baptists, recorded births.) It is perhaps worth stressing that baptismal registers continue down to the present day. While it is true that before 1837 you have to rely basically on church records, it is perfectly possible, especially in country areas where there might be only one or two local churches and where the influence of the clergy remained much stronger than in the towns, to trace a line of ancestors back to the sixteenth century by using parish registers alone. I have done it. The proliferation of churches in urban areas makes these registers more difficult to use in the nineteenth century, but town and county directories, as well as *Crockford's Clerical Directory*, should indicate the foundation date of each church, and the *National Index of Parish Registers* (Steel, 1968) will eventually provide the dates covered by the registers themselves.

Whatever your religion now, it is most probable that your forebears attended the Church of England if they lived in England over a century and a half ago. The further back in time the truer this becomes until, in 1700 and earlier, probably 95 per cent of the population are to be found in Anglican records. Strictly speaking, the phrase 'parish register' applies to the Anglican registers of baptism, marriage and burial, though it is nowadays colloquially (but incorrectly) applied to similar registers kept by other denominations (pages 78–80), the 'non-parochial' registers.

Whole books have been written about parish registers, so once again I do not propose to go into historical detail, which may be obtained from Burn (1829), Waters (1883), Steel (1968 ff.), Tate (1983) and Cox (1974). There are, however, some basic features of these documents which the genealogist should know, as without this information you cannot use the registers properly.

In common with most handwritten documents of the time, registers in the sixteenth and the greater part of the seventeenth centuries are written in a form of handwriting called secretary script. At first, the beginner may scarcely recognise the words as English, but with remarkably little practice it becomes legible without undue difficulty. *Amateur Historian* vol. 1, no. 5, Gardner and Smith (1956) vol. 3 and Hector (1980) may help at first with acquiring the skill, but there is no real substitute for attempting to read the real thing without guidance or transcription. Record offices will supply relatively cheap photocopies of secretary script of varying difficulty which you have identified. Distinguish between f and s, c and r, C and T and that is half the battle.

Another problem, which appears far worse to the beginner than it really is, is the fact that many of the earliest registers – up to the middle of the seventeenth century and a few beyond – are written in Latin. Surnames are not normally latinised, however, and the Latin words for the months of the year are easily recognisable. Days of the month are in roman numerals, with the final 'i' usually written as 'j'; the years themselves are in our own arabic numerals. The only problem, therefore, is in translating Christian names, occupations and such phrases as 'son of', 'widow' and so on. Even here, many are easily recognisable, but useful lists will be found in *Amateur Historian*, vol. 1, no. 10 and Steel (1968), vol. 1, pp. 110–112, 239–244.

Most textbooks on tracing family trees give forewarnings about spelling. Before the nineteenth century, officials were not very scrupulous about the way in which people spell their names; illiteracy was common anyway, and dialects stronger. The result is that the same person might have his or her name written in various ways, even in the same document, so that it will be a very unusual family tree which has a surname which never varies. Mander (1984) counted 36 ways of spelling Dixon, and one of my students, surnamed Pridgeon, has found 45 variations of his name (excluding one used by a lady who called him Mr. Prartridge!). Over time, variations of spelling and pronunciation might even change the name of a family. The grandfather of 'my' Sarah Hargreaves normally called himself 'Hargreave', but his grandfather was called 'Hargrave' which has quite a different origin. It is also possible that when names were very similar those who wrote the registers were more particular than usual about spelling in order to distinguish one family from another.

Until 1752, New Year's Day was celebrated on 25 March, not 1 January, so that December 1700 was followed by January 1700 in the registers. In a Christian country, of course, it was quite logical to use the day of Christ's conception as the beginning of the new year. In 1751, eleven days were lost at the time of changeover, with some odd results. May blossom has since appeared in June, and people alive on 2nd September 1751 could celebrate two birthdays a year. More pertinently for us, a child might appear to be born before the marriage of the parents, even though it was legitimate.

The information contained in baptismal records has varied over time and there was no standardised entry until 1 January, 1813. From their starting date in 1538, many contained the name only of the child, but perhaps this was the result of the order of 1597/8 which asked for all the older entries to be copied up in a book of parchment. As no pay was provided, it would be understandable if some clergymen copied only the barest essentials – the names of the children. Others took another easy way out; they seem to have done the minimum requested, and copied the old registers only as far back as the start of the reign of the then queen, Elizabeth I (1558); others did nothing at all. From the early seventeenth century however, if not before, parental names – the essential information for genealogists – begin to be included in the baptismal entry; as the next two centuries passed, other information also appeared. At first, we are perhaps given the name of the child's father, then of the mother, and later of the township within the parish, especially in the large parishes of northern England which contained several townships.

It must be stressed that this is not necessarily the way in which each register changed over time – there might be a regression to scant information when the incumbent changed, and there is often a wide discrepancy of styles between parishes. A typical baptismal entry from Whitegate in Cheshire reads: 'William, son of Jonathan and Mary Nickson, baptised 24 January, 1779'. At the same time at Witton, a chapelry in the adjoining parish of Great Budworth, the register is much fuller. 'Ellen, daughter of Samuel Walley of Witton, labourer, the reputed father (son of John and

Katherine Walley of Witton) and Betty Ravenscroft (daughter of Ralph and Ellen Ravescroft of Witton), born 13 December, 1778, baptised 6 January, 1779'. The north of England has a number of these very full registers, especially around York, following a directive from Archbishop Markham in 1777. They are, of course, a goldmine for demographic, as well as genealogical, research.

An Act of Parliament of 1812 (George Rose's Act) led to baptisms in the Church of England being entered on a standard form in printed books from 1 January, 1813. Most, though not all, parishes adopted the new forms, which are still in use to the present day, with significant amendments in 1978. Following the introduction of a stamp duty in 1783, and up to 1813, a few parishes were already using printed forms which provided a space for date of birth as well as baptism. For some parishes, standardisation in 1813 was a retrograde step, because the new forms required less information than the parish had entered in its pre-1813 registers. At Witton, however, a vestry meeting decided that their own system was so superior to the new one being introduced by Parliament that they would maintain the old in tandem with the new; they did so until 1862. A typical George Rose entry reads: 'Sarah, daughter of Thomas and Sarah Smith, joiner, of Witton, baptised 10 January, 1819'; the auxiliary register gives this as 'Sarah, daughter of Thomas Smith of Witton, joiner, (son of John and Betty Smith of Northwich) and Sarah (daughter of Samuel and Betty Wilcockson of Witton), born 20 December, 1818 and baptised 10 January 1819'. Thus, two entries from this register could cover six generations of the same family.

Entries for illegitimate children in parish registers before 1813 sometimes name only the mother. They often contain an additional term of disapprobation such as 'base', 'bastard', 'B', 'chanceling', 'illegal', 'lamebegot', 'merrybegot', 'nothus', 'spuriosus', 'viciatus', 'scapebegot' and even 'dratsab'. It is not uncommon for the name of the reputed father or fathers to be given also, especially after an Act of 1634 which required the recording of the names of both parents at baptism. In the seventeenth century, an illegitimate child might carry an 'alias' in his or her surname when an adult. Thus, John Smith alias Jones would have a father and mother who were not married to each other, one called Smith and the other Jones. John Smith alias Jones might then grow up, marry, and have children who themselves would carry the surname Smith alias Jones, and occasionally so might their children. In more modern times, illegitimacy has been the origin of some hyphenated surnames. An alias did not always denote illegitimacy, however; see Steel (1968) Vol 1, pages 89–96.

There were large numbers of illegitimate children in the days of our forefathers, and a great deal of research has investigated the phenomenon. It was once thought to be related to a high average age of marriage, or to other economic factors or social customs such as 'bundling' or trial marriage, a practice which lasted into the nineteenth century as a means of establishing whether a marriage would prove fruitful. However, the pattern of illegitimacy is one which has not yet been fully analysed, and the reasons for it seem to be more subtle than any of the above explanations. For one thing, it was more common in some areas than others – counties from Gloucestershire north to Lancashire had higher rates than the rest of the country, even long before the industrial revolution. The national rates have varied over time, with a peak of up to 5 per cent in 1590, a dramatic fall in the 1650s (the time of the Puritan ascendancy), a slow rise to 6 per cent by 1800 and to almost 7 per cent by 1845. (To put those figures in perspective, the 1984 rate was about 20%). It was unconnected with urbanisation, with the average age of marriage or with the ratio of men to women at any one time. The biggest mystery lies in the fact that the *proportion* of illegitimate children varied with the *actual* number of children born – the greater the number of births, the greater the proportion of bastards. Servants in rural areas were particularly likely to be mothers of illegitimate children; they were away from parental control and often denied the normal formalities of courtship. (See Turner, 1962).

If your ancestor was illegitimate, you can normally trace the tree only through the female line, but there are one or two ways to discover the father even if he is not named in the register. (It should be admitted, however, that most fathers who are named anywhere at all are to be found in the parish register entry, and occasionally more than one possible father is given!) The most common way is through bastardy papers, which are to be found among the parish poor law records. The mother of an illegitimate child who might require poor relief from the parish was interrogated in order that the father could be named, the onus of paying for the child's upkeep placed upon him, and even forced to marry, until the practice was made illegal in 1844. Quarter sessions papers and vestry minute books also refer to the problems caused to the parish by individual cases, and a few parishes have registers of bastards. For relevant legislation, see Tate, (1983), and the discussion of baptisms in other parishes on pages 58–69.

Until the Adoption Act of 1958, adopted children were sometimes (re) baptised as though the adoptive parents were the natural parents. Section 25 of that Act laid down that the entry should be marked "Adopted son or daughter of . . .", but I believe that this applies only to the Church of England.

With foundlings, unfortunately, you are almost always at a dead end. Such children had to be given names, and often these tell a little story in themselves about the child's circumstances. For example at Nantwich on 13 March, 1735 a child was baptised and recorded as 'Hannah Tuesday, a foundling'. I wonder how many other people whose names contain days of the week or months of the year are descended from foundlings. An entry for 1 February, 1593 in nearby Acton is the baptism of 'Matilda ignoramus' – 'Matilda [whose surname] we do not know'.

To look after these unfortunates, Captain Coram founded the nation's first foundling hospital in 1741. He accepted unwanted children who were left in a basket suspended from the perimeter wall, taking children from all over the country until 1760, when a grant from the government was discontinued.

The records of the more famous Dr Barnardo's begin in 1871 and are full from 1885. These are now deposited with the University of Liverpool, but only those over a hundred years old are available for research. For children 'adopted' before 1927 who assume a new surname (see page 24), the original parents are usually impossible to trace unless the family has preserved an individual record of the event.

Failure to find an Anglican baptism

Following a family through several generations in a parish register is often quite easy. Until the end of the last century, the baptisms of several children to the same parents, usually with an average of two years between each child, will have been preceded by a marriage which, in turn, arose from two baptisms twenty to thirty years earlier. It all sounds very simple until the genealogist is forced to conclude from his or her own research that long before the twentieth century – indeed long before the industrial revolution – there was much more geographical movement among the population than most people realise. There are several reasons why you might not find the baptism you are looking for and in each case, various possible courses of action to take. Sooner or later, however, you will encounter an insuperable problem, but the fascination is, of course, that you never really know whether it can be solved or not.

There is one important piece of advice which will help you to decide which course of action to take. You should make a note of all the occurrences of the surname you are looking for in the probable parish, and in those which surround it, building up their individual family trees just before and during the time when you expected to find your 'missing' baptism. The end papers of this book illustrate this stage of research into the origin of an ancestor whose baptism could not be discovered. This will establish the likelihood of a local birth and may reveal clues as to where the child had been baptised. Note also if the register provides evidence of mobility, and where the migrants had come from. A gap in the regular two-yearly production of children probably means an early death or miscarriage, but there may be other explanations. Conception was more likely if the mother was not breast-feeding the previous child.

Baptism in another parish

Do not be surprised if your ancestors moved from parish to parish even before the industrial revolution. Peter Spufford (quoted in *Local Population Studies*, vol. 4) concludes his research into seventeenth century mobility by suggesting that very large numbers did not live where they had been born, and that almost half the population did not die where they had been born. The most mobile appear to have been unmarried people aged over fifteen. Movement was largely limited, however, to a twenty-mile radius. Baptism in another parish is therefore such a common problem that before 1851, when the census began to include place of birth, it is worth looking at an actual case in order to see how it can be solved.

Thomas Darlington married Mary Houghland at Frodsham in

1745, but a search of the Frodsham register shows no baptism for him – indeed, there was no Darlington family in the parish when Thomas was probably baptised in about 1720. If only he had been given a more unusual name, like the Valentine Darlington who had been born at Whitegate nearby in the late seventeenth century! Alas, he had to be a Thomas, and several possible baptisms can be found in the notional twenty mile radius. (Fortunately, Frodsham is on the coast, which reduces the search somewhat.)

The first assumption to make is that he was born in a neighbouring parish and that his baptism took place in the parish of birth, although this rule, like so many others, was sometimes broken. Research through the registers of a series of parishes can nowadays be much easier than it used to be (just how easy depends on which county you are searching) by using the massive index being compiled by the Mormon church, about which more later. Even if you can find only one potentially correct baptism, you should then answer the following questions, in sequence, in order to reduce to a minimum the likelihood of error:

Did the child die before reaching adulthood?
Was the child later married in its parish of birth?
Did the child in turn have children in the parish of birth?
Did the child's father or other relative leave a will, making indentification possible?
Does your ancestor's age at death accord with this baptismal date?
Did other members of the family also move to the new parish?
Is there an MI (see pages 128–9) which would provide the names of other relatives?

In Tarvin, a parish bordering on Frodsham, one Thomas, son of Thomas Darlington, was baptised in 1719, twenty-six years before the marriage concerned. Was this the correct baptism? The Thomas baptised in 1719 did not die as a child; nor did he marry at Tarvin – so hopes rise that he is the right one. In the Tarvin baptismal register for the 1740s and '50s however, there he is, having children himself – so he has to be eliminated as he cannot be the man who married in 1745 at Frodsham.

Meanwhile, the Mormon index has produced three other possible baptisms, each of which will have to be checked in turn in the same way. This index is the start of a massive undertaking by the Church of Jesus Christ of Latter Day Saints (LDS) to computerise the extant records of birth, baptism and marriage of everyone who has ever lived. Members of the Church may then have the satisfaction of knowing that their deceased ancestors can, after the appropriate ceremonies, have the choice of becoming a Mormon or not. For most genealogists the end product of this indexing is a set of microfiche cards on which, in the case of England, each county is presented separately with the entries arranged in alphabetical order of surname. All Welsh entries are indexed together by surname or Christian name, and require some care in using – see Gibson (9). The computer updates the index daily, and the microfiche cards are reissued in expanded form every few years. Its name is now the International Genealogical Index (IGI). It was formerly known as the Computer File Index, and many librarians know it simply as the Mormon microfiche. Some family history societies and libraries have the fiche for the whole country, and it is available at LDS genealogical libraries, where the whole world's index can be consulted. Large public libraries and record offices normally have copies for their own and adjoining counties, and some (including Huddersfield) have facilities for issuing printouts of individual pages. Gibson (9) give the most complete list available for the location of IGI copies.

Using the index is very easy. If I am looking for, say, the baptism of a John Peatfield in Nottinghamshire in the 1750s, I look up the surname in the county microfiche, perhaps finding it mixed up with variations such as Peetfield, but nevertheless with the spelling identical to that in the original register. The information I expect to find against each entry is as follows: name; name of parents (or name of spouse in the case of a marriage entry); sex; husband or wife; date and parish of the event; type of entry ('A' for adult baptism, 'B' for birth, 'C' for christening, 'M' for marriage, and so on); three columns relating to the Mormons' religious ceremonies (the word 'cleared' in these columns means that the temple ceremonies were still pending at the time of computerisation); and references to the batch and serial sheet from which the entry has been taken. If the tenth column reference contains only digits, no letters, the first two will refer to the year (and the next three the day) in which the entry was computerised from information submitted by an individual. If the third number is less than 4, you can write to the Church for a copy of the original information sheet, which will include the name and address of the person who was interested enough in the entry to have it put into the Index, and perhaps get in touch with the person concerned to exchange information. You should send the relevant batch and serial number, with the county and name of the individual entry concerned, to the English Division, Genealogical Department, 50 East North Temple Street, Salt Lake City, Utah 84150, enclosing 25c for each sheet you require, (minimum $2). Following a long, unsuccessful attempt to find the deaths of my great-great grandparents, I have contacted relatives in the United States by using the IGI, who were able to tell me that most of the family had emigrated to Idaho in the early 1870s.

The IGI, however, has its drawbacks, and it is particularly important to know what these are if the entry you are seeking is not apparently on the Index. The proportion of surviving baptisms and marriages incorporated into the IGI varies considerably from county to county – in the city of London you can expect to find over 90%, but Herefordshire and Somerset only 4%. (The average is about 25%). See the *Genealogists' Magazine*, Vol. 21, No. 3 (Sept. 1983). Naturally, in an undertaking as large as this, human error is unavoidable; in the IGI, such errors can take several forms. Occasionally, entries from one parish are placed in the wrong county, such as those of Formby, Lancashire, which appeared to be across the entire north of England, and all the pre-1813 West Drayton entries, which were scattered elsewhere; in some cases, names are transcribed incorrectly – for example, Apolline Winstanley, who was married at Middlewich in 1686, appears as Apolonia Whinston, and is indexed under Whinston, with the result that no one looking for Apolline Winstanley would find her, except by accident. It has been estimated that up to 12 per cent of the Ilfracombe entries were incorrect. Part of the blame for this must lie in the employment of some transcribers who are not native English speakers.

Other problems for the genealogist arise not necessarily from faults within the IGI but from a failure to understand what it offers. The index contains almost no burials, so that, unless the word 'infant' appears in columns 5 and 6, there is no way of telling whether the person survived to marriageable age. No date of birth is included with a baptism, even when the original source provides both, so that an adult baptism could be overlooked by the searcher because it occurs at an unlikely date. The list of parishes included in the index, listed by county on a separate microfiche or print-out, can be misleading; for example, 'Runcorn baptisms 1700–1750' might mean that *all* the baptisms between these dates have been included, or only a few; you should suspect undertranscribing if the reference number in column 10 begins with a digit rather than a letter.

Finally, a word of warning about the arrangement of the names within the Index. I think that the surnames used to be admirably arranged, though even here the separate indexing of, for example, Tickle and Tittle, could be a reason for overlooking entries. So long as the transcript is correct, there should have been few problems in finding the surname you wanted if you searched the obvious variations. The 1981 edition was not arranged as conveniently as earlier ones, however, and many variants had to be checked separately in strictly alphabetical order. Fortunately, the 1984 edition returned to the 1978 format. Within each surname the Christian names are arranged alphabetically, and the events concerning each Christian name are presented in the chronological order in which they originally occurred. However, each variation in the spelling or even an abbreviation is treated as a separate Christian name. Eliz, Eliza, Elizabeth, Elizth, Betty, Liza, Betsy, Bess and so on are given separate lists, strictly as the transcriber had read the original register. Even Eliz and Eliz. are kept apart. Between Ino and John (two common forms of the same name) many other names would intervene, so that several names have to be passed over if you are to be sure that you have searched all the variations under which the entry you are seeking might have originally appeared. A considerable portion of the alphabet lies between Anne and Hannah, or Ellen and Helen.

It must always be remembered that, even when an entry has provided the correct answer, this is still only an index and not a substitute for looking up the record in the original parish register, where additional information will often be provided.

If the above methods fail to locate the baptism you are seeking, and there is no census or gravestone record to help you identify the place of birth, the search has to be extended geographically to cover even more parishes. This somewhat daunting task becomes very tedious and is an obvious danger point where the less committed may give up hope. However, even with a Smith or Jones (of which there were rarely a large number in any English parish before the industrial revolution) there are always ways of narrowing this search. Many of the documents dealt with in Parts II, III, and IV can help in locating families of the surname you are seeking when the baptism probably occurred. Your choice, of course, will depend on the period in which your missing baptism occurs, but the fullest are the GRO indexes. See Camp, 1987.

The earliest sources normally used by amateur genealogists to locate individual family names are probably the tax returns known as Lay Subsidies. These were paid by the laity from the late thirteenth to the seventeenth centuries and were levied by the monarch to pay for the armed forces in wartime. On certain personal property, the tax was fixed at the rate of one-tenth for townsmen and one-fifteenth for country-dwellers, but it is estimated that no more than one third of households were actually assessed as wealthy enough to pay. From 1290 and 1334, the returns provide individual names, but for the next two centuries only village totals are given. Then in 1524, when the annual value of land was taxed at 20 per cent and goods at 2/8 in the £, names reappear and continue until the Lay Subsidy died out.

Most of the returns are among the Exchequer records in the PRO. The earlier ones can be very difficult to read, but many have been printed by local record societies or in works on topographical history. Some have copies in CROs, surviving to the seventeenth century; (see *Amateur Historian*, vol. 3, no. 8; vol. 4, no. 3 for an historical introduction).

Additionally, several other documents which list inhabitants prior to the full 1801 census can give an indication of where families of certain surnames lived at different times. The earliest known is one for Ealing in 1599, but the first on anything like a national scale is the Protestation of 1642, an unsuccessful petition signed by most of the males in the country over the age of eighteen (occasionally females, and some over 16) which attempted to avert the Civil War. Those who could not write marked a cross against their name; those who did not wish their name to be given in support were also listed. The original petition is in the House of Lords, and the places covered are listed in the fifth report of the Historical Manuscripts Commission (1876), pp. 120–134, obtainable in the largest public libraries. Many of the returns have been published, and a list may be found in the *Genealogist's Magazine*, vol. 19, no. 3. (See vol. 21, no. 9 for the Collection for Distressed

Protestants, also in 1642.)

In 1694, a tax was imposed on all births and marriages, and on bachelors over the age of twenty-five, by the Marriage Duty Act. Many clergymen, who were responsible for collecting the relevant information, compiled lists of existing parishioners which could be used as their base line for assessing future changes; indeed, they were supposed to list all persons by name, social standing, marital status and property ownership. Lists have survived in relatively small numbers, however, and will be found with the other parish records either in the parish chest or in the Diocesan Record Office (DRO). The tax was levied until 1705.

The PRO contains the Association Oath lists of 1696, in which all MPs, freemen, military and civil officers of the crown, gentry and clergy in England and Wales swore loyalty to the House of Orange. Some areas have published their lists. See *The Genealogists' Magazine* vol. 21, no. 4 for a useful list of the areas for which the Oath rolls survive; see also Gibson (7).

In addition to the above, there are potentially a large number of other listings which may be available in individual parishes; local printed histories or the county archivist will be able to give you clues about which ones exist in the parishes and periods you wish to search. Muster rolls should list all able-bodied males between sixteen and sixty; militia lists can be found among the constables' accounts (see Tate, 1983). Muster rolls from the sixteenth century are usually in the PRO, but later ones may be found in the parish chest (see PRO leaflet no. 10). *Ad hoc* censuses are sometimes to be found on bases as wide as a county – for instance there was one in Westmorland in 1787; and pew rents, in the churchwardens' papers, give a very good indication of local surnames. Parishioners were allowed to have a choice of pew at a fixed rate, so that often plans would be drawn up, indicating who was entitled to sit in which part of the church – you can also infer social status from the distance of a pew from the altar or pulpit.

The hearth tax returns are a very useful source for finding families of particular surnames. They are also interesting, though indirect, evidence of your ancestors' wealth. (Probably about 80 per cent of people lived in a house with only one fireplace. This was especially likely to be the case in the countryside.) The tax was collected every six months at a flat rate of one shilling for each fireplace in the house occupied (not necessarily owned). For the period from 1662 until the mid-1670s, lists of assessments or actual taxes paid are in the PRO Exchequer records; those too poor to pay are listed separately at the end of each roll. Thereafter, however, until the tax was abolished in 1689, the government employed private tax collectors who were more interested in profits than making meticulous records. Many CROs have had microfilmed the lists associated with their area, so you need not rely on a visit to London; some even have contemporary copies of the returns, and an increasing number are being published. See Gibson (7).

This was a very unpopular tax because, in the words of the Act which abolished it, its collection 'exposed every man's house to be entered into and searched at pleasure by persons unknown to him', and one of William of Orange's actions *en route* from Torbay to London after his invasion in 1688 was to promise to get rid of it.

In abolishing it he also lost the revenue, and thus developed the window tax (1696 to 1852), which could be assessed without entering the house. There are two main difficulties in using these records, however. Very few are available locally – most are in the PRO once again; and the basis of assessment changed at frequent intervals, which makes interpretation difficult. For a full discussion of this tax, see Dowell (1965), who also lists an astonishing range of other taxes collected during the eighteenth and nineteenth centuries – taxes on people keeping male servants, on people keeping female servants (with bachelors charged double!), on persons possessing silver plate, carriages, horses and dogs (at a rate which is now ½p less than in 1877), on clocks and watches, on people wearing hair powder and so on. Most of the returns for these taxes are in the PRO. Rate books however (discussed on page 44) are more easily available for the purpose of locating families. See also the Poll Tax, page 86.

The Test Oath of 1723, which should have been signed by all male adults (except officials, who had already signed an earlier version) can be found in some CROs, probably arranged by main town centre in the order in which people came to sign it. Those who refused to do so are also listed, but it is clear that both lists are far from complete.

Of greater use to the genealogist looking for surname distribution and the wealth of known ancestors are the land tax records. Though started in 1692, the tax gave rise to easily accessible returns mostly from 1780 to 1832, when payment was a qualification for voting. They are normally to be found in the CROs and supply the names of landowners, land occupiers and the amount of tax payable; they are sometimes arranged in annual bundles for large areas, hence a search through the land occupation history of any one parish may be awkward. See Gibson & Mills, 1984.

Tithe schedules provide a slightly later source for similar information, but with the additional bonus of very large-scale maps which pinpoint exactly where your ancestors lived and perhaps worked. Tithe – an illegal (i.e. unparliamentary) tax of one tenth of a man's annual income, payable to the Church of England – had been a source of irritation for centuries, as Shakespeare and many other writers testify; the same feeling may be seen in Austria today, where tithes are still payable. With the growth of nonconformity and industrialisation, the reforming Whig government of the 1830s finally devised a way of eliminating it without suddenly undermining the financial support of incumbents. (Indeed, tithe still survives in a few small areas.) In establishing a firm basis for a gradual change over the next century, detailed maps were drawn for each parish in which tithes were payable, showing every house, garden and field. The accompanying schedule listed all landowners and land occupiers, the state of cultivation, acreages and the amount of tithe payment. Three copies were made during the next twenty years. One was eventually lodged in the PRO, one stayed with the incumbent of the parish, with whom it should still remain unless deposited in the DRO (though many are now lost), and the third went to the Bishop, who has normally placed his copy in the DRO. The last is the most convenient to use. Several parishes can be seen together; there are the facilities of a map room; and the schedules, which were originally stitched into the right hand end of the map, have in many cases been separated for ease of consultation.

In a few parishes, the clergyman's tithe account books have survived from long before 1836, giving the income from tithe payers in the parish (see *Local Historian*, vol. 14, no. 1).

Genealogists, incidentally, have another reason to be grateful for the tithe system – this is still the way the Mormon church funds its activities, including the IGI.

In parishes where tithe had already been changed into regular cash payments, about one-fifth in all, the tithe commissioners did not carry out this detailed recording procedure. (The East Midlands, for example, has fewer tithe documents than other areas.) But in some parishes enclosure maps and schedules might have survived. These, together with estate maps and any accompanying documents (which might go as far back as the seventeenth century) can provide very similar information about land use and surname distribution. They will probably be in local archive offices.

Among this long list of sources for locating the whereabouts of families of certain surnames at different periods, there are also voting documents. From 1694 until the introduction of the secret ballot in 1872, voting at general elections was open and the results were written down; many were even published, the largest collections being in the British Library and at the Society of Genealogists. These poll books list each voter, the candidate they voted for, and their address and occupation. Often, those who did not exercise their right to vote are also listed.

Original documents are in city or county records offices, and a list of all those in print was published by the History of Parliament Trust in 1953. See also Sims (1984). From these documents you can gather not only surname distributions, but also the way in which your ancestors voted – or perhaps the way in which their employers or landlords expected them to vote! Since 1832, there are also electoral registers (see pages 41–2).

For the rarer surnames, even modern telephone directories can be useful. Your public library should contain directories for the whole of the U.K., representing up to 80% of households in the country. If you put a dot on a map to represent each telephone rented by those with the surname you are tracing, you may be surprised how far this can be used for pinpointing the geographical origins of surnames. Most families will be represented in the main industrial centres, in London and across the south coast; but try to spot those parts of the country where the surname seems to be over-represented compared with the actual population size. You can examine areas as small as a county with useful results.

We have still not exhausted the ways of locating baptism in an unknown parish. If the mother's parish is known, you should try there for the baptism of at least her eldest children. This was a fairly common practice, perhaps because new mothers-to-be liked to 'go home' to have their first child, or because parents felt, particularly between 1662 and 1744, that it would give the child a little more security under the Act of Settlement.

This and subsequent Acts gave rise to another set of documents which may be useful to you in tracing the place from which a family moved. From 1662, each person 'belonged' to a particular parish, in the sense that it was responsible for poor relief payments if he or she fell on hard times. Normally, this was the parish of birth or place of real estate ownership, though other property could be provided as security by those who wished to change parish. Thus, births to paupers were a potential drain on the ratepayers and pregnant girls were often 'encouraged' to give birth elsewhere. This practice was stopped in 1744 by the simple device of recognising the legal parish of an illegitimate child to be that of the mother. Until this date, it was important to record births to 'strangers' (those not belonging to the parish) and some parents seem to have travelled to extra-parochial areas in order to avoid consequences of the settlement law. From 1691, legal settlement in a new parish could also be obtained through apprenticeship, being in service for a year, or paying rates in the new parish.

Settlement certificates were given to those leaving a parish, either temporarily or (after 1696) permanently, acknowledging the continuing responsibility of the parish of origin. The certificates were then lodged with the officers in the receiving parish and were sometimes copied into the parish books. If the new parish was later unwilling to give poor relief, and the pauper unwilling to return to his own parish, he or she would be examined by a magistrate and possibly removed by force. The procedure gave rise to Examination Papers, which sometimes contain extremely detailed biographical data and Removal Orders. These survive either in the parish chest or in Quarter Sessions papers (see Tate, 1983, Steel, 1968, Vol. 1, and Gibson (5). You should ask the county archivist's advice about where they are for any particular parish.

Sometimes, church or chapel membership lists will record where a new member had come from. Another way to discover where families migrated from is to look at other 'new' names appearing in the parish register and, in the nineteenth century, the census, in order to see if there is a clue pointing to where others had come from. This is a bit of a long shot, of course, but not too difficult if the register has good indexes. I have the impression that agricultural labourers tended to move in single families or as individuals, but that industrialisation could bring about the movement of many people engaged in similar trades at about the same time when major new developments such as canals were being undertaken. In more rural areas, it has been possible to find the place of baptism by discovering which other parts of the county were held by the local lord of the manor, and searching there; manorial records (pages 89–90) can sometimes also contain lists of freemen and tenants for individual years. Certificates of baptism had to be produced when couples took out a licence to marry between 1 August, 1822 and 26 March, 1823, and should be found with the bonds and alligations; see pages 109–11; see also the *Genealogists' Magazine*, vol. 21, No. 3 Sept. 1983. Ordination papers of clergymen should include baptismal certificates, and the PRO has parentage for most solicitors from their articles of clerkship, 1730–1835.

Parliamentary Sessional Papers (1843, Vol. XLV) list a couple of thousand individuals who had moved from specified agricultural areas to industrial centres, but such numbers are, alas, only the tip of the iceberg.

Baptism not recorded

Some children were simply not baptised, even before the industrial revolution. This seems to have been particularly true of the very large parishes in the north of England in which families might be living several miles away from the parish church. Of course, many of these missing baptisms were of children who died young anyway. (Probably between 2 per cent and 5 per cent of children died within the first few days of life in the sixteenth and seventeenth centuries.) However, as we shall see, others were baptised together as a whole family and it is difficult to escape the conclusion that some families never got round to baptism at all. Many others were baptised in non-Anglican churches (see pages 78–80). A few parish registers recorded births in the early eighteenth century, and they are much more numerous than baptisms; see, for example, the register of Childwall, published by the Lancashire Parish Register Society, where only 75% of those born between 1700 and 1725 were baptised.

Additionally, some Anglican baptisms were not recorded. The

scribe either forgot, or was too lazy to enter the event in the register. Steel (1968) notes that illegitimate children were commonly not baptised, or did not have the ceremony recorded. Scraps of paper which the clergy used for a 'first draft' of the entries were sometimes lost. In the 1806 register for Woodhead in the Pennines, there is a note to the effect that the previous baptisms, from 1780, were 'taken from the Notes found amongst the papers of the late Reverend Joseph Broadhurst, Minister of Woodhead, dec'd'. The very act of writing up the register from daily notebooks could cause difficulties. In Frodsham, all the entries from 5 July to 1 December, 1727 (twenty entries) are identical with those from within the period 28 June to 1 December, 1726 (twenty-four entries), and it is evident that six months' baptisms, or thereabouts, are missing.

Some registers have deteriorated over the centuries to such an extent that parts are either illegible or missing altogether. Through poor storage conditions, fire damage, or the eating habits of rodents, illegibility is an all too common problem, but in many cases an ultra-violet-light reader, which record offices usually possess, will help. Unfortunately, these machines are often too small to use with bulky parish registers, and perhaps such repositories should consider a mobile UV light such as those used by veterinary surgeons for identifying skin complaints.

Vandalism has affected registers as well as the church fabric. It has been known for visitors to cut out entries while the clergyman has his back turned. Stories from the nineteenth century include the parson who threw away an old register because no-one could read it, a parish clerk who was a local grocer and who used some of the leaves of the register as wrapping paper, leaves being used to back books in the church school and so on. Whole registers have disappeared. A useful list was produced as part of the 1831 census, which investigated the state of each parish register. However, registers continue to be lost through fire, negligence, and (especially after 1812 when wooden chests holding the parish documents were replaced by iron ones) dampness. Lord Teviot reported to the House of Lords in 1976 that 2,400 volumes had been lost since 1831 – one every three weeks! Gatfield (1897) told some sad stories of how this was happening.

One of the objectives of the 1978 Parochial Registers and Records Measure is to give greater security to these documents.

As a general rule, if a register was missing in the 1831 list, it is most unlikely to turn up now; if, however, it was there in 1831 and is now missing, seek the advice of the relevant county archivist. He or she will either tell you that it has been lost through some known disaster, or that its loss is news – in which case the CRO will almost certainly search for it. This has happened to me twice over the last few years, and the registers have been found.

'The gap' is the notoriously difficult period in the 1640s and 1650s during and after the Civil War. It has been estimated that about one-sixth of all baptisms are missing in this period. The war itself is often blamed for the fact that whole years are omitted from the registers; and during the 1650s registration was taken out of the hands of the clergy, and civil clerks – often schoolteachers, for example – were required to record births as well as baptisms; indeed, an ordinance to do so had first been passed in 1645. Although Wrigley and Schofield (1981) have shown that baptismal registers in the 1550s were twice as defective as those of the Civil War period, in general the quality and survival rate of the registers does decline at this time, and some of the main ways to overcome the problem in other periods (see the discussion of alternative sources to parish registers, pages 81–5) are not available.

Since the revised canons of 1948, the Anglican church will not marry a couple if neither party has been baptised, and may make stipulations in cases where only one party has been baptised. Before this time, however, I can find no rubric on the matter, so that an Anglican marriage does not necessarily imply baptism of the bride and groom. Even since 1948, so long as the baptism is in the name of the Trinity, it has not mattered *by whom* the child is baptised, and private baptism has long been held to be just as acceptable as church baptism – indeed, private baptism (or 'half-baptism') is sometimes distinguished in the records from public christening. According to Canon 70 in 1603, a clergyman should have recorded *all* baptisms in his parish, and indeed it is not uncommon to find the letter P or 'Priv.' in the margin of a register of baptisms. The 1801 census listed private baptism as one of the major reasons for deficiencies in parish registers and estimated that up to one-third of entries were missing in Northimberland for this reason. However, private baptism saved many children from being refused a proper burial (see pages 137–9). Some clergy evidently waited for the public baptism before making the entry, but paupers, it is said, could not afford the cost of either the ceremony, or the party which was expected to accompany it. The registration of private baptisms is supposed to have improved after 1812.

Occasionally, odd pages of the original register may be missed by the technician doing the microfilming – page numbers or sequence of dates should be checked if omissions are suspected.

For solutions to all the problems thrown up in this section, see the alternatives to registers discussed on pages 81–90.

Entry missed by searcher (see also page 21)

There are several potentially dangerous circumstances in which a baptismal entry can easily be missed:

if you are reading the same set of records for more than an hour continuously;

if you are using registers in which baptisms, marriages and burials are not separated, but written in the chronological order in which any of these events took place. Sometimes the clerk puts small marks in the margin in order to distinguish baptism, marriage and burial entries from each other. Baptisms are occasionally written as burials and *vice versa*; and in many registers the odd few entries are written entirely out of chronological order, or even on the fly-leaf of the register book;

if you are using a microfilm copy of the register; it is all too easy to forget that some entries are too difficult to read, and to fail to check them later in the original register. In fact, once a register has been microfilmed, you might have some difficulty in persuading the archivist in charge of the original to allow you to use it;

if you are looking for entries of families of more than two surnames at the same time;

if you have eyesight that is less than perfect. Muscular strain is automatically relieved by a temporary alteration of focus without the sufferer being aware of it, until the fault is corrected by an optician. The result is that the eyes do not allow sufficient concentration on each entry on the page.

Base information incorrect (see also pages 22–3)

You will normally be searching for a baptism with no positive indication of the place of birth, unless it has been obtained from the census. The first assumption must be that the baptism occurred in the parish where the marriage, or birth of later children, took place. There are two basic reasons why your search might not prove fruitful. As we have seen, the population was quite mobile, even in pre-industrial times, and the twenty- or thirty-year interval between birth and marriage was ample time for a family to move, perhaps more than once; and the registers themselves might be faulty. You might also be looking in the wrong direction if the base of your information is misleading you.

There is, for example, a period between about 1780 and 1837 when some clergymen, particularly but not exclusively in the new industrial areas, stated incorrectly that the bride and the groom were both 'of this parish' when they married, the real place of residence being concealed. It is not clear why this happened, and it did not affect marriages by licence as much as marriages by banns. You should also bear in mind that many of the sources which have given you a clue to the date of birth – age on a marriage bond or gravestone, for example – are not necessarily accurate, especially for those who claimed to be centenarians, and for those who claimed to be twenty-one at the time of marriage. Even knowing this, it is not easy to accept a baptism in, say, 1722, when the age given at marriage in 1748 is '22 years and upwards', and the strategy adopted on pages 58–9 should be adopted as a test of identification.

At a census, teenage girls and women in their late twenties show a tendency to present themselves as being in their early twenties, but on the whole, people under thirty do not overstate their age. On the other hand, many over thirty pretend to be younger than they are, and research suggests that women are five times more likely to do so than men. Probably under 1 per cent of ages given in censuses are wrong by more than five years, but up to 10 per cent show an error of over one year. (Coincidentally, 10 per cent of people entering hospital twice in the 1960s gave a different date of birth on each occasion, and most of the errors involved the year of birth.) People over the age of fifty show a tendency to overstate their age, a tendency which increases with age! Be careful to note whether an age in the census has 'mo' against the age figure, indicating months instead of years – the 'mo' is sometimes placed inside the next column, and can be missed. Ages given on marriage licence documents can also be wrong; a study of these suspects that ages are overstated and has spotted a curious tendency to give an age divisible by two, especially thirty. Demographers call this tendency 'heaping'.

There are many other reasons why your base information may be misleading. Have you automatically assumed that a John Smith junior must be the son of the local John Smith senior or that Robert Jones the younger is the son of Robert Jones the elder? It is not necessarily so. Place of birth given in the census should not be taken for granted any more than age. A comparison of answers by the same people in the 1851 and 1861 censuses shows a 14 per cent discrepancy – always look in more than one census, if the individual was still alive, and if the census is accessible to you. Another odd feature of the census is that, when people moved parish, they tended to give their new parish as their place of birth at the next census – then tell the truth in later ones. The name given in a census schedule might be a nickname or second Christian name. Before the twentieth century, 'Mrs' might refer to social rank rather than marital status – hence, 'Mrs Taylor' might have been a spinster. Similarly, 'cousin' might mean 'relative' rather than 'child of aunt or uncle' and 'widow' could be simply an 'old woman'. 'Son-in-law', even as a census entry, might mean 'stepson'. The spelling of distant and therefore unfamiliar placenames by a clergyman or census enumerator sometimes leads to curious variations, and therefore false conclusions about the place of birth. 'Parish of settlement' can also be misleading, because it was not always the place of birth; (see page 68). Do not assume that anyone leaving a will must therefore be over twenty-one; before 1837, testators could be fourteen (males) and twelve (females); since 1970, the lowest age has been eighteen, (even if the testator is married), unless on active military service. If you are looking for the baptism of a bride, remember that she might have been a widow already (see also page 98) and that the marriage register would not necessarily record her marital status before 1754. See page 115 for minimum age at marriage. The 1841 census can suggest misleading information because relationships and marital status are not given.

Remember that earlier registers sometimes latinised Christian names, but not always. If you have found the marriage of a Silas, you might need the baptism of a Silvanus – or *vice versa*.

After the start of the industrial revolution, and until birth certificates give more specific information, the following type of baptismal entry can give quite a misleading direction to your search: 'John, son of Charles Hardwicke and Jane Stilling.' The obvious inference is that John was illegitimate; but if you cannot find the earlier baptism of a Charles Hardwicke, it is probably because the father's name was Charles Hardwicke Stilling and Jane was his wife. The entries for John's siblings would probably clear up the mystery.

Change of name after baptism (see also pages 25–7)

I suspect that informal changes of name after baptism were at least as common two hundred years ago as in our own day. Case law built up concerning the legality of banns, marriage licences and even marriages using names with which the bride or groom had not been baptised in the first place. Logic dictated that using the original baptismal name for banns could subvert their purpose if the person was normally known by another name, so that marriages were not always in the same names with which the people had been baptised. Both names could, of course, appear in the marriage entry, though I am not sure what to make of 'Sarah Richardson, commonly called Peter' who married Maria Sprosten at Middlewich in 1750. Often, however, the change would have been one of those common alternative versions – Peggy instead of Margaret, Bill instead of William – which can be found listed in the *Oxford Dictionary of English Christian Names*. This book also provides an indication of when individual names were first used or were fashionable in this country. (See also Steel, 1968.)

There have been many motives for changing a surname. The Churchill and Cromwell families acquired their names in order to associate with a well-known set of ancestors; others have changed name, or introduced a hyphen, in order to avoid racial or foreign overtones, to facilitate inheritance, or to break with another part of their own family.

Late baptism

With the exception of Mormons, Quakers, Jews and Baptists, almost all sects in Britain baptise in early infancy. Collective baptisms, however, in which several brothers and sisters may be baptised on the same day, are not uncommon, a phenomenon especially noticeable when families moved parish or a more zealous incumbent took up his post. Baptism at the age of twenty-one, or just prior to marriage, was not unknown, and at Rochdale in 1659 we find baptised on the same day James Chadwick and his own great-grandfather, James Stocke.

The 1662 Prayer Book said that infants should be baptised within fourteen days of birth, but detailed local studies suggest that parishes continued to differ quite markedly in how rigidly they adhered to this guideline. The number of adult baptisms rose after 1660, and it was also common in the last few days before civil registration began on 1 July, 1837. The median age at baptism seems to have increased from about one week to one month between the middle of the seventeenth century and the eighteenth. In Bedfordshire there were mass baptisings once a year on the day of the saint to whom the parish church was dedicated. To be safe, you should assume that only 75 per cent of those born were baptised in the first month of life. (See *Local Population Studies*, vol. 24 for a series of articles and references on this subject.) My own analysis of seventeenth century Lancashire registers indicates that children who were illegitimate and children of the gentry were the two categories most likely to have been baptised late. Before 1813, the age of people being baptised as adults is not always given, but a good indication is that the name of the parent is not supplied. Such an entry needs to be treated with caution, however, because it might be a burial which has been entered in the wrong part of the register!

Finding more than one possible baptism

The techniques used to solve the problem of baptism in another parish (pages 58–69) will sometimes lead you, as we have seen, to more than one possible candidate for the honour of joining your family tree. You might, on the other hand, have already met the problem in the parish where you expect to find the baptism, and genealogists are normally grateful when one, and only one, such child comes to light within the probable timescale of between twenty and thirty years before a marriage. Believing that you should never look a gift horse in the mouth, few bother to check whether the child baptised and the adult married were one and the same person. The professional searcher would never dream of such a casual approach, and if you are looking as closely as possible for 'the truth', you must exploit all the evidence before confirming the identification.

Such evidence must be employed when two or more baptisms

are found in the right place at the right time, a problem not uncommon in genealogy. When looking for the baptism of Thomas Darlington's bride, Mary Houghland (pages 58–9), it was somewhat disconcerting to find Mary, daughter of William Houghland, baptised in 1715, and Mary, daughter of William Houghland, baptised in 1717. Because the children both had William as their father, they might have been sisters; but there was more than one William Houghland with a wife of a child-bearing age living in the area at this time.

The first way through this sort of problem is to study the burial register for a parish for the days, and if necessary the years, following the date of the two baptisms. Until the end of the nineteenth century, it has been estimated that up to half the children born did not live to be adults. The figure was especially high in the early eighteenth century. The easy solution, therefore, is to find that one of the two Mary Houghlands died as a child. One of my students had a similar problem, followed this strategy, and found that both had died! In the case of Mary Houghland, however, neither was buried in Frodsham, so I had to have recourse to other methods. Did a William Houghland leave a will after 1745 naming Mary Darlington as his daugther? Do other Darlington or Houghland wills provide sufficient evidence for identification? If the marriage had been after 1753, a relative might have been named as a witness. Did the 'other' Mary Houghland marry in such a way as to provide evidence? Does the Bishop's Transcript (pages 82–4) include the burial of the first Mary, missing from the register itself? Can any of the other documents listed below on pages 81–90 be used to help? Was either Mary buried in an adjoining parish? Does the burial entry for Thomas Darlington's wife indicate her age at death? Between 1696 and 1832, Jurors' Lists in Quarter Sessions Papers provide the ages of those qualified to serve, as well as their occupation, place of abode, and location of estate.

When all other possibilities have been tried and found wanting, try ignoring the two children for a moment, and concentrate on the ancestry of the two fathers. If you have men of the same surname living in the same parish at the same time, it is quite possible that they were brothers or cousins. If you can accept a temporary fork in the trunk of your family tree, you can thus bypass an otherwise insurmountable obstacle, which is surely far better than the record coming to an early end.

If the problem occurs immediately prior to 1841, the census might provide the name of a brother or sister or your ancestor who was born after 1 July, 1837. In this way, discovering two possible baptisms, as well as a missing baptism, can be overcome by tracing known siblings instead. For an earlier period, the relevant wills might provide similar evidence. It should also be pointed out, however, that it was not unknown for couples to have more than one child alive with same Christian name as each other, especially before the early eighteenth century.

Occasionally, children were baptised twice, and not always by two denominations. There are instances of a private baptism being recorded first, and then a public christening some weeks later or when the mother was 'churched' after childbirth. The two baptisms might even be in different parishes, if the parents had moved, or if they had property in the second parish. Illegitimate children, admitted to the London foundling hospital between 1756 and 1760, are known to have been baptised twice with different names on each occasion.

Some genealogists advocate a careful study of the sequence of Christian names among the children in a family in the belief that choice of name might have been determined by the Christian names of their parents and grandparents. Such a closely defined system is most common among the Sephardim Jews. It is certainly true that the eldest boy was sometimes given the name of his father, or grandfather; but it is equally true that many families followed no such pattern. If there is really no other evidence, I suppose it is something to fall back on; and it is certainly useful when the Christian name in question is an unusual one.

Non-Anglican baptism

Whatever your own religious persuasion, it is increasingly likely that, as you trace your ancestors back over the last four hundred years in Britain, you will find them in Church of England records. It should always be remembered, however, that some parts of the country remained staunchly Catholic, despite the Reformation of the sixteenth century, and that Protestant nonconformity was common in other parts from the middle of the seventeenth. It soon became impossible for the Anglican clergy to obey

Canon 70 of 1603, which directed that they should register *all* baptisms in the parish. In the main, however, nonconformist registers become numerous only after 1780. Wrigley and Schofield (1981) suggest that nonconformist baptism tripled in the last thirty years of the eighteenth century, from about 2 to 6 per cent of all baptisms.

Even in south Lancashire, where the gentry ensured the relative continuity of Catholicism through the sixteenth and seventeenth centuries, the earliest surviving Roman Catholic registers (those of Wigan) date from 1732. Nonconformity grew with the industrial revolution, so that by the early nineteenth century, a large number of non-Anglican churches and chapels flourished, especially in the swelling towns of the midlands and north and also in certain rural counties such as Cornwall, Norfolk and in Wales. By 1812, in settlements with over 1,000 inhabitants, there were normally more dissenting places of worship than Anglican.

The records of these different denominations have been very well described by Steel, 1968, vols. 2 and 3, who covers Jewish, Roman Catholic and a host of Protestant nonconformist – or 'non-parochial' – registers. Subsequent volumes in this series will indicate which such registers are known to exist for individual counties. See also Palgrave-Moore (1987). With the main exceptions of Jews and Baptists, most denominations record parents' names at the baptism of infants. (Quakers recorded birth rather than baptism.) Some registers supply additional data such as the names of the godparents. The fullest records are probably those made by some Lady Huntingdon's chapels – eighteen entries to a page, and noting the names and parish of parents, the maiden name of the mother, her parish before marriage and the date and place of the birth and baptism. Additionally, there were some private chapels, often Anglican, attached to large manorial estates, which gave baptismal facilities to estate workers.

There are several ways to discover the existence of these nonconformist places of worship. Some books, for example, advocate a careful study of the number of baptisms and burials in the local Anglican registers; where the number of baptisms falls to the same level as, or below, the number of burials, that can be taken to be an indication of nonconformist baptisms in the area. (The odd year or two in which this happens normally indicates a higher than normal mortality rate, or a failure to record the baptisms which had been celebrated.) For most genealogists, however, this is too complicated. Early town or county directories (page 42) will provide the dates at which most churches or chapels were founded, as will the year-books or directories of the denominations concerned. Even simpler, however, is to ask the advice of the local history librarian in the nearest large public library, or the archivist in the relevant CRO, who should have this knowledge at their fingertips.

The local record office, indeed, should be able to tell you not only which non-parochial registers exist, and where they are; it might even have some of the original registers, and will almost certainly have a microfilm copy of most surviving pre-1837 registers. Following the start of civil registration in 1837, all non-Anglican denominations were approached with a view to having their registers centralised with the Registrar-General for safe keeping. This had already been suggested by some nonconformists as a way to give more authority to their records in an age when evidence of birth and baptism was becoming more socially desirable (*Journal of the Society of Archivists* vol. 2, pp. 411–417). By 1859, over 8,800 were in the General Register Office; they were transferred to the PRO in 1961. Jewish and most Catholic churches declined to deposit, and on the whole their records, together with the modern non-parochial registers, are still in their churches. Even some Catholic registers, however, have been transferred to CROs, via the diocese; many early Baptist registers are with the Baptist Union, and some Congregational registers are in the United Reformed Church headquarters at 86, Tavistock Place, London. Registers of closed Methodist chapels usually go first to the safe in the relevant Circuit headquarters, and are *not* in the Methodist archives in the John Rylands University library, Manchester, contrary to popular belief. A number of recent booklets describe the search for ancestors of particular denominations; see, e.g. Milligan & Thomas (1983) for Quakers.

As with the Anglican registers, modern transcripts sometimes exist locally, though there are almost no Bishop's Transcripts (for which, see page 82); few non-parochial registers have been printed, though the Catholic Record Society has published a number of early Catholic registers for Lancashire and Hampshire.

The Mormon IGI (pages 59–62) contains a very large number of entries taken from the non-parochial registers, including those in the PRO.

Registers not accessible – alternative sources

The Parochial Registers and Records Measure of 1978 (affecting only the Church of England) will have the effect of hastening a development which has been going on for many years – the centralisation of parish registers and other documents from the parish chest to Diocesan Record Offices (DROs). The public already has right of access to those registers which are housed in local authority institutions – most commonly where the DRO and CRO share the same organisation and facilities.

As in register offices, genealogists can help themselves to get better service in record offices by taking certain precautions. Current cuts in local government spending, and the substantial increase in the public's use of CRO's in the last few years are resulting in deteriorating services and increased charges for access to records. Check hours of opening and let the archivist know in advance which documents you will require or send a small, specific search enquiry by post. Be as specific as possible, and book a place in advance if necessary. Always use pencil, never ink. Learn how to use the document reference system yourself. Occupy an archivist's time as little as possible. And never eat or drink in the search rooms!

There are three private DROs, however, which are allowed to charge the same search fee as incumbents (see below): Canterbury (in the Cathedral Library); York (at the Borthwick Institute); and Oxford (in the Bodleian Library, which has begun to charge fees). As time goes by, you will be expected to consult more of these registers on microfilm rather than handling the original. Any earlier difficulties concerning access to registers deposited in DROs can now be overcome by reference to Section 20 (2a) of the 1978 Parochial Registers and Records Measure which allows searches to be made 'at all reasonable hours'.

This Measure will still leave some old registers, perhaps in up to 10 per cent of parishes, in those churches whose parochial church council has decided to invest in the equipment necessary to keep the records at the appropriate temperature and humidity levels. The incumbent retains the right in these cases to make a charge for inspecting the registers or even, by judicious timing of his religious and social calendar, effectively to deny access altogether.

Crockford's Clerical Directory or the current diocesan handbook in your local library will provide the name, address and telephone number of the incumbent (and a little about his career). You should include a stamped, addressed envelope in your request for an appointment to view his registers. Better still, telephone for an appointment at his convenience – do not ask to visit for this purpose on a Sunday! If the incumbent is not accessible, the diocesan handbook also provides the names of the churchwardens and the secretary of the parochial church council. Ask about fees, for whatever textbook you are consulting may well be out of date.

Some genealogists may be deterred by the fees alone. To search registers remaining in church you can be charged £4.00 for the first hour in which you search the registers for any baptism or burial, and £3.00 for each subsequent hour, or part thereof. This fee applies to marriage registers only before 1837, but the incumbent may make any charge for inspecting his marriage registers later than that year. A certified copy of an entry of baptism or burial is included but this is not normally required by the genealogist, who needs only the information. Each additional copy costs £4.50 and the fee for a copy of a marriage entry after 1837 is £5.00, the same as the Registrar-General's fee. You might even find that some parishes make an extra charge as a churchwarden's fee, but I am not sure about the legal basis of such a levy.

It is thus still important to find alternative ways of acquiring information about baptism, even when the register still exists, and as we have seen, there are many other circumstances which make the quest for such alternative sources essential.

Bishop's transcripts

By far the commonest way around these difficulties for Anglican registers are bishop's, or episcopal, transcripts, occasionally called 'register bills', and affectionately known in the trade as BTs. Some date from as early as 1561 when at least the Diocese of Lincoln believed that annual copies of the parish register entries should be sent to the bishop. The order to do this eventually came in 1597, from which date a large number of parishes in England and Wales provided such duplicates, each year's entries being written onto a single sheet of parchment. 'Peculiar' parishes (exempt from many normal procedures) had to return them only after 1812, however, when all returns should be found on standardised forms, though many had sent in BTs earlier.

There are advantages and problems in using BTs. Bishops have their own record offices which, in many cases, but not in all, coincide with a CRO. Most Welsh BTs are in the National Library of Wales at Aberystwyth. At these institutions you can see, usually free of charge, copies of a succession of parish registers, and all this in the comfort of an office which is purpose-built, equipped and staffed. Before the nineteenth century, BTs regularly contain entries which are not in the original parish register, and indeed it is suspected that some registers are actually a copy of the BT, or that they are each copies of an earlier rough draft. Whatever the cause, the extra entries and the extra information sometimes found in BTs make them well worth consulting, whether the local register is missing or not. Remember the important general principal – if the evidence is there, use it.

Unfortunately, there are snags. As usual, the church provided no extra money for this work, and the result is an intermittent rather than a continuous series, especially before the eighteenth century. Postage was supposed to be free, at least between 1812 and 1840, but if Post Office officials did not recognise this exemption, the parcel was destroyed because no-one would pay for it to be delivered. Even worse, there were several dioceses where the submission of annual BTs never became an established practice. The worst offenders were Bath and Wells, London, Rochester and Salisbury. In contrast, the diocese of Canterbury has transcripts from 1558 to 1870, with a duplicate set of transcripts to 1812. Some clergymen submitted BTs during an episcopal visitation, which was not necessarily held at the start of a new year; notice therefore which months are covered – some entries may be missing for that reason. Even after 1812, the BT could be submitted within two months of the year's end. From 1754 to 1812, marriage BTs record the names of the bride and groom, not the full parish register entry. It also goes without saying that the transcripts are subject to individual quirks. Some baptisms of illegitimate children are known to be omitted from the BTs, and at Kencot in Oxfordshire, marriages where both parties were not 'of the parish' were not included. Incidentally, entry in a BT was never accepted as legal evidence of baptism, a fact which led to some curious legal wrangles concerning legitimacy and inheritance.

In those dioceses which did have a tradition of sending in the

BTs, the practice continued for most of the nineteenth century, dying out gradually rather than ending suddenly, with some parishes sending returns well into the twentieth century. The exception to this seems to have been marriages, entries for which do not continue long after civil registration began in 1837. The BTs are no automatic solution to 'the gap' in the 1640s and '50s, for bishops themselves were abolished in 1646, and BTs are often missing for some years before that. However, some bishops, including those of Carlisle, Lincoln and Chester, when they were reappointed in 1660, ordered that some or all of the missing BTs should be submitted. See Gibson (3).

Other copies of parish registers

According to George Rose's Act of 1812, the bishop's registrar who received the BTs should have compiled alphabetical indexes for each parish, and made them available to the general public. J. S. Burn (1829), however, complained that this part of the Act was not being complied with because of shortage of money. These registrar's transcripts do exist in some areas, and are to be found in the DROs. You might find, however, that the names of only the children are entered.

A few parishes, as we have seen, possess their own second copy of the registers, In London at least, there are parish clerk's (or sexton's) transcripts, which appear to be the rough notes, day books or memoranda books from which the registers and perhaps BTs were compiled. As such, they are sometimes more detailed than the register itself (*Genealogist's Magazine*, vol. 20, no. 2). George Rose's Act in 1812 tried to stop such rough registers being compiled.

It is also possible that the register has been published, and in this case you will normally have the advantage of a name index. Counties vary widely in the extent to which their registers have been published because in some there are parish register societies which have been undertaking this task for a century or more. The most fortunate counties are Bedfordshire (where all pre-1813 Anglican registers have been printed), Cornwall, Cumberland, Durham, Lancashire, Lincolnshire, London, Northumberland, Shropshire, Staffordshire, Sussex, Westmorland, Worcestershire and Yorkshire. The current parish register project in Cheshire should soon improve the situation immeasurably in that county.

When using these printed registers, you should note whether the dates in the title apply to baptisms, marriages and burials, whether the index is comprehensive (at baptism, for example, some name only the children, not the parents) and whether the register has been collated with the BTs before publication – the preface should inform you. If an entry you are expecting to find is not indexed, it may be worth looking through the text itself to double check. Indexing a parish register is not only a time-consuming and thankless task; it is also prone to errors of omission and, I guess, is rarely checked against page proofs before submission to the printer. When a register has been published, the baptisms and marriages will be entered in the next edition of the IGI, we may hope.

If the register you are seeking has not yet been published, it might have been transcribed already with this in mind, possibly with an index added. Such transcriptions are widely scattered. Many are in private hands and some are in the possession of the local parish register society. The county archivist should be able to advise you on which exist. Occasionally, you will find an index available without transcription.

An increasing number of registers are being microfilmed, but these are indexed relatively rarely. Any difficulty in reading the original because of natural wear and tear is quite literally magnified on microfilm and it is therefore much easier to miss an entry, so extra care should be taken during the search and you should make a note of the location of the illegible entries. Microfilming was originally started during the second world war to help to preserve the records from enemy action – but ironically, any lists made of those parishes where it was done seem to have disappeared and the films themselves have been scattered. In more modern times, microfilming is done to protect the original registers from over-use; individual incumbents and DROs can make use of convenient microfilming facilities, often in large public libraries which then keep a copy themselves for their readers. Microfilming is also an essential part of the programme of the Mormon church as part of the compilation of their IGI (page 59).

Military records and school registers
These have already been discussed on pages 30–6.

The poll tax

Governments are fond of taxing essentials, rather than luxuries, but records concerning taxation (see above, pages 63–6) normally provide no direct genealogical evidence. One exception to this is the poll tax – 'poll' being an old word for a head. It was first used in the fourteenth century, when each person over the age of fourteen had to pay a groat (four pence). Raised intermittently for another three centuries, the poll tax was revived by Charles II is his desperate search for money after the puritan rule of the 1650s; it was collected several times until 1698 when it died out. The original returns are in the PRO, but their survival rate has been uneven across the country. Copies can sometimes be found in CROs, and a few have been published.

The tax returns list families together (wives and children are named as such), the different rates they paid whenever it was collected and exemptions given to those too poor to pay. Normally, the children listed are over fifteen.

The poll tax, of course, was no more unpopular than any other form of taxation; it is therefore hard to believe the story found in the diary of Oliver Heywood, a nonconformist preacher, who wrote in 1678, 'In Cheshire, not far from Maxfield (Macclesfield) a woman killed too of her children, the third run to his father in the barn, who coming in met his wife in the doore, who sd I have saved thee two shillings and if the other had stayed I had saved thee three, meaning she would have killed that lad, for fear of paying the pole-money for them, wch at that time was imposed'. (Turner, 1881–5.)

Records of the College of Heralds

From 1528 to 1686, a tour of the nation's gentry was made on behalf of the College of Heralds, county by county, on average every thirty years or so; this was used by the Tudor and Stuart monarchs as one means of maintaining their political control over that class by verifying claims to gentility. After 1583 lists of gentry were drawn up from the jury lists kept by the county sheriffs. All who had the right to bear arms were listed, together with their ancestry for three generations; a list of disclaimers for those families who had descended from grace or fallen on hard times was normally included, though not always printed. They are preserved by the College of Arms. These county visitations are listed in

Sims (1856). Richard Sims, who worked in the British Museum, also made an index to the pedigrees included in these Heralds' Visitations. This index has been reprinted (Sims, 1970). A large number of the Visitations have themselves been printed, often by a record or historic society within the county concerned (Mullins, 1958, lists these society transactions; Squibb, 1978, lists the printed Visitations). These family pedigrees are not infallible by any means because of the sources of information on which they are based, but gift horses in the shape of a 'free' set of parents and grandparents must never be overlooked. Of course, the information they provide should not be taken for granted, but checked wherever possible. Remember that as well as the families concerned directly, these records also contain input on the female side from many other ancestors; on the other hand, they are rarely comprehensive even in their coverage of the immediate family of the 'key-man' on whose status the pedigree was based.

From 1567 until the eighteenth century, it was also the practice for any herald from the College to record the details of all the funerals which he attended. The record included the date of death, place of burial, the deceased's parents, spouse, in-laws, children (their ages and to whom they were married) and their arms and crest. Lists of mourners and friends in the funeral procession are also provided.

Once again, these are records which concern only the wealthier classes; indeed, after the late seventeenth century, they are confined to royalty and a few great noblemen. Not a lot survive; but once again many have been printed by local societies devoted to the publication of old records.

Inquisitions post mortem

These somewhat grim-sounding documents provide useful genealogical information from the thirteenth century until the late 1640s, when they decreased in use until they were finally abolished in 1661. They describe investigations into land-holding when a landowner had died, and were instigated by the crown because, in certain circumstances, the land could revert to the monarch. The inquisition recorded evidence concerning the original acquisition of the land, the deceased owner's family, his heirs and age. If the heir was a minor, there is often a 'proof of age' document.

There is a typed index to inquisitions in the PRO, where most of these documents are housed; but because a copy was kept by the family concerned, many are also in CROs. Inquisition summaries have been published by local record societies, and the archivist or librarian in the county where your ancestor lived should be consulted for advice – some will be very difficult to read in the original form (see *Amateur Historian*, vol. 1, no. 3).

Freemen rolls

From the middle ages until modern times, cities or corporate towns have had the power to grant 'freedom' to certain categories of people who were not necessarily confined to those who lived in the borough concerned. They could be: the sons of other freemen or, after 1835, direct descendants of freemen along the male line; anyone who had been an indentured apprentice in the borough (though not all trades seem to have used the facility); anyone who wished to purchase such a freedom; and those who had received an 'order of assembly' for the freedom to be given as an honour. Benefits to the freemen included being allowed to be self-employed in the town, exemption from tolls, business protection, a share in the borough administration influencing the price and quality of goods; and the right to vote, all of which made it an attractive proposition, you would think, for any tradesman to take up.

Ideally, the rolls record parentage, date of admission, the name and trade of the master (in the case of a former apprentice), the amount paid, the father's residence and whether the master or parent was dead. It should be stressed, however, that their quality varies considerably. They are normally kept in town halls or archive offices, if they have survived at all. Those for London are in the possession of the City Chamberlain. Some have been printed, and if so they are worth consulting; but annual admissions cover under 1 per cent of the borough's population, so do not be surprised if your ancestor is not among them.

Apprenticeship records

From 1563 until about 1835, a seven-year apprenticeship was the normal period and method for training craftsmen, though each trade developed its own set of regulations governing the entrance of its members. Records have survived in large numbers from 1710, when a tax was imposed on the indenture, and include the boy's name, his father or mother and, occasionally, their trade, the master to whom the boy was being apprenticed, the trade and the fee. They became briefer after 1760 when the poorer boys were exempted from the tax, along with those paying less than one shilling for the indenture.

Apprenticeship indentures have survived in many places, a surprisingly large number remaining with individual families. These family copies have often found their way into libraries and record offices, and some may even be bought in antique shops. During the period when the tax was levied, a copy of each indenture was kept by central government and many thousands are now recorded in the PRO, indexed by the name of the master and the apprentice (see PRO leaflet 26). Additionally, Crisp's Bonds, held in the Society of Genealogists' library, cover some 18,000 apprentices' names from 1641 to 1888.

Unless the genealogist has access to London, or to a London searcher, these records are very much a hit and miss affair – mostly miss. In more modern times, however, when it becomes possible to identify the firm for which an apprentice worked, the firm's own records should be searched – some, such as Metrovick's in Manchester, have even been printed as an index. (See also trade union and friendly society records, pages 39–40, and *Family Tree Magazine*, vol. 1, no. 3, 1985.)

Manorial records

It has been argued that for the genealogist this class of record is second in importance only to parish registers. This may well be the case in those areas where access to them has been eased. They are most useful in the period before the industrial revolution, though many continue into the nineteenth century, and some into the twentieth. Manorial documents are scattered in a number of private and public repositories. The National Register of Archives (Quality House, Quality Court, Chancery Lane, London WC2) will give advice on their present location, though you should be specific about the parish(es) and dates which are the subject of your enquiry. Even when you locate the records, you will find that, apart from the period of the Protectorate (1653–1660), they are written in Latin until 1732. Anita Travers suggests that one third of manors have no surviving records, and that less than one

fifth have a good sequence from before 1700; see *Genealogists'*
Magazine, vol. 21, no. 1.

The luckier searchers will find that the manorial records they
want have been translated into English; some are even published.
Then you can see the old manorial courts at work. The records
sometimes provide lists of tenants (including absentees from the
court, or Essions) and of jurymen in the court-leet, which dealt
with a wide variety of minor offences. Most important from the
genealogist's point of view, they also record the transfer of property and leases as they affected the interests of the lord of the
manor in the Court Baron. Leases for a number of lives are
especially useful as they record relationships between them. Any
tenant's death since the previous meeting led to an investigation
into his holdings, his heir (including age) and whether any forfeit
was due to the lord upon transfer. The information contained in
the records of such cases can be used to distinguish between
people in the parish who have the same name.

III—Looking for marriages

Introduction

There are basically two reasons why genealogists need to search for the marriage of their ancestors. Before 1 July, 1837, a record of marriage is normally the only way to discover a bride's maiden name, which you need to have in order to find her own birth or baptism. Recourse to a marriage might also be needed in order to confirm the age of one of the parties or the name of one of their parents.

Marriage records are among the more satisfying which genealogists use. Among the birth/baptism, marriage and burial series they are probably the least susceptible to omissions. The reasons for this are that marriage establishes the legitimate rights of future children and widows and that the number of entries you have to search is far smaller than the number of births, as it takes two to marry, and many never did. The discovery of a marriage brings evidence of a whole new family series which can then be linked to your own – indeed, it is your own.

Marriage Certificates, 1837 to the present day

Since 1 July, 1837, the Registrar-General has had a duty to record all valid marriages in England and Wales, no matter what the form of ceremony involved. Since that date the state, represented by a Superintendent Registrar of Marriages, has been able to conduct marriages itself. However, the fact that both church and state can conduct marriages complicates the recording and indexing process considerably at the local level.

In the case of civil ceremonies, the recording process is similar to that for births (see pages 12–13). There are again two entries, one kept locally by the Superintendent Registrar, the other centrally at St Catherine's House. If the wedding takes place in church, the same will apply when a registrar is present, and both church and civil certificates are completed immediately after the ceremony.

The latter is kept by the registrar and a copy is sent to St Catherine's House. However, registrars have not been present at Church of England, Jewish or Quaker marriages since 1837, and since 1898 other denominations have been able to apply for this relatively privileged status for individual church buildings. In this case an 'Authorised Person' (usually the priest or a member of the congregation) is the sole recorder and sends copies of each marriage quarterly to the Superintendent Registrar and the GRO. Relatively few Roman Catholic churches have applied for 'AP' status, though the number is now increasing as a consequence of recent industrial action by the registrars. The 1985 Efficiency Scrutiny Report recommended changes to this and other aspects of the registration service, but require legislation.

Civil marriage, available in this country before 1837 only for a short time in the 1650s, grew slowly in popularity, though surprisingly large numbers used this option after 1837 in the far north of England, the south-west and Wales. In 1841, under 2 per cent of all marriages were by civil ceremony (about 90 per cent were Anglican). By the 1970s, most brides and grooms went through a civil wedding though the balance has now swung back.

Sooner or later, therefore, the state receives two copies of each marriage celebrated since 1 July, 1837, one in St Catherine's House, the other locally. Indexing is by the names of both bride and groom, in alphabetical order strictly according to the spelling on the entry. At the GRO, the index is national, covering England and Wales; in the Superintendent Registrar's office, however, each church is normally indexed separately, which makes the task of locating any one entry extremely laborious unless you know in advance where the marriage took place – or at least which denomination it was likely to be. Only in the large cities, starting with Manchester in 1950, are marriage indexes now unified annually; in most districts, there are still many indexes to search.

In these circumstances access to the GRO indexes saves even more labour in the case of marriages than it does in the case of births. They are far fewer in number, but still occupy about 180 yards of shelving. They are bound in green, in contrast to the indexes for births (in red) and deaths (in black). Each quarter is contained in only a few volumes – in only one for certain years for which the original indexes have become so worn that they have had to be typed and rebound; and, unless you do not already know the names of both parties, it is very rare that you will be faced with more than one possible marriage. The normal technique is to search for the rarer of the two surnames; each time the full name occurs, look for the name of the spouse in the same index in order to see if the reference numbers coincide. If they do, then almost certainly that is the entry you require. You can then apply for the certificate, using the green application form. From 1 January, 1912, both names are given against both bride and groom, so that cross-checking is no longer necessary. This normally applies only to the GRO national indexes, though occasionally (e.g., Liverpool, 1837–54) you can find such cross-referencing in local indexes. In the case of the remarriage of a widow, her earlier married name will be indexed, but not her maiden name; the certificate, however, should provide both.

Yet another advantage of using the indexes in London is that they can be consulted free of charge, whereas the local indexes may be searched for only a five-year period without incurring the prohibitive 'general search' fee. Normally, you will know the names of both parties from the birth certificate of one of their children, but this will not have told you whether that child was the eldest or the youngest in the family, so that a long search may be needed before the entry is found unless the marriage ended in divorce; (see pages 100–1). It is particularly at this point that family 'information' about the probable year of marriage can be very misleading. The cost of searching for, and purchasing, marriage certificates is identical with that for birth certificates (see pages 13–15). It should be remembered, however, that an application to a Superintendent Registrar's office in a large city may require a long search unless you can provide the denomination or sub-district in advance. Do not be surprised, therefore, if you are politely advised to do the search yourself, or apply to St Catherine's House instead.

The certificate itself provides the following information for both bride and groom: date and place of marriage, age, condition, rank or profession, residence, father's name and occupation and the names and signatures of the bride, groom and witnesses. Witnesses can be minors, so long as they appear to be 'of credible age'. They are usually of the same age group as the bride and groom. 'Condition' in this context means marital status – bachelor, widow, etc. – rather than weak at the knees. This entry is usually correct as stated, but occasionally, widowers or divorcees will describe themselves as 'bachelor'. Between 1858 and 1952, a divorced bridegroom should be described as 'the divorced husband of . . .', his former wife's maiden name being given; a divorced bride is 'the divorced wife of . . .' with the additional phrase 'from whom (s)he obtained a divorce' *only* in the case of the respondent. Since 1952, the condition of a divorcee is simply 'previous marriage dissolved'. A divorced woman, by the way, must remarry under the surname by which she is then known, which is not necessarily her earlier married name or even maiden name. After an annulment of marriage, the parties normally reverted to their previous status until 1971, when their stated condition became 'previous marriage annulled'.

The entry in the age column is all too often given as 'full', meaning twenty-one or over. Giving the correct age was not compulsory, and a few did not provide it even in the mid-twentieth century. (Giving the wrong age or condition does not in itself invalidate the marriage, though wilful deception might lead to a prosecution for perjury.)

'Minor' or 'under age' meant between twelve and twenty for a girl, and fourteen and twenty for a boy, until 1929 when the lower age limit was raised to sixteen for both parties. A consent form should be signed by the parents of minors but the system involved is still easy to subvert. No one already widowed has been classed as a minor, no matter what their age.

In the first decade of civil registration, over three-quarters gave their age as 'full'. The average age of marriage was partly related to social status, the upper classes having a higher average marriage age. Professional men married at almost thirty in 1871, but manual workers at about twenty-four. Women have always tended to marry, on average, about two years younger than men during the last few centuries, and also to be two years younger than the groom. The father's occupation column will sometimes indicate that he was already dead; but sometimes the occupation of a dead father is given without indication that he had died. It is not uncommon to find that the father's surname is different from that of the groom or spinster bride; this probably implies illegitimacy, remarriage or foster parenthood. When an adopted child marries, the father on the entry can be the adoptive or the natural father.

Relatively few marriage entries at the GRO contain original signatures of brides, grooms and witnesses. If it is important to check a signature, you should therefore approach the Superintendent Registrar or the minister of the church/chapel where the marriage took place to see if he will consult the records for you. Remember that many Anglican registers have now been microfilmed, in which case the signatures are easy to check for yourself. (Superintendent Registrars can issue photocopied entries only to solicitors.)

Failure to find a marriage entry in the indexes

This problem is rarer for marriage than for birth certificates, but even so it does happen, and once again there are many reasons why. Some of the reasons are similar to those which sometimes make birth certificates so elusive. If the marriage was terminated in divorce (pages 100–1), many of these problems can be solved through the record of a decree absolute.

Registration in another district

If the national indexes are being consulted, this will not be a problem. If you are sure where the bride and groom lived or worshipped and cannot find the marriage indexed in the area(s) concerned, then it is almost certain that the marriage was elsewhere. There are several ways to discover where, though access to the national indexes it is by far the easiest.

The solution may be found in the Anglican books of banns (pages 107–8) in the known parish of the bride or groom. All marriages other than Anglican have their equivalent of banns, known as 'notices of marriage' which are publicly posted before the ceremony. In the years following 1837, they were sometimes read out at the Board of Guardians' meetings, so may be found in their minute books. There is no obligation on the Superintendent Registrar to keep these notices longer than five years, but many do so. The notices must, in any case, be written up into permanent notice books. The public's right of access to the old notices remains an unresolved question, however. The Superintendent Registrar also issues certificates as an 'authority for marriage' which have been an alternative to Anglican banns since 1837. These are returned to the Superintendent Registrar in all cases where a registrar was present at the marriage ceremony – the certificates from 'authorised person' marriages (page 92) are returned to the Registrar-General quarterly. They are kept for a minimum of two years, but again many districts keep them much longer. The Superintendent Registrar's licence, which is quicker than a certificate, is not acceptable for a Church of England marriage. A Registrar-General's licence since 1970 allows for a marriage to take place in an emergency or unusual situation – i.e., at a deathbed – and is somewhat akin to an Archbishop's special licence; (see page 109). Other ways of discovering a 'missing' marriage involve trying to find the parish of the partner, as this is where it was probably performed. In the nineteenth century, the place of birth of an adult is available from the census (pages 45–6) or military records (pages 30–1); in more modern times, place of birth has been on death certificates since 1 April, 1969. Even if place of birth is discovered, of course, there is no guarantee that the marriage took place there. The date of a Roman Catholic marriage can sometimes be found in the margin of a subsequent baptismal entry.

Discovering which churches were licensed for marriages is not easy. A town or county directory should help, and the Registrar-General regularly publishes an official list of certified places of worship which celebrate marriages.

If the marriage was in the Jewish or Quaker faiths, it should be remembered the marriage can take place anywhere in the country (whether registered for marriages or not). Thus, a person authorised to register Jewish marriages in Leeds may record a Jewish marriage in someone's front room in Penzance, provided that the *groom* is a member of the synagogue in Leeds.

Marriage not registered

While this is a theoretical possibility, it is more likely to be the refuge of a bad amateur genealogist, or at least one without much wit or stamina. The exception will be the unfortunate bride and groom who, perhaps unwittingly, have gone through an unorthodox marriage, a rare practice which is still alive in the 1980s. On the whole, if the marriage was not registered, it was not performed; and there were plenty of couples who simply lived together as man and wife knowing that the law puts the burden of proof on those who would challenge such a 'marriage' as invalid. If you are looking for a second marriage, make sure that the first spouse was actually dead or divorced – living in sin was perhaps preferable to committing bigamy.

Marriage incorrectly indexed – see pages 19–20

I have been told that the first priority of brides and grooms is not to check that the spelling of their names is correct, and of course many in the last century were unable to do so; if the entry is wrong, the index will be wrong also. Standards in this century are, of course, much better, and recently prevented the marriage of one Elsie Dawn Hobbs being entered as Elsie Doorknobs!

Marriage not in England and Wales – see pages 20–1, 123 & 139–41

Scotland, Ireland, the Isle of Man and the Channel Islands each have their own registration system, and if your ancestor lived in Britain but married outside it, there will not be an automatic copy returned to the national records. Marriages of Britons abroad are, of course, subject to the laws of the country where the ceremony takes place. However, the couple can voluntarily inform the British consul, who will then include the marriage in the consular returns, which are at St Catherine's House. They sometimes include a version of the banns system, and one of my students discovered such a record which post-dated the marriage itself! If a British chaplain conducted the ceremony, the entry should be in the Chaplains' Returns, again at St Catherine's House. They have been housed with the Registrar-General since July 1849. The indexes, together with those of military personnel marriages, are on the open shelves. See Yeo, 1984.

Index entry missed by searcher – see pages 21–2

Base information incorrect

If the spelling of a parental name on a birth certificate is incorrect, then you might be looking the wrong part of the marriage index. Even if you have the correct name, however, you might still be misled. For example, the bride or groom might have had a double forename of which you are not aware; your John Smith might be James John Smith. In 1866, and from 1 July, 1910, only the first of a bride or groom's forenames appear in full in the GRO indexes, other forenames being only initialled. Do not make the mistake of thinking that a marriage should be at least nine months before the birth of the child – search all quarter years, including that of the birth concerned – indeed, it might be found dated after the birth of the eldest child(ren). In the first half of the nineteenth century, almost one third of all brides were pregnant (Wrigley and Schofield, 1981). Do not make the mistake of thinking that the births of siblings occur within a twenty year period; a teenage bride could have given birth at any time during the next thirty years. Do not make the mistake either of thinking that the maiden name of the child's mother is the name she married under; the further back in time, the greater the proportion of weddings which involved the remarriage of a widow – 10 per cent in the middle of the last century. The birth entry of one of her children might indicate both her maiden name and her earlier married name, but a space for this information was introduced only in 1969. A later census, which might include her children by an earlier marriage, should also provide useful clues, because those children should have the surname of the mother's former husband. Again, the marriage will not necessarily be found just prior to the birth of the eldest child recorded from the census; it often happened that teenage children were not living at home when the census was taken, thus making a 'middle' child look like the eldest. If a father had married more than one wife with the same Christian name, and had children by each, the marriage to the woman whose maiden name appears on the birth entry of his younger children will not be found before the birth of his eldest! Similarly, the census will not tell you how many children of a father were born to the wife named in that census. Since 1953, a registrar can supply a new birth certificate for a child, making it seem to have been legitimate, upon the subsequent marriage of the parents; such a certificate would give a misleading clue to finding the marriage. In this case, the new certificate should contain the phrase 'on the authority of the Registrar-General', and a copy of the original entry (marked 'reregistered on. . .' with the date) cannot then be issued. In these cases, however, the original NHS number of the child is retained, a direct reference to the first entry.

Change of name before marriage – see pages 25–7
If marriage followed a change of name by deed poll, the fact would be recorded by the registrar, if it was declared, as 'Name

changed by Deed Poll'. 'Formerly known as . . .' and 'otherwise
. . .' can also indicate change, but will be entered only if the
registrar was informed at the time of marriage.

Finding more than one possible marriage

Once again, this misfortunate is much rarer with marriages than
with births, and normally the place of the marriage given in the
index should resolve it anyway. You can confirm the correct entry
by checking the name of the father of one of the parties to the
marriage against their birth certificate or other source such as the
census, and supplying this information when you apply for the
marriage certificate. A signature can be a very useful means of
identification, but normally you can see these on only an original
or microfilmed 'AP' marriage entry, not from the GRO. Confusion can arise very occasionally because the reference number
given in the index refers to a page of marriages in the register
book, not to an individual entry. If your friend John Smith
married Elizabeth Jones, and on the same page in the register,
another John Smith married Elizabeth Taylor, then John Smith,
Elizabeth Jones and Elizabeth Taylor will all be given the same
reference number.

In the rare event that you find more than one possible marriage
in the index, the verification fee is £2.50 per entry. Marriages
known to be bigamous are not so marked in the registers, and
certificates may be issued as though the marriage had been valid.

Occasionally, presumably in a fit of enthusiasm, a couple will
remarry each other. When this happens the date and place of the
previous marriage should be found in the second entry.

Indexes or certificates not accessible – alternative sources; (see also pages 19–20, 28–40, 86–8 and 101–6)

The options open to those who cannot afford the cost of going to
London, or even the cost of locally obtained marriage certificates,
are fewer than in the case of birth certificates. However, marriage
certificates are sometimes cheaper from the incumbent of the
church where the ceremony took place. The marriage might also
be recorded in local newspapers (see pages 40, 131), which will
often provide evidence of denominational preference and place in

a sequence of siblings. Churches retain their own records of marriages, unless they are so few in number (as in the case of small nonconformist chapels) as to make the keeping of a marriage register something of a luxury. However, the church entry would be difficult to locate unless the approximate date and place are known (see pages 91–2). As duplicates of the civil ceremony do not exist outside the registration system, apart from a copy which may be retained by the couple themselves, recourse should therefore be made to any other documents which supply the name of the bride, such as a child's birth certificate. In this way the marriage can be simply by-passed altogether. To the genealogist the marriage certificate is only a means to an end – and sometimes that end can be reached more quickly and more cheaply.

Mormon branch libraries (see page 45) are microfilming the national indexes of marriages, and members of the public can see this index free of charge. So far, indexes from 1837–1980 are available to the public.

Records of divorce may provide another means by which information about the original marriage may be obtained. Before 1857, the only legal means of obtaining a divorce were by Act of Parliament or (except for Jews) through the ecclesiastical courts – for the latter, the bishop's registers should be consulted in the DRO. (See Steel, 1968, vol. 1, p. 323 for acceptable grounds for divorce). However, very few people actually obtained a divorce before 1857 (a situation which led some desperate men to sell or exchange their wives), and until 1858, the Registrar-General did not even issue instructions on how to describe the condition of a divorced person at remarriage. The number of divorces after 1857 remained small – some hundreds each year – until the present century when, from a few thousand per year between the two world wars, they jumped to over 50,000 afterwards (McGregor, 1957, and Latey, 1970).

Case records are kept in the Court where the divorce proceedings were heard, and (if they result in a decree absolute), copies of the final certificate may be obtained, by post or in person, by any member of the public. This decree absolute includes the names of the two parties, the date and place of the marriage being terminated and (until recently) the name of any co-respondent in the case. Many other documents, including a record of the hearing, dates of birth of any children to the marriage and the final settlement, are confidential to the two parties concerned and their solicitors. Despite this, I would recommend making an approach to the court for access to these papers if you can show that the parties have given permission or are dead. These files are kept for fifty years, and are then destroyed, but the Lord Chancellor's office has directed that files on cases over fifty years old can be preserved if they relate to matters of general public concern, throw light on social or economic change, illustrate new or revised legal procedures or legislation, relate to cases published in the annual all-England law reports, or are generally of wide public interest.

Records of all decrees absolute since 1857 are kept by the Record Keeper of the Divorce Registry, Somerset House, through whom copies may be obtained. There is a fee of £2.25 for a three-year search, and the full forenames of both wife and husband are needed. There may be a few days' delay because the copies are issued by the court where the proceedings had been heard.

There are no geographical boundaries to the jurisdiction of each court, so it is by no means obvious where the divorce took place; Somerset House will tell you, for their index is national. It seems extraordinary that the public has no direct access to any indexes of divorce, either local or national, and I believe that a good social case can be made for divorce being registered and indexed also by the Registrar-General.

Marriage in church, 1538 to the present day

Marriage records of the Church of England form a very useful series indeed, whatever your religious persuasion nowadays. They start at the same time as the baptismal records (pages 52–7) and have a similar history before the mid-eighteenth century. They are subject to the same vicissitudes, especially in the 1640s and 1650s when it has been estimated that over a third of all marriages were unregistered. In Mary's reign a century earlier, the figure was almost as high (Wrigley and Schofield, 1981). In 1653, the right of performing marriages was removed from the clergy altogether and temporarily given to justices of the peace. Between 1657 and 1660 either JPs or clergy could marry people. From the late seventeenth century, the Anglican church was ignored by an increasing number of nonconformists as well as Roman Catholics, though sometimes their extra-parochial activities are reported in the Anglican parish register. The Vicar of Bowdon, for example, recorded that Roger Simpson and Mary Harrison 'of this parish married about 21 November 1699, but do not tell where, when, or by whom they were married. This said by Mr John Brown, not in Holy Orders'.

Until 25 March 1754, marriages are normally entered into the same book as baptisms and burials, usually in a separate list, but sometimes in the same list with each event written in chronological order. Since 1754 until the present day, marriages have been entered in a separate book, consisting of printed forms. This change was brought about by Hardwicke's Marriage Act (1753) which was passed in order to prevent a series of abuses (especially in the 'marriage shop' parishes) which had scandalised the more socially responsible for decades. The most notorious were the marriages conducted within the area of the Fleet prison in London by laymen who were not particular about who were being married so long as the fee was forthcoming. Until 1754, even canon law recognised vows before witnesses, and subsequent consummation, as the only necessities for a valid marriage. The centre of these abuses shifted to the Gretna Green area after the passing of the 1753 Act. Gretna retained its popularity until the Marriage (Scotland) Act of 1939 (though Brougham's Marriage Act of 1856 introduced a three week residential qualification for at least one of the parties). Scotland and the Channel Islands were exempt from Hardwicke's Act so that, for example, the marriage of a minor which took place there remained valid without parental consent. All such areas advertised their liberties, with some success. Hardwicke's Act had several other important consequences for the genealogist.

From 1754 until the Marriage Act of 1836, only Church of England, Jewish and Quaker marriages were valid. Statistically, Quakers formed a tiny minority falling from 1.1 per cent in 1680, to 0.2 per cent in 1800 and 0.7 per cent in 1861 (Wrigley and Schofield, 1981). In effect, other denominations had to go through an Anglican marriage ceremony if they wished to live in lawful wedlock, to have legitimate children and if a widow was to be able to claim pension rights. Any bastard dying without children himself could have his property revert to the crown. These penalties made it very desirable for couples of all persuasions to go through a valid ceremony. Thus, James Livesay of Walton and Ellen Riding of Houghton, Lancashire, who married in Brindle Roman Catholic Church on 2 February, 1755, also married in Walton le Dale Anglican church the next day in order to legalise their union. Statistically therefore, deficiencies in Anglican registers between 1754 and 1837 must be very small indeed.

Hardwicke's Act also limited the number of buildings in which marriages could be performed. It is thus quite common to find chapels in outlying townships having marriages before 1754 but not afterwards unless they achieved parochial status. To retain the facility for marriage, an episcopal licence had to be obtained. For the genealogist, this requirement means that the search for a marriage entry in the two generations following 1754 is easier than before or after, though a few clergymen, such as Mr Hadfield in Mellor, Derbyshire, continued to conduct marriages without such a licence.

Thirdly, having a printed form normally ensured that, in addition to the names of the bride and groom, a certain amount of additional information was recorded. This was the first time that the form of entry in a parish register had been laid down by law. Before 1754, only the names of the bride and groom were normally given, sometimes with their township of residence. It is very rare to find marriage registers such as those of Glossop in the early seventeenth century in which the names of the bride and groom's parents were also recorded. Hardwicke's printed forms were of two kinds and can be found with either three or four entries to a page before 1813 and three to a page afterwards until 1837. One kind incorporates a space for banns (see pages 107–8), the other does not; each asked for the names of both parties, their parish, whether the marriage was by banns or licence and the names of the witnesses, who might be relations, but equally might be the parish clerk or other 'regular' witness who performed this function for many couples. The form was modified on 1 January 1813 to include a consent section for the marriage of minors (those under twenty-one). Consent by guardians, by the way, does not necessarily mean that both parents were dead; guardians could be appointed while the mother was still alive – for example, by the court of probate (see page 153). Subsequent to 1 July, 1837, the

Anglican marriage register takes a similar form to the record of civil registration (pages 93–4) and includes the name and occupation of the father of both bride and groom.

Occasionally you may come across chapels which continued to use the old style of register book after 1754, without the printed forms – this happened at Daresbury and Waverton in Cheshire.

Over the years, several students have asked me variations on the same basic question which has arisen during their researches – which categories of people were not allowed to marry each other? From Archbishop Parker's statement of 1563, adopted as Canon Law in 1603 and written into the 1662 Book of Common Prayer, the list of 'prohibited degrees' remained unchanged until 1907:

A man was not permitted to marry his:	*A woman was not permitted to marry her:*
Grandmother	Grandfather
Grandfather's wife	Grandmother's husband
Wife's grandmother	Husband's grandfather
Father's sister	Father's brother
Mother's sister	Mother's brother
Father's brother's wife	Father's sister's husband
Mother's brother's wife	Mother's sister's husband
Wife's father's sister	Husband's father's brother
Wife's mother's sister	Husband's mother's brother
Mother	Father
Step-mother	Step-father
Wife's mother	Husband's father
Daughter	Son
Wife's daughter	Husband's son
Son's wife	Daughter's husband
Sister	Brother
Wife's sister	Husband's brother
Brother's wife	Sister's husband
Son's daughter	Son's son
Daughter's daughter	Daughter's son
Son's son's wife	Son's daughter's husband

Daughter's son's wife	Daughter's daughter's husband
Wife's son's daughter	Husband's son's son
Wife's daughter's daughter	Husband's daughter's son
Brother's daughter	Brother's son
Sister's daughter	Sister's son
Brother's son's wife	Brother's daughter's husband
Sister's son's wife	Sister's daughter's husband
Wife's brother's daughter	Husband's brother's son
Wife's sister's daughter	Husband's sister's son

These rules can be circumvented by the parliamentary personal bill procedure, though many are not to everyone's taste. Against the first in the list, one wit wrote, 'Lord have mercy upon us and incline our hearts to keep this law'.

It was thus not only possible for first cousins to marry each other; it was also quite common, having been legalised in the 1540s. Perhaps two or three in every hundred marriages were between first cousins, though this figure seems to have varied with place and time (see *Genealogists Magazine*, vol. 8, no. 6). I have no doubt that it was not only the Quakers who frowned on such unions, but it was probably more common before the industrial revolution improved the facility for mobility among a much increased population. The absence of a satisfactory system of medical record linkage means that the genetic effects of close-kinship marriages are still a matter of some controversy, but the need for such a system will surely increase with the development of embryo technology. The risk of genetic malformations in children of a cousin marriage is twice that of a normal marriage.

The only addition to the list of prohibited degrees in the twentieth century is that of a child with its adoptive parent, though marriage with an adoptive sibling is permitted.

In 1907 for the first time, a man was allowed to marry his deceased wife's sister, though a clergyman can still refuse to conduct the ceremony. From 1921 he could marry his deceased brother's widow and, from 1931, nephews and nieces by marriage.

Until 1835, any marriage which had been inadvertently contracted within the prohibited degrees was voidable; Lord Lynhurst's Marriage Act made void any contracted after 1835.

Not until 1837 were Jews and Gentiles allowed to marry each other.

Many genealogists like to be precise about stating cousin and cousin-derived relationships. Children of siblings are first cousins, their own children second cousins, and so on. Each generation gap between cousins is denoted by a number of times 'removed'.

Failure to find an Anglican marriage

If you are interested in tracing only the male line, failure to find a marriage really does not matter, especially before 1837, when there is little hope that the entry will give the groom's parents. However, there are many genealogists, including the Mormons, who wish to trace all their recorded ancestors, so that the mother's maiden name, normally obtainable before 1837 only from a marriage entry, is very important. There are several reasons why a marriage entry may be hard to find.

Marriage in another parish

This is a very common problem, though one good authority has suggested that almost all pre-industrial marriages were within a fifteen mile radius. I suppose that, in the days before bicycles, most courting couples relied largely in shanks' pony for transport. Evidence points to the 1850's being the decade which marks a large rise in the mean marriage distances, especially over 30 miles, as trains improved on the inter-city cart and (more expensive) stagecoach facility. Normally, you will know in advance the surname of only the father of a baptised child, and you will need the marriage record to discover the maiden name of the mother. Now, if a man married a woman who lived in the same parish, and they had their children there, the marriage should be found without much difficulty. Even in this simple case, however, it was not unknown for the couple to marry elsewhere. It sometimes happened even when the marriage was by banns. William Darlington married Betty Cookson by banns at Daresbury in 1803 (an entry omitted from the IGI, by the way), despite the fact that they both lived in Frodsham. The marriage took place two months after the baptism of Betty's illegitimate child. Speculation suggests that William had been the father; but why the need for secrecy, I wonder, implied by holding the ceremony at Daresbury? Had they incurred the wrath of the vicar at Frodsham? Had William's parents forbidden the marriage – but he was married twenty years and eleven months after his baptism, so perhaps he was already twenty-one?

Much more commonly, however, the problem of a 'missing' marriage arises because the groom married in the bride's parish, though occasionally they marry in the groom's parish, then live in that of the bride. The resulting problem is still the same, though the possible solution is slightly different. Often, they married in the nearest large town.

If the marriage took place after 1753, there should be a record of the banns or licence, either of which should lead you to the parish where the marriage took place. However, only from 1823 has the law compelled banns to be read in both the bride's and the groom's parish where these were different (except during the period 1941–1947). Also, not all books of banns have survived; and in some of those which have, banns might have been recorded only where the marriage was to take place. In the middle of the nineteenth century, there were complaints that some clergymen were increasing their revenue by marrying persons (even minors) neither of whom were their parishioners, and not bothering to check the addresses which the parties gave; but the abuse continued long after that.

Both banns and marriage licences have been used since the middle ages as means by which the church protected itself from performing invalid marriages, particularly those which involved close relatives (see pages 104–5) or bigamy. At a time when the reading of banns – the intention to marry a named person – over three consecutive Sundays would be heard by the majority of the population in the parish of the bride and groom, it would normally be expected that someone would know the parties sufficiently well to be able to inform the clergyman if the ceremony should not take place.

From 1653 to 1660, banns were read from either church or market place, and normally these readings are noted in the parish register itself. Apart from this short period, however, it is very unusual to find banns recorded at all before Lord Hardwicke passed his Act of 1753 making the recording of banns compulsory. Hardwicke himself had wanted all marriages to be by banns, but fortunately for genealogists, licences were continued.

From 1754 until 1812, banns were recorded on printed forms, which may be found in a number of different places in the parish records. Sometimes they are in separate books, or in a separate section of the main marriage register, each entry recording names, parishes and dates of publication. Some marriage forms, however, have a space for banns to be entered at the top, and I suspect that in this case, clergymen were reluctant to 'waste' a whole form on marriages which were to take place in another parish, and so did not enter them, being content to send a certificate to the church where the marriage was to take place. Occasionally, on the other hand, a parson would fill in one section of such a book with banns only, and use another part of the book for the marriages. Also from 1754, the marriage had to take place in one of the churches where the banns had been called.

After 1 January, 1813, it is normal for banns to be in separate books, and in the mid-nineteenth century the Society for the Propagation of Christian Knowledge tried to prevent certain abuses of the marriage regulations by issuing books of banns forms which contained space for street names and house numbers. Any separate surviving register of banns is usually kept with the parish register itself, so that when the latter is centralised to a DRO, the associated books of banns will probably go with it. No search fees are laid down. There is, however, no legal obligation to preserve banns books permanently, which has allowed some incumbents to throw away older ones if they were thought to be cluttering up the vestry.

The existence of a set of banns does not prove that the marriage took place, but if the prospective bride's Christian name is the same as that of the later mother, then in the absence of any other evidence, they should be accepted as one and the same person. This cannot be infallible, but it may be all the evidence you can find. You are the only person who can decide whether to accept it as sufficient proof; but note that it would not be accepted in a court of law! Sometimes the banns system was effective in preventing a marriage; for wasting the time of the church, a fine could be levied if the marriage did not take place after the banns had been called. From 1837, banns could be replaced by a certificate from a Super-intendent Registrar (see pages 95–6).

Marriage licences, or 'dispensations', could be obtained as an alternative to having the banns read. They were issued at a number of levels within the church hierarchy: by archbishops (whose special licences have been issued since 1533 for marriages which cannot be performed between 8 a.m. and 6 p.m.; these licences enabled marriages to take place at any time and in any place, but the weddings should nevertheless be entered in the local parish register); by bishops, archdeacons, surrogates (deputies) or clergymen in a 'Peculiar' parish exempt from normal procedures, though the last were barred, in theory, by the Canons of 1603.

The licence has always been a rather more expensive method of ensuring the legality of marriage, and for that reason it has never been as popular as banns. I believe however that a licence was more popular if the bride and groom came from different parishes. The 1603 Canons said that licences should be issued only to those 'of good state and quality'; it is still discretionary for the church to issue one, whereas banns must be read for those who request them. Nowadays, the issuing of licences tends to be discouraged unless banns appear to be inappropriate – for example, for a marriage between a British citizen and an alien.

The proportion of marriages arranged by licence has varied considerably over time and by area. In seventeenth century Bowdon, up to 30 per cent of marriages annually were by licence rather than banns, but elsewhere the figure was much lower. A licence was popular with certain families, especially those who did not wish to have their domestic affairs paraded before the other parishioners on three consecutive Sundays; it also had the advantage of relative speed and secrecy, and seems to have been particularly popular with sailors! A licence also facilitated a marriage during Lent, when banns should not have been called, and avoided embarrassment for dissenters having them called.

A marriage of minors by licence (but not by banns) without the consent of parent or guardian, was null and void after 1753.

A visit to the clergyman issuing the licence resulted in three separate documents. An allegation (or affidavit) was sworn out, normally by the groom, to the effect that there was no lawful impediment to the marriage. By the seventeenth century, these are on printed forms, with spaces for the relevant details including names, ages, marital conditions, residence and occupations of the parties wishing to marry, the name of the church(es) where the marriage was to take place and sometimes even the name of the clergyman who was to perform the ceremony. Secondly, there is a marriage bond, which was a promise by two people – normally the groom and a friend or relative, though the second name is often fictitious – that if the marriage proved to be invalid in the eyes of God or the law, they would pay to the church a very substantial sum of money, usually amounting to tens or hundreds of pounds depending on the place and period. Such bonds became compulsory from 1579. Unfortunately, not all dioceses asked for bonds, which were no longer required after the Marriage Act of 1823. The details were often written up into the bishops' Marriage Act Books, which are now in DROs. Although the evidence from surnames suggests that relatives often acted as bondsmen, it was unusual for the relationship to be stated on the bond itself.

Finally, there was the marriage licence itself, but as this was given to the parties concerned it has not normally survived. The church kept the allegation and the bond which, when they are now in DROs, can be consulted free of charge (see Gibson, (3)).

There are three ways to discover whether a marriage took place by licence. The easiest is to search the indexes which have been compiled and often printed in the last hundred years by a local record society – see Gibson (3) for a list of those which have appeared in print. These indexes often supply the relevant details from the allegation and bond, so that reference to the original document sometimes adds nothing to what you already know. Secondly, for those areas or periods which have not yet been indexed, a long search through boxes of dusty documents, usually arranged chronologically or by year, will be necessary. Finally, the parish register itself will normally indicate (by the letter L, or 'Lic.', or *per lic*') that the marriage had been arranged by licence rather than by banns; in this case, the diocesan papers should be searched because of the extra information which the allegation and bond will give you. However, the diocesan record has not always survived, especially when the licence was issued by a surrogate.

If the register does not indicate banns or licence, it is worth spending time searching the relevant period to see if a licence was taken out. William Hallows and Eleanor Grice were married at Frodsham in 1763, and for some time I searched for Eleanor's baptism in the neighbouring parishes. The nearest I could find was Ellen Grice, baptised at Runcorn, an adjoining parish, in

1748, only fifteen years before the marriage. Though this would have been legal at that time, it seemed unlikely; perhaps she was two or three years old when she was baptised? This was clutching at straws, which should only be done when all other evidence has been consulted. In this case, the marriage was by licence, and the allegation told me that William was a thirty year old miller from Kingsley in Frodsham, and Eleanor was twenty-four years old and already a widow – so she had not been baptised Eleanor Grice after all!

It may be helpful to point out that changes in the rules governing the use of licences are relevant to the genealogist. Until Hardwicke's Act of 1753, for example, although a church and even a clergyman could be named on the documents, the licence was used for any church and any clergyman. I once searched in Bowdon for the marriage of Joseph Walton and Jane Ashley. Both had been born in the parish; the licence, dated 2 December 1709, mentioned St. Mary's Bowdon, and all their children were baptised there; but, there was no marriage record. It was only years later that I came across it, quite by accident – they married at Daresbury on 4 October, 1711. It was not unusual for couples to take out more than one licence. Presumably they had had second thoughts about marrying the first time. However, after 1753, the church named on the licence has been the only one for which the licence is valid. Other odd situations arose before Hardwicke's reforms; for instance, in 1631 John Meredith took out a licence to marry Ellen Nield four days after marrying her!

During the civil war, the office of bishop was abolished, so there is a gap in the marriage licence series between 1646 and 1660.

The next set of solutions is identical with that for missing baptisms (see pages 57–72); that is to say, searching the marriage registers of neighbouring parishes, especially those which seem to have attracted a very large number of marriages compared with the population of the place. If that search fails it has to be widened, turning first to those parishes containing families of the surnames you are looking for. Try looking also in the churches in the nearest town where marriage licences were issued. Once again, the Mormon IGI (see pages 59–62) may be a great help.

If the marriage is in the IGI, you will learn the name of the spouse, the date and place of the event and a reference to how the information was included in the Index.

The IGI is the largest of many marriage indexes which have been compiled over the last century or so. Of these, the most famous is that of Percival Boyd, which covers sixteen counties, being especially useful for Cambridgeshire, Cornwall, Durham, Essex, Northumberland and Shropshire; (see Steel, 1968, vol. 1). This is now being largely incorporated into the IGI anyway. There are many others, often on a county basis; there are, for example, excellent ones for Hertfordshire and the Isle of Wight; sometimes there are copies in CROs, but others remain in the hands of the compilers as a source of profit. A fairly recent list of these indexes will be found in the *Genealogists Magazine*, vol. 16 nos. 6 and 7. See also Gibson (6), and *Family Tree Magazine*, vol. 1, no. 5.

A word should be added about 'missing' marriages during the period between 1653 and 1660, especially before 1657, when only JPs conducted marriages; couples might have had to search for a parish in which a JP was available, so that some parishes consequently had far more marriages than in normal times; others had far fewer. Again, in the decades before 1754, some small parishes have far more than their fair share of marriages; were some clergymen accepting reduced fees, I wonder?

Marriage not recorded

Steel (1968, vol. 1) reports a remarkably high estimate of one quarter to one third of marriages in the first half of the eighteenth century were 'clandestine'; the figure was especially high in London.

There can be no doubt that, even in the relatively complete period from 1754 to 1837, some marriages in the Church of England were unrecorded through the negligence of the clergyman. Before 1754, many seem to have been in the habit of keeping the relevant notes on scraps of paper and entering the marriages *en bloc* later. Since 1754, fortunately, the bride and groom have been required to sign or mark the entry immediately after the ceremony. Even so, however, these printed forms were not universally adhered to, as we have already seen.

There are several standard ways to overcome the problem of a missing marriage entry. If the Bishop's Transcript (pages 82–4) does not yield the information then, before 1837, you must use more indirect evidence, mainly sources which relate to the preparation for the event rather than the ceremony itself; (see banns and licences, pages 107–111). The marriage, perhaps, never took place. Some of the early census draft returns record certain couples as 'not married'. (See also Steel (1968) for more information on unrecorded marriages.)

Entry missed by searcher – see pages 21, 72

Apart from the usual causes (tiredness, searching too quickly, failure to decypher handwriting correctly and so on) there is a further cause which can sometimes be easily rectified after 1753. If the clergyman wrote down the name of the bride or groom incorrectly, you might still be able to check through the signatures themselves, which occasionally show discrepancies between the names signed and those written by the clergyman. Many, of course, marked rather than signed; but if you have good reason to think that the marriage should have been in a register, and you have not found it, try going through the signatures at the end of the forms, just in case. John Handford apparently married Nelly Ashton at Mottram in 1790; but her signature – actually written under her mark – gave her real name, Nelly Ashworth. (Some brides, applying impeccable logic, signed with their new married name.)

Marriage not in England and Wales – see also pages 97 and 139

Occasionally, you may find the phrase 'married abroad' in a parish register. This almost certainly means married in another parish rather than in another country.

Base information incorrect – see also pages 97–8

The three main elements in a marriage entry, from the genealogist's point of view, are names, a date and a church. We have seen already how a marriage licence document earlier than 1754 may be misleading if it names the church where the marriage was to take place. It is also possible that, if you cannot find the marriage you are looking for, you have been misled about the date and even the name. The spelling of an unfamiliar surname by a clerk in a distant parish can result in some extraordinary variations; and if the wife's maiden name has been obtained from a birth certificate, remember that your ancestor might have married her when she was already a widow.

Probably the commonest garden path up which you may choose

to walk, however, arises from an interpretation of an unusual Christian name among the children of the marriage you are seeking. One of my great-great-grandfather's children was baptised John Hignett Rogers, and my first assumption was that Hignett had been his mother's maiden name; but I was wrong. Then I thought that the child, like myself, had been given his paternal grandmother's maiden name; but I was wrong again. That left only his maternal grandmother's maiden name; but I was still wrong! Then by chance, I came across Miège's account of the manners and practices in early eighteenth century Britain: 'Tis rare for the English to have two Christian names . . . but it is not unusual with them to Christen Children with the Godfather's surname'. Samuel Taylor Coleridge is a later example. Arthur Barlow Stubbs, born 29 April 1912, was given his middle name because both parents worked at Barlow Hall. On this subject, see Steel, 1968, vol. 1.

Incidentally, the use of a surname as a Christian name implies that the parents were mainstream protestant rather than puritan or catholic. It is a pity, genealogically, that more parents did not follow the example of one Thomas Smith, a schoolmaster in early nineteenth century Cheshire, who was clearly so frustrated at having a common surname that he christened one of his children Edmond Frederic De Courcy Moleneaux Gerard Swinchatter Smith. There is no chance of getting *him* confused with someone else of the same surname.

If you have inferred a marriage from the 1841 census, you should bear in mind that no relationships were stated therein, and a 'couple' might have been, for example, a brother and sister.

Another cause of going astray is to make assumptions about the date of the marriage from other evidence. A licence, as we have seen, was sometimes not used, and a further one had to be taken out. We all assume that people are likely to marry in their early twenties, but the average age of marriage seems to have fallen from about twenty-eight (for men) and twenty-six (for women) in the early seventeenth century to about twenty-five and twenty-three respectively by the mid-nineteenth century. This average varied across different periods and different social classes, there being some evidence that the gentry married earlier yet had fewer children than yeomen; labourers married even later and had even fewer surviving children; but by the second half of the nineteenth century, the reverse was true.

Before Hardwicke's Marriage Act of 1753, there was no lower legal age of marriage, except during the 1650s when it was sixteen for 'men' and fourteen for 'women'. In 1753 it was fixed at fourteen for men and twelve for women, and remained at those ages until the Age of Marriage Act in 1929, which raised it to sixteen for both. Of course, marriage below the age of twenty-one (eighteen in 1969) should have had the consent of parents or guardians recorded on banns or licence, and on the marriage entry itself, but it was often omitted. A consent section on the standard form was introduced only in 1813. After 1835, marriage of minors without consent was not invalid, nor was the minister conducting the ceremony punishable if he had not been informed that one of the parties was a minor. There were, in fact, very few child marriages (Laslett, 1971); but it must be remembered that any first assumption about age at marriage can be wildly inaccurate for a specific event. (See *Local Population Studies*, vol. 3, for an account of a virginity test on a widow of thirteen who wished to marry her own brother in law!)

At the other end of the scale, births to women aged 45 and over were not unknown – the oldest mother in my own family gave birth at 48. In 1980, one legal abortion in 240 was to women in this age group, and births to women in their 50s have been authenticated.

Sometimes, when recording a baptism, a clerk will repeat the child's name in error instead of entering the name of the father or mother. Check the baptisms of siblings before seeking the marriage of the parents – it is unlikely that the error would have been repeated.

Finding more than one possible marriage

If the names of both parties are known in advance, it will be very rare indeed for two possible marriages to be found. If it happens before 1837 you should find the parents of all four people and see if any subsequently left a will which provides a clue towards the solution – naming grandchildren or places of abode, for example.

Before the middle of the eighteenth century, it is possible that you will not discover even the Christian name of the mother from the baptismal entries of children, which sometimes give the names of only the child and the father. In this case, the burial register or one of many other documents discussed in this book might help. Up to half the offspring of the marriage probably died as children anyway, and one of the burial entries might give the mother's Christian name; and the mother herself should be buried as the named wife or widow of the husband. Note, however, that widows were sometimes still called 'wife', which can add considerable confusion to the reconstruction of a family group.

If only one marriage of the right groom's name can be found, you will have to assume that the entry is the correct one, especially if it was within twelve months of the first child's baptism. At Davenham in 1748, Richard Greenaker married Mary Shaw, and in 1756 at the same place, Richard Greenaker married Mary Nickson. I am descended from Mary, daughter of Richard and Mary Greenaker, baptised in 1761; but which one? The first thing to check, once again, is the burial record, for it is quite possible that there was only one Richard Greenaker who married twice. Luckily for me in this case, his first wife died in 1756, buried on 10 May, less than four months before his second marriage. By modern standards, this interval between the death of a first wife and the remarriage of the widower seems very short, and is often taken to indicate a certain coolness towards the first wife's memory. In the seventeenth century, however, the average interval was only three months (a bit longer in the eighteenth century), as men who had been left with young children to raise clearly looked for an early remarriage as the easiest, most socially acceptable way out of their predicament. Needless to say, the average interval for widows to remarry was considerably longer. Men remarried twice as quickly.

If, however, there had been two Richard Greenakers, each of whom had married a Mary, it would require a careful study of the baptismal register in order to distinguish between them, unless they lived in separate townships. Once again, a will provides important clues if one was left by any of the eight parents, or even by the parties concerned. From 1754, comparisons of signatures on the two marriage entries can provide further evidence, as can manorial records. (It was, however, considered unlucky for a bride to sign if the groom had marked with a cross, or, in the case of Jews, a circle!)

It should be observed at this stage that the pattern of second marriages has changed dramatically over time. In the sixteenth and seventeenth centuries up to 30 per cent of all marriages was a remarriage for one of the partners. By the mid-nineteenth century, it had fallen to 10 per cent and after the second world war to less than 5 per cent, but it is now rising as a result of the increasing number of divorces. The decline is not fully understood, but the type of remarriage which became less popular, oddly enough, was that of a bachelor marrying a widow. In Peter Laslett's analysis of 100 English communities, there were four times as many widows as widowers.

One more word of warning about remarriage; a study of the Bowdon marriage licence documents from the seventeenth century shows that some widows were entered as 'spinster' in the parish register itself.

In the late seventeenth and early eighteenth century, and especially in the Commonwealth period in the 1650's, it was not unknown for couples to marry each other twice, in two different Anglican churches on different dates. I do not know the reason for this, unless the couples were from the two parishes concerned; occasionally, but not always, it may be a case of one clergyman making a note of a marriage in another parish. John Wilcoxon of Over and Ann Young of Whitegate took out a licence on 19 February, 1695/6, the wedding to take place in either church; but two days later, they married at both Whitegate and Witton, a chapelry in a neighbouring parish. On the other hand, the reason for the remarriage of John Stringer and Eleanor Ashbrooke at Daresbury in October, 1769, was clearly given in the register: 'heretofore married on the 14th day of April, 1768, as appears on the 81st page of this Register, by one S Jones an Impostor who took upon himself the Office of a Minister not being in Holy Orders.'

One possible explanation for 'double' marriage entries is given in a Mottram register entry: 'John Hollinworth of this parish and Mary Ann Holinworth or Sidebottom of this Parish having been married at the Parish Church of Doncaster on the 8th of January 1827 but as they were then and still are generally resident in this parish it has been deemed expedient to repeat the ceremony were married in this Church by Licence this sixth Day of April 1831'.

Non-Anglican marriage

The location and extent of non-parochial registers have already been briefly described (pages 78–80). Until 1837, most of them contain baptisms and burials only, but a few churches of all denominations included marriages also. Between 1754 and 1837, marriages other than the Church of England, Jewish or Quaker ceremonies were not illegal; they were simply not valid.

Marriage registers from closed Methodist churches are usually sent to local record offices. Often, however, marriages in nonconformist churches were not recorded if the 'authorised person' was absent and the registrar attended instead, or if there was no 'authorised person' at all; this has not been true of Roman Catholic marriages.

Where Roman Catholic registers survive, even from before 1754 the names of formal witnesses are given, a practice which was extended by the Quakers to include all present at the wedding, with relatives and friends on separate lists. Unfortunately, relationships of witnesses to bride and groom are very rarely stated. In 1837, Jews and Quakers adopted a printed marriage form, providing for information identical to that in the civil registers; but the Quakers maintain their earlier tradition by issuing another, much fuller and larger certificate to the people concerned, which still lists all those present at the ceremony.

It may be possible to find transcripts of Catholic marriages with the relevant Catholic diocesan authority after 1850. Subsequent baptisms often provide the mother's maiden name.

***Registers not accessible – alternative sources;* see pages 81–90**

IV—Looking for deaths

Introduction

Death is of less importance, genealogically speaking, than birth or marriage. Once you have been born, married and had children, your life is over, the remainder being of no direct genetic consequence. Death is no more than a vestigial triviality, except for the release of pressure on resources. (When my time comes, of course, I reserve the right to change my mind.) Certainly, you can trace your ancestors without knowing anything about the death of any of them, and the absence of date of death is a normal feature of family trees.

Why, then, are genealogists known for that peculiar perversion, an attraction to things which normal people consider morbid? Who but a genealogist would ask for a death certificate as a birthday present? I remember receiving a most odd stare from a lady living opposite to a graveyard where I was feverishly clearing snow from a set of stones (though I must admit to going a bit too deep to find a stone which was not actually there!); and more than one of my students has found it hard to get used to the idea of looking at other people's wills. Yet such records are not only interesting in themselves; they can save you a great deal of time, effort and money, and can provide information which is unobtainable elsewhere.

I had a good start: my father-in-law was in the death business with a fleet of hearses. He was fond of bringing his wife flowers until she discovered where they came from; he used to talk about Burningham and Droppingham, and for a long time I wondered where they were! In other words, he had developed that hardness towards death, the degree of realism which insisted on extra-strength handles on his own coffin and which comes to all those professionally involved with it; the genealogist soon feels the same.

Death creates probably more records than any other event in our lives (if you see what I mean). There is the doctor's certificate (centralised to the GRO); possibly a hospital record; the bills of the undertaker and other tradesmen involved; the state regist-ration of death, duplicates of which may be found in the Medical Officer of Health records; a grave register entry; an order for cremation, with the cremation record; a burial or funeral service entry; the gravestone itself, with the monumental mason's copy; the will and associated documents; if the death was in any way unusual, a coroner's report; and perhaps memorial records – cards, newspaper entries and so on. It would not be exceptional if my death generates over a dozen different documents.

Death Certificates, 1837 to the present day

Since 1 July, 1837, the recording of deaths in England and Wales and the location, cost and accessibility of the certificates are similar to those for birth certificates (pages 12–15). Deaths, however, must normally be registered within five days of the event, instead of the six weeks allowed for births, unless the coroner is involved, and the national indexes are now rehoused in St Catherine's House, Kingsway, London (from Alexandra House, where they were until 1985).

The certificate gives the following information: the date and place of death; the name, sex and occupation of the deceased; the cause of death; the signature (see page 16), name and address of the informant (often a close relative and living at the same address as the deceased); and the date of registration. Sometimes, the name of a dead woman's husband is given. In the case of a legitimate child under school leaving age, the name of the father should be given in the occupation column. From 1 April 1982, the name of the mother is also entered. Since 1 April, 1969, the date and place of birth of the deceased, the usual address, and the maiden name in the case of a married woman, are also given. Cause of death is notoriously inaccurate, particularly in the nineteenth century; phrases such as 'act of God' do not inspire confidence, whether correct or not! From 1874, a doctor's certificate has been necessary before a death certificate can be issued, but even thereafter – alas, even to the present day – medical opinion is not infallible. Until 1874, entering the cause of death was not a legal requirement, though it had been partly pressure from the medical and insurance professions which had led to civil registration of death in 1837;

from that date registrars were simply asked to request a medical statement, and were even encouraged to use popular, rather than medical terminology on the entry. The registrar collects much more information than appears on the final entry, but it is used for statistical purposes only.

There are two main reasons, apart from interest, why the genealogist applies for a copy of a death certificate. Age at death will suggest the approximate year of birth; and the addresses can be used to locate the family in the census.

The indexes are used in exactly the same way as those for birth, with one important difference; from 1 January 1866 to 31 March 1969, age at death is given in the national (not the local) indexes, so that a copy of the certificate itself need not be bought if that is the only information you require. (From 1969, the date of birth is given instead.) The main problem is to know which years to search, for often you will have no clue to pinpoint when the death occurred, especially if you cannot find a will.

Be careful what you do with a death certificate. A number of statutes, including Section 36 of the Forgery Act, 1861, are in force, allowing for fines and imprisonment for destroying, defacing, injuring or falsifying the register or a certified copy with unlawful intent.

Stillbirths, by the way, have an entry which combines the characteristics of birth and death entries. Compulsory registration of stillbirths and their indexing started only in 1927, cause of death being added only in 1960. Before 1874, no certificate was needed for the burial of a stillborn child, which encouraged infanticide and underregistration of live births, especially the illegitimate. I believe that the registration system still lags behind public opinion in its attitudes towards stillbirths. The local registrar does not retain a copy, there is no public index, and the Registrar-General will normally issue a Certificate only if it is needed for legal proceedings. Before 1983, the baby could not be named (and still cannot be named retrospectively). Perhaps the Stillbirth and Neonatal Death Society will put some pressure on the GRO to have the system liberalised and humanised from the parents' point of view.

Failure to find a death entry in the indexes

By now it should come as no surprise that sometimes a death entry is difficult to find in the indexes, but in many cases the reasons are the same as those which create difficulties in the search for birth and marriage entries.

Death in another district

Deaths should be registered in the district where the event takes place, not necessarily in the district where the deceased lived (see page 18).

Death not registered

A minute number of deaths continue to be registered without the individual being named; most of these cases involve a body which cannot be identified. In 1840, over 500 unnamed corpses were registered, a figure which has fallen to about 50 *per annum* today. A registrar of my acquaintance was once called in by the police to register an unidentified body. They advertised for anyone to help with their enquries and eventually contacted the wife of a local publican who had been missing for some time. She went through the traumatic experience of having to visit the mortuary and identify the body; my friend filled in the missing name on the certificate, and the body was duly cremated. Several weeks later, the publican turned up, large as life, and they had to tell the police what had happened. When asked how she could have made such a mistake, she said that she had not been wearing her spectacles at the time! So, the death entry was changed again and some poor man's death entry is anonymous. Since then, the police always photograph an unidentified customer for the crematorium.

Even in the first decade after 1837, registration of deaths was always more complete than that of births. Contemporaries believed that no more than 2 per cent were missed – but, in the circumstances, this still seems a high figure. Research suggests that this under-registration is worst in the period 1841–1846, and that the majority of those missing were probably young infants. Relative completeness is encouraged by the requirement, since 1837, of a certificate from the registrar or coroner before the body can receive a normal burial or cremation.

A death cannot be registered for a person 'missing presumed dead', even when (after seven years' disappearance) legal death is pronounced by a court of law.

Death incorrectly indexed – see pages 19–20, 97

Death not in England and Wales – see also pages 139–41
Deaths of British citizens abroad should be recorded in the same way as births and marriages (pages 20–1 and 97). Soldiers killed in the first world war are listed by the War Office (1920–1921). Any will (page 144) leaving property in England and Wales should be proved in this country. There is no rule governing whether death at sea near the coast should be registered by the local registrar or by the Registrar-General of Shipping and Seamen.

Information about deaths abroad of members of the armed forces in active service may be supplemented by contacting the Commonwealth War Graves Commission which will answer postal enquiries if relevant details are provided. See also Gibson (6) and Yeo, (1984).

Index entry missed by searcher – see pages 21–2

Base information incorrect
As indicated earlier, genealogists often have no clues about when an ancestor died, and looking for him or her in the death indexes can mean a very long and tedious search. It can also be expensive if the name is fairly common, because you must pay to have certificates checked to see if they are the ones you want.

In 1866, and since 1 July, 1910, only the first of a deceased's forenames is given in the GRO indexes, together with others initialled.

If you have obtained information from a will or burial record, it should be accurate enough; but bear in mind that any other source of information is distinctly fallible. Just because your ancestor no longer appears in a set of records such as an electoral register or trade directory, it does not mean that he or she had died; on the other hand directories are notorious for including information which is out of date by a year or two. Even today, electoral registration officers usually repeat the previous year's entry if

Form A is not returned, rather than prosecute the offender. Search the death indexes for the years immediately before the name disappears from these sources, especially if the deceased was likely to give his name to a firm which might have continued after his death. Finding more than one possible death

Finding more than one possible death

This is a very common problem, especially when the date cannot be identified from a burial or probate record. It is necessary to provide the registrar with more information than simply the name and approximate age in order to distinguish between possible certificates (there is a verification fee of £2.50); this is one of the reasons why most genealogists prefer to search burial records first. The extra information required would be an address, or perhaps the name of the probable informant – the widow or widower.

Very rarely, between 1837 and 1874, a death could be registered twice; this happened to William Goodess of Hulme in 1838. The introduction of medical certificates in 1874 (designed to reduce infanticide) made this impossible. See pages 27–8.

Indexes or certificates not accessible – alternative sources

You can often get the information which you want from a death certificate more cheaply from other records. In addition to the following, see also church burial, pages 133–44. Some libraries have microfilmed copies of GRO death indexes; see pages 19–20.

Local Authority burial records, 1827 to the present day

The population explosion during the late eighteenth and early nineteenth centuries put so much pressure on the Anglican church that its documentary seams burst, as we have seen many times already. That same pressure was also being felt by Anglican graveyards, which were expanded in area wherever possible. Otherwise graves were dug even deeper (some thirty feet deep and holding eighteen bodies) or the old earth and corpses were simply removed to make room for the new. These were the days of the body-snatchers and cheap fertiliser for gardeners.

Early private graveyards were opened in the eighteenth

century. They relieved the pressure but cashed in on other people's misfortunes. Then, in 1827, London opened the first of the public graveyards, to be called cemeteries, followed by other large cities. The Metropolitan Interment Act of 1850 gave burial powers to local Boards of Health, which could also close down disused churchyards. Since then, the public cemetery has been a local authority responsibility, usually run by a parks and cemeteries (or even recreation) department. Unlike places of marriage, which have had to be licensed since 1754, place of disposal requires no formal approval so long as it is neither offensive nor dangerous to health.

The choice of burial in a church graveyard or public cemetery lies with the family of the deceased, but, unfortunately, there is no formal link connecting the state's death certificate and the place of disposal of the corpse. I believe this to be a serious defect in our registration system, yet one which could so easily be rectified. It is true that a registrar of deaths issues a disposal certificate to the informant, and that (except in the case of stillbirths) this must be returned within fourteen days, showing how and where the corpse has been disposed of; but the counterfoils need be kept by the registrar for only five years. (A 'certificate of no liability to register' can be issued for disposal in this country of a person who died abroad.) Unless you have information in advance, for example from an obituary or will, you will therefore have to search both church and state burial grounds in order to find the entry. To complicate matters still further, most cemeteries have sections which are used by different religious denominations. Copies of burial entries in ground consecrated for Anglicans may sometimes be found in the diocesan archives. If you have any problems locating cemeteries, seek the advice of the local undertakers (see page 127).

Cemetery records, in my experience, are excellent, and so is the service which those in authority offer to genealogists who wish to consult them. You should go first to the office attached to the cemetery, not to the graves themselves, making sure you know the hours of opening. A telephone call will clear this up, and, indeed, if you know the date of death or burial, the official will sometimes search the register for a specific dated burial while you are on the telephone. This register normally contains the following information: name of the deceased; address; occupation; date of death and burial; age of the deceased; and the place of the grave in the cemetery, or a grave number. If you are lucky you might find an alphabetical order arrangement, but, usually, the entries are in chronological order of burial. This means that, unless you know at least the year of burial, you might have a long search ahead of you. There is no statutory search fee laid down, but you can find some authorities making a small charge, perhaps £1, for answering queries by post. If the index refers to a grave number rather than a place in the cemetery, there should be a grave map available showing the location of those numbers; failing that, ask the official where the grave is – the number should be marked on the stone itself.

A third document available in a cemetery office should be a grave – as opposed to a burial – register; this should tell you who owns the grave, when it was bought and who is buried in it; this is especially useful for those graves without a stone.

If the cemetery has been closed, the records should have been transferred to the local authority's archives office – the town clerk's department or librarian will advise you.

Cremation records, 1884 to the present day

Public cemeteries often include crematoria, and a separate register of cremations is kept in the office concerned. This provides the same information as a burial register (except, of course, relating to the grave) but also marital status of the deceased, name and address of the persons who applied for the cremation and signed the certificates, the district where the death was registered, how the ashes were disposed of, and sometimes other family data.

The hazards to public health from overcrowded graveyards, plus the fact that many bodies removed from graves to make room for new ones were being burned anyway, led Dr William Price to cremate his own son, Jesus Christ Price, on Caerlan Hill in Wales in 1884. It was suddenly realised by a shocked British public that cremation was not illegal, though a Cremation Society had pointed this out since 1874. The first crematorium opened at Woking in 1885, followed by Manchester in 1892 and Liverpool in 1896. There is a directory of crematoria, some of which are private. From this small beginning, the number of cremations rose very slowly. Until the first world war, there were few more than a thousand per year; by the second world war, this had risen to ten thousand; and since 1968 over half the people dying in England and Wales each year have been cremated. You are unlikely to find a Roman Catholic cremated before 1965.

If someone is cremated, of course, there will be no grave, though there may be a plaque giving name and date of death. The ashes may be disposed of in the grounds of the crematorium; but they may be kept at home, if desired, by fond relatives. A funeral service will not necessarily be recorded, because the 1902 Cremation Act gives clergymen the right to refuse to conduct such a service before, during or after a cremation (unless the ashes are subsequently buried in the consecrated ground of a churhyard, a practice first allowed by the Church of England in 1944). In that case, the scattering or burial will be entered in the normal church burial register (page 133). However, ashes are the property of the next of kin, and have been put in a wide variety of places – on the mantlepiece, awaiting the death of the spouse; in an egg-timer 'so he will do more work dead than alive'; and on to the 'holy' Kop end of Anfield, though Liverpool Football Club, alas, keeps no register of those whose support survives their death.

Undertakers' records

An act of genealogical desperation which has been known to pay off when the place of burial cannot be found is to approach the undertaker nearest to where the deceased lived to see if his records go back as far as the burial you wish to locate. You will find undertakers in directories or the 'Yellow Pages' listed under 'Funeral Directors'. The National Association of Funeral Directors publishes a directory of members. You will find undertakers' records in chronological, rather than alphabetical order, but they can include name, address, age, occupation, relationship to the person organising the disposal, place of death and disposal, and sometimes a list of people attending. However, note that undertakers are under no obligation to preserve their older records.

Gravestones, and failure to find them

Most of our ancestors have no gravestone. Either they could not afford one, or the stone has not survived the effects of weather, church rebuilding or, in our own day, environmental improvement. It is worth looking, however, because if they do exist, gravestones can provide certain clues to a family's history which are unobtainable elsewhere. For example, those dating from before 1813 can be the only evidence for age at death. Members of the same family are often buried in the same grave, with relationships stated on the stone; and it is quite common for units within an extended family to have adjoining grave plots. In every case, you should copy down all the information on each stone, even about those whose relationship with your own ancestors is not clear; one day, it might help. Gravestone transcription can be time-consuming and open to error, so a photograph is much better.

Finding a particular grave is by no means as easy as it sounds, unless the church or cemetery keeps a map or key which will connect a burial to a grave number or plot. Always ask if such a map exists but never be surprised, in the case of a churchyard, if it does not. Tell the clergyman, verger, sexton or other official which gravestone you are seeking; they are around the graveyard quite regularly, and the position might have stuck in their mind. If the church does have a map or key, it might take the form of a grave register in which each grave is either listed in turn, possibly in the order in which the graves were started, or by its position in the graveyard, in which case the register will simply indicate the names of the people interred in each. The grave register is kept by the sexton. A comparison of a grave register with the gravestone inscriptions can indicate that there are often more people buried in a grave than appear on the stone; that many graves have no stone, including the 'public' or 'common' graves in which large numbers of corpses – without coffins until well into the nineteenth century – were cast; and occasionally that a corpse is not buried directly under the stone on which the name is recorded.

I fear, however, that you will have to search most graveyards without anybody or any document to help you find individual plots. Without wishing to be discouraging, I must warn that it can be a dirty, frustrating, time-consuming task, with no guarantee of success at the end of the search. For this reason, genealogists and family historians have, for many years now, undertaken the wholesale transcription of gravestones. These records are often referred to as monumental inscriptions, or MIs. One of the earliest and most famous is that of John Bigland, who is said to have copied most of the inscriptions in the county of Gloucester in the late eighteenth century. Most MIs are far less ambitious and usually include only one graveyard. It is the custom, and certainly an invaluable service to others, to place a copy of any MI into the local library and CRO, as well as in the church itself. The Society of Genealogists also possesses a very large collection, and the Federation of Family History Societies is undertaking the immense project of transcribing all extant MI's. Such a transcript should certainly always be made if there is any possibility of the gravestones being moved in a modernisation project. In the case of the Church of England and local authorities at least, MIs must be submitted before the stones can be removed. Those deposited with the Registrar-General are transferred to the PRO.

Failure to find a gravestone is common. You may be looking in the wrong graveyard anyway, and your ancestor quite possibly had no stone. Some have not survived, particularly early graves very close to church buildings which have been extended, and in areas where only soft sandstone was available. At Bowdon in north Cheshire, the church was rebuilt in 1859/60 when the parish clerk, one Eli Morgan, was also a housebuilder; some of his houses are still standing, and have gravestones embedded in them as cellar floors or hearthstones. It is always worth looking at MIs, especially when they are old, as they contain inscriptions from graves which have since disappeared.

There are other reasons for failure which you might be able to overcome. One of the commonest is the sheer size of the problem, especially round an old parish church near a large town. You can, however, eliminate many areas of the graveyard by noticing the style of the gravestones. Broadly speaking, any before the early nineteenth century is likely to be fairly close to the church and flat on the ground. Those before about 1730 also have more crudely carved lettering compared with the later ones, and those before about 1700 are likely to be entirely in capital letters. These flat slabs were used until after 1850, but the older ones can contain more modern inscriptions as fresh corpses were added. Genealogists will note that directors of horror movies pay little regard to such detail and have seventeenth century witches cavorting around Victorian gravestones.

The large, upright stones, probably blackened with pollution, will be nineteenth or early twentieth century; and the smaller, cleaner uprights will be quite modern. It should be said, however, that the size, shape and type of stone used vary considerably, not only from one part of the country to another, but also across social classes. The most disappointing are slabs which contain only the initials of the deceased. I hope, however, no one follows the example of one vicar who searched the registers for a reported eight years in an effort to find who 'HWP' had been, only to be told that it stood for Hot Water Pipe!

Gravestones earlier than 1600 are very rare, and most from before 1700 have disappeared. The flat, ground-level stones are often overrun with weeds, which are sometimes packed so closely together that the lettering can be seen clearly in mirror image in the tangled roots when they are lifted. In contrast, some of those exposed to the weather are difficult to read, and should be viewed in a slanting light if possible. Many stones have sunk too deeply to be easily recoverable. Visit your graveyard with strong gloves and suitable implements (trowel and secateurs are useful). Make sure that you search all possible hiding places for the six by two slabs. Usually, graves in churchyards lie east–west, arranged in rows with inscriptions legible from the east. Variations from this norm can hide some interesting stories; and although the heads of most corpses are at the western end, clergymen have been buried the other way round so that, when we all rise to face the dawn of the Day of Judgement, they will be facing their congregations!

If a few seem to be missing from the line perhaps they are below the present surface. Others may be inside the church itself, together with memorial plaques to more prominent citizens. It is still permissible to bury inside a place of public worship, except in the case of churches built in urban areas outside London since 31 August, 1848.

Monumental masons' records
Monumental masons, like funeral directors, are not obliged to keep their records beyond the needs of Her Majesty's Inspector of Taxes, but many do so; and because there are certain skills and equipment involved, firms of masons are both fewer in number and longer lasting than those of undertakers. They will usually search their records if you can provide an approximate date, and if their records go back that far.

Obituaries

Like notices of births and marriages, notices of death and obituaries ('obits') have appeared in newspapers for the last two hundred and fifty years. They often include a reference to where the deceased was buried. The main difficulties are knowing which are the right newspapers for *your* ancestors and getting access to them. *The Times* (1920) lists national and local newspapers for different periods during the nineteenth century. By far the oldest obits in newspapers are to be found in *The Times* itself and in *The Gentleman's Magazine* (1731–1908), each of which has indexes. However, only your richer ancestors are likely to be found in them. The era of mass obits and notices of death is much more modern – the late nineteenth century in most cases, by which time local newspapers were quite numerous. You should ask the local history librarian of the large public library nearest to where your ancestor died which of these old papers exist, and where copies are accessible. (The newspaper office itself is usually the last place you should try!) Again access to London eases matters considerably, for the newspaper section of the British Library has most regional and local papers. Obituaries should also be sought in trade and professional journals and parish magazines. See Gibson (8).

If your ancestor was of any substance, or notoriety, or if the death was unusual, the local newspapers should be consulted anyway, in order to acquire information unobtainable from the matter-of-fact records of birth, marriage and death. Searching local newspapers will not take as long as you might imagine because most appear weekly rather than daily, and notice of deaths and burials (which can even include paupers when they were buried at public expense) will be in the same place in each edition. However, you will probably be asked to look at old newspapers on microfilm in order to preserve the originals.

Hospital records

As in the case of births, deaths in these institutions are recorded in the hospitals' own archives (see page 37).

Trade union and friendly society records

The records of many trade unions (page 39) contain details of death benefits paid to relatives of deceased members and give dates, addresses, causes of death and sometimes a copy of the death certificate. Friendly society records (pages 39–40) covering individual membership are not as numerous, but again can provide a clue to the time and circumstances of death. It should be noted that whereas early British trade unions were normally created around workers in individual trades, and in many cases were true descendants of the craft guilds, friendly societies were usually based on a geographical area, and contained labourers and skilled craftsmen from many occupations.

Coroners' records

Any indication of death in unusual circumstances should be followed up in local newspaper reports; the records of a coroner's court may also be available, followed by a second newspaper report. The burial register and, from 1837, the death certificate should indicate whether the coroner's office had been involved. County directories will give you the names of contemporary coroners. See Gibson & Rogers, 1988.

The office of coroner was founded in 1194 and many of their early surviving records, for Bedfordshire and Nottinghamshire, for example, have been published. A considerable amount can be gleaned from these records. One of the most famous cases was that of the dramatist Christopher Marlowe, the discovery of whose inquest report of 1593 threw a whole new light on the political aspect of his life and death. For reasons which do the legal profession little credit, coroners' inquests fell in number between 1837 and 1860. After 1860 coroners were salaried, and the number of inquests returned to normal. In the present day, the coroner is even notified by the registrar of deaths if the deceased had not seen a doctor within fourteen days of the death, or had suffered a recent accident, violence, industrial disease or medical operation failure. Stillbirths can be referred, if the registrar suspects that the child might have been born alive.

Coroners' records, which include the depositions of witnesses, contain minute details of events leading up to the death, the name, age, address and cause of death of the deceased, and the verdict. They also contain some gruesome items of evidence from the hearing. Until 1926, the jury had to view the corpse; the coroner himself did so until 1980.

Apart from those which have been published, I have seen no set of indexed records, so a long search might be involved for any one entry; normally, however, you will know the approximate date of the inquest. Indexing the surviving records would be a straight-forward and worthwhile task for any family history group looking for projects to undertake. The PRO holds many of the early records, sometimes from as far back as the fourteenth century and, for a few areas, right up to the nineteenth. They are kept in the records of the Clerk of Assize.

These records, however, present one of those annoying difficulties which serve to remind us that, as far as public archives go, we still live in a very paternalistic society. In this instance confidentiality is carried to ridiculous lengths. All coroners' records earlier than 1875 are now preserved. The coroner keeps his current records until they are 15 years old, at which point the Home Office has directed that those relating to treasure trove and any deemed to be in the public interest should be transferred for permanent deposit to a specified local archive office. The remainder may be destroyed, despite the fact that inquests are held in public, and interested parties can buy a copy of the case notes.

Unusual deaths should be followed up in newspaper reports, of course, both immediately, and after a possible coroner's inquest.

Professional body records

Registrars of deaths are required to send copies of death entries (or form 111 which provides the same information) to certain professional bodies if the deceased was a practising or retired member. These include pharmaceutical chemists, druggists, solicitors, opticians, midwives, doctors, dentists and veterinary surgeons. Similar documentation is forwarded to the appropriate organisation if the deceased was in receipt of a pension from British Telecom, the Ministry of Defence, the DHSS, the Police, and Civil Service. If you have trouble locating the death entry of a member of any such profession, it may be worth approaching the professional body concerned for information

Church burial, 1538 to the present day

Until the second world war, burial was the most common means of disposing of corpses. It was normally preceded by a funeral ceremony, and indeed some old church registers refer to funerals rather than burials. With the rise of nonconformity towards the end of the eighteenth century, the events in the register may be burials, but not funerals. The funeral ceremony is always religious; a burial is not necessarily so, and since the advent of Local Authority cemeteries about 150 years ago, the state will record the burial of a corpse without a religious ceremony having been performed.

The history of Anglican burial registers follows very closely that of baptisms (pages 52–7). Until 1 January 1813, the entries are normally in the same parchment books as baptisms, but since that date they have been entered on printed forms in separate books, eight to a page. During the previous three centuries, the entries were subject to all the weaknesses and difficulties already described. At first, only the name of the deceased and date of burial are entered; further information was added in most parishes during the seventeenth century: the name of a dead child's father, and even its mother; the township within the parish where the deceased had lived; the name of a deceased wife's husband (very rarely that of a deceased husband's wife); and the marital status of the deceased – widow, spinster and so on. For a short period between 1645 and 1660, you might find the date of death as well as of burial. The age of the deceased was not entered regularly before the last quarter of the eighteenth century, and it was not done in every parish even then.

In 1813 George Rose's Act introduced the standard form on which the following information continues to be given to the present day: name, abode, date of burial and age. You will see that in some ways, a burial entry on the standard form is often less helpful than one in an earlier register. In particular it normally contains no information about the parents of dead children and the marital status of women. However, the lucky genealogist can still come across more complete registers even after 1812 (see church baptism, page 55). Witton continued to give much more detail in its auxiliary register until 1862. A typical entry reads, 'Elizabeth Wilcoxon, widow; died of natural decay, 20th April, 1824; buried on the north side of the churchyard on the 24th; daughter of John and Mary Shepley of Macclesfield; aged 69'.

Although you are very unlikely to be descended from anyone described in the burial register as 'son of' or 'daughter of', information about the burial of your ancestor's siblings can be very useful in supplying clues to the previous marriage, as we have seen. Before the nineteenth century, child deaths accounted for almost half the number of burials in normal times, and well over half during epidemics of such diseases as measles or diphtheria. Forty-four per cent of 29,000 burials in Lancashire during the 1620s were of children (Rogers, 1974). Infant mortality (the death rate of children before their first birthday) was at least one hundred times higher than in our own day, particularly in towns; it was still 15 per cent at the end of the nineteenth century and was especially high among illegitimate children. At the end of the eighteenth century, half the children born in some large towns died before they were five, and in London before they were three.

Searching for one particular burial entry in a parish register can be a long exercise unless the parish is small or the register has been correctly indexed. The baptism of children in a sequence will provide a general guide to the date of marriage and a good base for estimating the date of birth of the parents. There is no such clue concerning the date of death, however, unless the couple stop having children significantly before the mother reaches the age of forty. If, for example, the couple marry in their early twenties and appear to produce children for only ten years or so, you should look for the father's burial up to one year before the baptism of the last child, or for the burial of the mother to about three months before the last baptism, as well as for the following couple of years. (Of course, the couple might have simply moved parish.) If, however, the mother gives birth into her forties, then you might have to cover half a century in the registers and even then not find the burial you are seeking. One of my ancestors, Thomas Blain of Norley, fathered at least eight children in the 1720s and '30s. His wife died in 1763, but if the register had not been indexed I would probably never have found his burial in 1791, 'aged 102', as I would not have considered searching so far forward in time. Death at such an age was considered a rare enough event for a memorial to be placed in the churchyard, even though he had been 'only' an agricultural labourer.

Failure to find an Anglican burial

Burial in Anglican graveyards has never been universal, though there are many rural areas where it was almost so. Even in the seventeenth century, when you should expect to find at least 90 per cent of all burials in the Anglican registers, many were buried elsewhere. Into the eighteenth and nineteenth centuries, the percentage of Anglican burials declined dramatically, especially in the growing industrial towns.

There are several reasons why you might fail to locate the burial of an individual in the registers.

Burial in another parish

Any person was entitled to be buried in the parish where they lived or in the parish in which they had died; additionally, the clergyman or churchwardens could consent to bury anyone who had expressed a desire to be buried in 'their' parish, though fees for burying 'strangers' were often higher than those for parishioners. Presumably, the right of burial would also be extended to the owners of grave plots, even if they had neither lived nor died in the parish. From 1807, shipwrecked bodies had to be buried by the parish where they had been washed ashore. By the nineteenth century, many churchyards were full and the deceased sometimes had to be taken to a neighbouring parish for burial. Finally, it has been quite common for people to want to be buried in their parish of birth, with an irrational, though understandable, feeling for the idea of 'dust to dust'. My mother was buried in her parish of birth, having left it almost thirty years earlier.

Thus, there could be several reasons why our ancestors might not be buried in their own churchyards, and even after 1837, when the national death indexes begin, there is no easy way to discover where someone is buried. Searching one burial register is time-consuming enough; having to search many parishes in turn is sometimes not worth the effort. Is it not time that the place of disposal be included in a permanent document such as the death certificate itself?

Some of the other documents listed earlier might indicate when the death took place, which does then narrow the search considerably; until the eighteenth century, it was particularly common for testators to indicate in their wills where they wanted to be buried. In 1882, however, it was held in *Williams* v. *Williams* that such an indication is not binding on the executors. Heralds recorded place of burial in their Funeral Certificates (see page 87), and so do many obituaries.

Burial not recorded

Needless to say, parsons sometimes forgot to enter a burial, especially in the smaller benefices where they might not be resident. In the 1550s and 1640s, about one quarter of all burials seem to have gone unrecorded. It is always a good idea to consult the bishop's transcripts (pages 82–4) if they are available. Remember, however, that most printed registers have already been collated with the transcripts anyway – the introduction to a volume should inform you. Additionally, entries such as 'a man found drowned in the river', 'a poor woman found dead in the snow' are familiar enough to most searchers to suggest that many people's burials had to be recorded anonymously.

There were, however, certain categories for whom a normal Anglican funeral service was (and still is) forbidden by Canon 68, confirmed by statute under Charles II. Registration and burial were both affected. Those who had not been baptised (by anyone, not only by the Anglican church) could not receive Christian (i.e., Anglican) burial, and evidence suggests that numbers in this category increased into the eighteenth century. Baptist children, who were not baptised until the age of fifteen, were particularly affected, though their parents disliked the idea of consecrated ground anyway. It was high Anglican feeling against this sect which led to the notorious Akenham burial case of 1878 (see Fletcher, 1974). According to the 1801 census returns, however, most Baptists did bury their dead in the parish graveyard.

It sometimes comes as a surprise to learn that the Church of England used to excommunicate, and quite frequently at that, for what seem to us today to be trivial offences; but excommunicate she did, and exacted a penance or collected a fee for the excommunication to be lifted. Excommunication could also be accompanied by up to six months in jail. Although it became obsolete by the twentieth century, the power still rests with the Consistory (bishop's) Court. Anyone who had died excommunicated for some 'grievous and notorious' crime, if no-one was prepared to testify that he or she had repented before death, was deprived of a normal Anglican burial. However, from 1745, relatives of an excommunicant could compel burial in a churchyard, and a modified form of service was available following the Burial Laws Amendment Act of 1880. Even before that date, however, any sympathetic clergyman could absolve the deceased, and subsequently read the normal funeral service anyway. Canon 70 of 1603 had directed that all burials within the parish should be entered within the register, but the Anglican clergy have a reputation for independence of action in such matters.

Another category not entitled to burial service were those who, being sane, had nevertheless killed themselves (as judged by a coroner's jury). These unfortunates could be buried in an unconsecrated part of 'God's acre' only from 1823; before that, they were buried in the public highway, often at crossroads, with a stake through the heart. In 1961 suicide ceased to be a criminal offence, but ecclesiastical law remains unchanged; only the goodwill of the clergy, plus the fact that the corpse has probably been buried long before the jury brings in its verdict, gives a *felo de se* a normal burial.

In the sixteenth and perhaps early seventeenth centuries certain other persons could also be excluded – heretics, anyone not receiving Holy Sacrament (at least at Easter) and anyone killed in a duel, tilt or tournament. Executed criminals were also so deprived, and after 1861, murderers had to be buried with the prison walls if space was available.

It is to be hoped that all such persons were few in number; but that is no consolation to the genealogist whose ancestor was a rare exception. Fortunately, except in the case of the unbaptised, the offence often gave rise to documents which can provide more interesting information about the individual concerned than those which are available for more law-abiding mortals. (In the same way, the court cases of those refusing to complete their census form nowadays will probably be more interesting than the census returns themselves!) For example, excommunications will be in the proceedings of the ecclesiastical courts, which are normally in DROs. The cases were often started in the churchwardens' papers, for they had a duty to 'present' to the archdeacon or bishop those whom they suspected of having broken church law. Lists of such cases sometimes appear in churchwardens' accounts; the courts themselves kept the presentments. Summonses were drawn up in citation books, and the cases were then heard. They could involve immorality, marriage, probate, church finance, unlicenced teachers and midwives – a very wide variety of mortal fallibility. The record of any subsequent punishment, whether it was excommunication, a fine or penance, will be found in the 'correction books' (or Comperta and Detecta). See, e.g., Hair, 1972. Slowly the growth of population, urbanisation and nonconformity reduced the powers of these church courts. Divorce, matrimony and probate cases were lost to the civil courts in the 1850s, bigamy in 1861 and incest in 1908; but I believe that a church court could still try a case of adultery, if it so chose!

Burials often went unrecorded during epidemics, and indeed a diseased body could be refused admission to the church. (In this context it should be remembered that institutions such as hospitals and workhouses sometimes had their own graveyard and that their burials might not be entered in the local parish register.) It does seem natural that the normal obsequies would be cut short or cut out and, if the clergyman himself were ill, that even the burial of the healthy might go unrecorded. In Lancashire in 1623, for example, the registers of Brindle, Croston and Garstang were not written, and the clerk of Stalmine acknowledged that forty had been buried 'the tyme that I were sick'.

There were other causes of underregistration of burials. Large numbers died abroad (see below), mostly soldiers and sailors rather than travellers; and some people give their body for medical research, though the corpse has to be disposed of within two years. Nowadays, any burial in an Anglican graveyard (even the scattering of ashes) will be recorded, whether there has been a funeral service or not; but formerly, the register seems to have been a record of funerals rather than burials. The *Abstract of Parish Register Returns* (1801), which was associated with the first census, analysed briefly the causes of deficiencies in burial registers. The list of causes includes interment without ceremony, and London, Bristol and Newcastle-on-Tyne are singled out as particularly faulty in this respect. Writing in 1829, J. S. Burn said that more unregistered burials took place in the unconsecrated burial ground called Ballast Hills in Newcastle than in all the local churches and chapels put together, simply because the poor could not afford the burial fees. Other burials took place in non-Anglican graveyards (see pages 142–3).

Burial not in England and Wales – evidence for emigration
It is much easier to discover evidence for the fact of emigration of named individuals in the country to which they travelled, where

most documentary sources, research, and publications will be found. The last, of course, may be found in the larger libraries in the UK, and the Society of Genealogists. (See also Gibson (6).) Even in 1985, no British government department compulsorily records the emigration of individuals, and although the National Health Service tries to remove them from lists of doctors' patients, the information is not open to the public.

The evidence for transported convicts has survived more completely than for the free emigrants who were about a hundred times more numerous before the end of the nineteenth century. Convicts were sent to America until 1776, and Australia from 1787 to 1868, with some to South Africa between these periods. Transportation was generally an alternative to the death penalty, and cases, with sentence, can be found in Quarter Sessions papers (in CROs) or Assize records (PRO). Only a minority of men, but most women, so sentenced actually went abroad. Criminal registers and transportation registers are also in the PRO which houses a large number of other sources for individual transportees (see Cox and Padfield, 1981, PRO Leaflet No. 7, and *Family Tree Magazine*, vol. 1, no. 3, 1985). The latter should be consulted first if you know that the individual was transported, but not the area from which he came.

The free emigrants included those who were lured out of Britain by the promise of full bellies, gold, freedom of worship, or a host of other attractions; many were encouraged to leave because the colonies were desperate for labour, and because of the belief, which filtered into government circles once Napoleon had been beaten, that these islands were overcrowded. Thus, the state, and also local authorities on whom the burden of the relief of unemployment and pauperism fell, began to offer assisted passage.

For these emigrants, the evidence is thin and scattered. Passport registers, in the PRO, show name and date of issue, and are relatively full only after 1915. There is a thirty-year access rule, and the application forms, showing address and intended destination, are destroyed after only eleven years. There is sometimes a record of a farewell service in church, and especially chapel, minute books, and a note concerning emigration in the list of church members. My favourite among these is from Tintwistle in 1858: 'Samuel Harrison, to New Zealand; Mrs. Samuel

Harrison, to the USA'. Men would quite frequently go some years ahead of their wives.

Records of passage assisted by HM government are found in the PRO, the earliest being 1815. Poor Law Unions were allowed to support emigration from the rates after 1834, including children under 16 from 1850. Counties varied widely in the number of parishes involved in this assistance; see *Genealogists' Magazine*, vol. 20, no. 11 (Sept. 1982). Some Boards of Guardians' records are in the PRO, some are in CROs. Others had a passage assisted by the lord of the manor, trade unions, or voluntary societies such as Dr Barnado's. Passenger lists are rare before 1800, and most before 1890 have been destroyed. They are in the PRO, complete from 1890 to December 1960, arranged by port and year, name, age, occupation and approximate address.

Finally, some records survive in this country even once the individuals had emigrated. The PRO has censuses taken in Australia in the first half of the nineteenth century; some Anglican registers of parishes abroad are in the Guildhall Library (see Harvey, 1983 and Yeo, 1984). If an emigrant disposed of property in England and Wales, the will should have been proved in the PCC (see page 150) but many are in the diocesan probate registries.

Entry missed by searcher – see page 72

Base information incorrect

Bear in mind that some people were not buried, or even married, under exactly the same name with which they had been baptised; a few were even buried under their nickname. My favourite is the widow Marrowbone Roeby, buried at Witton in 1769. If you cannot find the burial of a widow, check for a possible remarriage (pages 116–17) – you might have been searching for the wrong surname. Occasionally, remarriage of the husband did not follow widowerhood or divorce, but separation followed by bigamy, especially before 1857. Equally, some clerks recorded burial of "the wife of" when it should have been entered as "the widow of".

Finding more than one possible burial

Additional information will be required in order to identify the right one. Was the subsequent burial of a wife that of a widow? Did the deceased leave a will which might identify him? Is he missing from other wills in which you would expect to find him if he were still alive? In other words, information from a variety of sources should be used in order to identify the correct entry or to eliminate the wrong one(s). For example, perhaps the gravestone or grave register will identify the burial you are seeking by linking it with other members of the same family, or to a known address.

Non-Anglican burial

If a systematic search of the Anglican burials proves fruitless, it is useful to bear in mind that other denominations have had burial grounds for centuries, the oldest probably being those of the Roman Catholics and Quakers. The law gave everyone the right to be buried in their local Anglican graveyard (though some, as we have seen, had to be in unconsecrated ground) and the Burial Laws Amendment Act of 1880 even legalised Catholic or any other Christian rites in the Anglican graveyard. Such burials should be entered in the register, and the name of the person giving the incumbent notice of burial will appear in the column for the officiating minister. However, there has never been any compulsion to be buried in the parish churchyard. Welsh parishes in particular have large nonconformist, as well as 'established' graveyards. For any one area, the archivist in the CRO should be consulted for advice about which non-parochial burial grounds existed at particular periods, and which have registers extant. Much that has been written about non-parochial baptismal registers (pages 78–80) also applies to burials, though not all chapels conducting baptisms had graveyards. Much of the legislation which makes the Anglican records so useful did not apply to other denominations – there are no bishop's transcripts, for example, and the entries are not always on standard forms.

Non-parochial burial registers vary widely in the amount of detail they provide. The fullest are probably those of the Quakers, which give name, description, abode, date and place of death and burial, and the age of the deceased. In my experience, the least conscientious have been the Methodists; their burial registers are often non-existent, even when they had their own burial ground, and even after the Registration of Burials Act of 1864, which compelled them not only to keep such registers, but also to send copies to the Anglican registrars. I do not know why this is and Methodist archivists I have approached on the subject have been unable to offer a satisfactory explanation. Even when they do survive, nonconformist burial registers are often incomplete. It is common for services to be conducted by visiting ministers who, if the chapel safe is not unlocked at the time, do not always remember to enter the interment later.

The quality of the other non-parochial burial registers lie on a spectrum between the Quakers and the Methodists. Each sect has its own peculiar, often convoluted history, which should be examined in *The National Index of Parish Registers* (Steel, 1968ff) vol. 2. On the whole, nonconformist burial grounds are rare before the end of the seventeenth century, and it has been estimated that even in Manchester in the 1770s, under 5 per cent of all burials were in dissenters' graveyards. This proportion increased in the nineteenth century, however, especially as their burial fees were normally lower than those of the Church of England; by 1831 almost 75 per cent of all Manchester burials were in non-parochial graveyards, a figure which included many Anglicans.

Registers not accessible – alternative sources

Many of the records listed earlier in Parts II and IV may be of assistance if the burial register is not available (see especially pages 81–90, 124–33). In addition to documents concerning graves and probate, several of the alternative sources for baptismal registers (pages 81–9) also apply to burials.

Following the Burial in Woollen Acts of 1666–1680, some parishes kept copies of burials in the churchwardens' accounts, or in a separate affidavit volume. Reference to this affidavit often occurs in the normal parish register, but although the Act remained in force until 1814, it fell into disuse between 1750 and 1780.

These accounts can refer to burials when a fee was paid to the churchwardens, and can contain more information than the parish register entry. The original affidavits themselves have occasionally survived.

Probate records

Wills form such an easily accessible and important source of information that genealogists have written entire books on the subject of their location (Camp, 1974; Gibson (1) and (2)). In many ways, a will tells you more about the living and about the deceased during their lifetime than about the death; but, after all, this is the reason why you are looking for records concerning death. The probate record can also provide the first evidence for the date of death.

11 January, 1858 marks an important watershed in the history of wills. For over three hundred years before that date, the right of proving wills had lain with the Church of England, and before that with the Roman Catholic church. Since 1858, the state has had the right of probate. Wills have also become more jargonised and shorter, perhaps reflecting the increased influenced of solicitors.

Wills proved since 11 January, 1858

If the executors of an estate wish to have the will proved, which gives a legal basis for the transfer of goods and property in cases where ownership has to be recorded, they arrange for it to be done in any one of two dozen or so district probate offices established in the major cities and towns of England and Wales, or through a subsidiary office. Since 1926, there have been no geographical boundaries to the jurisdictions of probate offices, which is convenient for distant executors. Once this process has been completed, a second copy of the will is sent to the Principal Registry of the Family Division, Somerset House, Strand, London WC2R 1LP, which thus houses copies of all wills proved in England and Wales since 1858. Because of pressure of space, wills more than fifty years old are now being removed from the district probate offices, and some are even being transferred to Somerset House. It seems a great pity that both copies of what is essentially a local document should go to London, but I understand that most probate offices are finding ways of housing their old wills nearby. You are advised to telephone the relevant probate office in order to discover the present whereabouts and accessibility of such records before you make a wasted journey.

According to a spokesman for the Principal Probate Office, each district office can decide on future location and accessibility for their wills over fifty years old. Genealogists should therefore press for continued public local access, but some archives have already been closed. In Manchester, for example, you can see wills proved in the late 1930s, but not in the 1920s.

Additional, registered copies of the original wills were made until 1940 in most districts, handwritten into large volumes and separately indexed. These copies and their indexes should be found in the relevant CRO. For lost wills, see page 152.

The existence of a will is quite easy to discover. Each probate office possessed a printed index of all wills proved in England and Wales since 1858, arranged annually by surname of testator. This index, or calendar, gives the name of the deceased, the address, date of death, sometimes the place of death, date of probate, the names of executors or administrators, the value of the estate and the name of the office in which the will was proved. Do not be surprised if your ancestor's will was proved at Llandudno during the second world war – the Principal Probate Registry was evacuated there from London. The GRO went to Blackpool.

As with the wills themselves, calendars over fifty years old are also being moved. It is said that the reason is again pressure of space, but this seems difficult to accept because, since 1973, calendars have been produced on microfiche (which usually omit the names of the executors, by the way). It is to be hoped that each town concerned will be able to retain these older calendars (and in circumstances more accessible than some of those being used at present), perhaps in the relevant CRO. Even more valuable (and rewarding for Somerset House) would be to make all the calendars available on microfiche. These could be sold to the many libraries, record offices, societies and individuals who would be interested in acquiring copies. For the present location of calendars see *The Local Historian*, vol. 15, No. 3 (November 1982).

Once you have access to these calendars, it is quite an easy though dusty job to search many years for a particular individual or family. Remember to search the addenda at the end of some volumes. District offices have photocopying facilities or, if it is still there, you can ask to see the will itself in the office where it was proved, free of charge. You are allowed to make notes, but not to take a full copy yourself. Ask to see, in addition to the will, any other document in the same file. There might be nothing; on the other hand, there could be bonds, oaths, powers of attorney, renunciations and other legal documents which cast light on the family concerned.

If there is a reference to a firm of solicitors, the Law Society can advise whether the firm still exists, albeit amalgamated with another. Contact with such a firm may produce extra data about the family, though you may have to pay for the privilege. Solicitors' archives, of course, contain large numbers of wills which were never proved.

Because the indexes are national, it is easy to discover the existence of a will, no matter where it was proved in England and Wales. Even death abroad should be followed by probate in Britain if the will involved the transfer of property in this country. If your search is fruitless, it almost certainly means that no will was proved, even though a will might have existed. The survival of unproved wills normally depends on the individual family concerned. Such a situation does not necessarily imply that the family was guilty of carelessness or even worse.

A will can be proved between seven days and six months following the death, so that probate might be indexed in the calendar year after the death itself. Indeed, the will could give rise to further proceedings which extend over a number of years.

If a thorough search has failed to reveal a will in the indexes, there is another avenue to explore for the period 1858–1870. If the deceased died intestate, or if the will was for some reason invalid, or if all the named executors renounced their office (any single one among them can have the will proved), then the probate court can issue Letters of Administration which give to named individuals, normally the next of kin, the right to administer the estate. Since 1870, these Letters of Administration have been indexed together with the wills themselves; but from 1858 to 1870 inclusive, they are indexed in a separate set of volumes. Administrations, however, are something of a disappointment. Admittedly you will learn the date of death and the occupation of the deceased, but there is none of the detail of a will which can bring your ancestor to life. Before the Administration of Estates Act of 1925, not even the

next of kin or relative had to be appointed as an administrator –
indeed, a statute of 1357 compelled the appointment of close
friends. Since 1926, if a close relative cannot be found, the estate
of an intestate can be appropriated by the Crown through one of
the Duchies, or the Treasury Solicitor. In the case of administrations over 75 years old, it is useful to follow the cases through the
Estate Duty Reports; (see page 152).

Wills proved before 11 January, 1858 and failure to find them

The proving of a will before 1858 was the prerogative of the
Church of England, and it is because there were so many courts
carrying out this function that the location of earlier wills can be a
complicated undertaking. Camp (1974) and Gibson (1) and (2) are
the basic guides for finding them. Sooner or later, every genealogist should consult one or other of these books; additionally, a
very full account of the law of wills prior to the nineteenth century
is in volume four of Burn (1824); for modern times, see Bailey
(1973) and Holoway (1979).

The tone of most of these early wills is very religious. They
begin with the phrase, 'In the name of God, Amen, I, A.B. of the
parish of C. in the county of D. . . .'; the occupation is normally
given, then some observations on the future of the deceased's soul
and the disposal of the mortal remains; the testator claims to be
sane (otherwise the will would have been invalid), but very often
admits to illness; finally at length, the will indicates how the
worldly goods are to be distributed among the living. Children,
grandchildren, other relatives and even servants are often named.
A common technique was to divide the estate into three parts,
giving one to the widow and one to the children. The final third
paid any debts and the funeral expenses. Any remainder would be
redistributed.

Most wills were proved by an archdeacon of the diocese in
which the deceased had lived and died. This was certainly the
normal court to which executors were expected to turn, though
there were many areas where the bishop himself undertook probate. According to Richard Burn, Chancellor of the diocese of
Carlisle, 'Archdeacons as such have no power to grant probate;
but they do not do it as archdeacons, but by a prescriptive right';
(Burn, 1824, vol. 4, p. 231). For the genealogist, the right is less

important than the fact; and Richmond in Yorkshire, a neighbouring archdeaconry to Burn's own diocese, enjoyed a jurisdiction extending over four counties.

The wills themselves are now normally to be found in the DRO,
and where this is combined with a city or county record office,
they can be consulted free of charge. All the offices with which I
have had contact are prepared to send photocopies of specified
wills for a relatively modest (but perhaps minimum) charge.
When sending for photocopies, you should be as explicit as possible about what you want – for example, indicate whether you want
only the will copied, or only the inventory (see page 154), or all the
associated documentation. Dioceses do not have the same geographical boundaries as counties, of course, and this is one of the
reasons why the reference books quoted above are so useful – they
answer the basic question about the location of wills left by
testators in county areas as well as in dioceses.

How do you discover whether any of your ancestors left a will?
The first step is to locate indexes to the wills. You will normally
find that an index of testators, giving the name and date (perhaps
also with the occupation, residence, and date or probate) is available at the record office concerned; many have been printed.
Details of available indexes are to be found in Camp (1974) and
Gibson (2), but more have been printed since those books
appeared.

The indexes are usually in alphabetical order of surname within
groups of years. There is no specific starting date nationally, and
many areas have wills surviving from as far back as the middle
ages, before parish registers began. Most testators were men or
widows; until 1882 married women could make a will only with
the consent of their husbands, sometimes following a formal
agreement or settlement at the time of marriage. It was normal,
before the nineteenth century, for a testator to mention all his
children (or all except the eldest son, who might have received his
inheritance already) and often grandchildren. In consequence, it
is possible to use wills to trace generations of a family without
having to use the parish register. A recent study of 350 wills left
between 1500 and 1800 found that an average of ten persons was
mentioned in each, most of whom would be relatives.

The index may refer to specific types of document associated
with probate – tuition bonds, or inventories for example (see pages

153–4). 'Nunc.' or nuncupative wills were unsigned declarations before witnesses, but in 1837 were made invalid for all except those on active military service.

Access to the index is only the first step. Which of the many testators having your surname were your ancestors? There is no simple answer. Sometimes you will be looking for the will of a man whose name and date of death you already know. Sometimes you know the name, but not the year he died, so that the index will be the main clue to the latter. Sometimes, you will know only the surname and probable place of residence. For example, if you have not been able to find a baptism, you may be searching for possible parents, hoping to find mention of a son or daughter-in-law which might confirm another generation for you. In this case of course, you must search all the wills left by anyone of that surname in as wide a radius as possible.

In each of the above cases, it is strongly recommended that you look not only at the most obvious candidate among the list of surviving wills, but also at any others left by testators with the same surname in that or adjoining parishes, or even further afield in the case of a rare surname. It is possible to build up an extensive network of relationships when the genealogical information has been extracted from these wills and reconstituted into family groups.

If you have any difficulty with the terminology of probate records, there is a useful glossary and abbreviation list in Gardner and Smith (1956), vol. 2, pp. 28–35, and Gibson (2).

There are a number of reasons why genealogists fail to find a will which they are seeking. Some we have met before, but others arise from the peculiar nature of wills and the way in which they have been proved and indexed. More than anything else, it should be remembered that, although a surprisingly large number of people left wills, most did not do so. Gibson estimates that, on average, each household left a will which was proved in court just once every 150 years. The following sections suggest reasons why a will which *was* made might now be difficult to trace; later sections describe other probate documents which may be available if the will cannot be found.

Wills proved by another jurisdiction
The law on the probate of wills before 1858 was somewhat

complicated, and although probate by archdeacon or bishop was the norm, circumstances might dictate that another type of court was used. Furthermore, whatever the law said was often ignored in practice, especially if the executors or next of kin lived in a diocese different from that of the deceased.

If the testator held property in more than one diocese, or even lived in one but died in another, the will should have been proved by an archbishop. In the northern parts of England and Wales, this would be the Archbishop of York, unless the property was partly in a diocese coming under the Archbishop of Canterbury, whose court had the superior jurisdiction. These series of wills are known by the names of the courts themselves – the Prerogative Courts of Canterbury (PCC) and York (PCY). The PCC had the sole right of proving wills from 1653 to 1660, when there were no bishops.

For all their pride of place in the genealogical textbooks, and their clear advantage in offering to most executors a more remote, and therefore more confidential, jurisdiction, I have always been disappointed by the PCC wills, concluding in my more cynical moments that they were made largely by the rich, south-easterners and sailors! Be careful about asking for the printed PCC indexes in your library – they can be listed either under the Index Library, or the British Record Society, and have different volume numbers in each case.

In the diocese of Chester, a will could be proved by an inferior court if the value of the property was under £40. These wills, just as valuable genealogically, are still stored separately, and are separately listed in some of the printed indexes. Tell the archivist that the will you are applying to see is 'Infra' in this case.

If the testator lived and died in a 'peculiar' jurisdiction, the will would be proved by a small local court which had powers relatively independent of the bishop. Anyone having property inside and outside the peculiar, however, had to go to the relevant archbishop's court.

According to Canon 126, those below the level of bishop who claimed to be able to prove wills should have sent copies every year to the diocesan registry, on pain of having their prerogative suspended; but it is evident that many did not do so.

Wills not proved

Until the Court of Probate Act of 1857, wills containing the disposition only of land (i.e., not goods) were not subject to ecclesiastical or to any other probate and have not normally survived, except among family papers. In the early middle ages, when wills in the modern sense started, the Crown jealously guarded its interest in land, so the civil courts retained sole decision in disputed cases. Such a will was nevertheless valid without probate and could be used in a temporal court of law. Again, wills involving only cash or personal property such as clothing, jewellery or furniture need not have been proved. Such wills were originally called 'testaments' and were in separate documents until 1540, when the 'last will and testament' became one.

Some wills were not proved because they were invalid or because the executors renounced their duties (see page 146).

Wills poorly indexed

Much of what has been written about the problems of indexing (page 19) applies to wills. Before the spelling of most surnames was standardised in the early nineteenth century, these problems are acute so it is important that the indexes should be arranged either phonetically, collecting together all spelling variants which sound the same (the technique used by the IGI for surnames), or alphabetically, with an efficient cross-referencing system so that all variants can be consulted. You should have little trouble with the former type, but not all cross-referencing is as good as it might be.

Wills proved late

If the indexes which you are using are arranged by groups of years, remember to search for two or three years after the date of death. Although most wills were proved within a few months, there was sometimes a long delay, and the wills are listed by date of probate, not date of death. There are also cases of second probate. These were caused, for example, by the death or late renunciation of an executor. Second probate in a diocesan court can follow an initial grant of probate in the PCC or PCY. The will of a man leaving a life interest to his surviving wife might have been proved decades later when she died. Disputed cases may be followed in the consistory court papers in the relevant DRO; these papers are normally indexed, and can be extremely useful to the genealogist.

Lost wills

There can be no doubt that, over the centuries, wills have been subject to the ravages of time as much as other documents, for they have not only been moved from one part of the country to another, but also stored in sometimes unsuitable conditions. Wills left by anyone whose surname began with A, B, C, D, E or F in Cheshire or south Lancashire in 1670, for example, have rotted away through being stored in a damp attic; other have been eaten by rats, destroyed by bacteria or lost in transit. Early wills in the probate registry at Exeter were destroyed by enemy action in 1942, though many have been replaced by the estate duty copies for 1812–1857 (see below).

Until 1858, there is some hope that you will find abstracts of the missing wills in the bishop's Probate Act Books, or even copies of the wills themselves in his enrolment books, sometimes known as th Bishop's Register. The Act Book abstracts normally include the name, marital status, occupation and names of executors, and can occasionally supply information additional to that contained in the original will. You should consult the diocesan archivist for advice about the years for which the Act Books are available. Ask if there are also registered copies of wills, made for consultation.

Abstracts of all British wills proved between 1796 and 1894 can be found in the PRO, compiled as a result of the stamp duty which became payable during the Napoleonic War. The abstracts are indexed by each court separately until 1812, and nationally thereafter. However, only those registers over 75 years old can be seen by the public – yet another illogicality within our system of preserving and giving access to records. You can see an original will, and even buy a photocopy of it, but you cannot see the summary! These estate duty registers in the PRO, often the easiest way to find a will in the nineteenth century, are described in the *Genealogists' Magazine*, vol. 20, no. 8; see also PRO leaflet no. 34. The registers can provide additional information on events subsequent to probate, including disputes.

Letters of administration (see also page 146)

It is also possible that even if there is no will (and occasionally even when there is one), there is a grant of letters of administration for the estate of the deceased. Circumstances in which such a grant was made were: intestacy; if all the named executors renounced their duty; if all the executors were under twenty-one; and if the diceased had died in debt and his creditors were granted the administration. Oddly enough, although the grant was made by the Church of England, the bishop was in this case acting as an officer of the civil law.

Sometimes you will find these 'admon bonds' ('admon' is a blanket term for administration documents) indexed with the main series of wills in that jurisdiction, but not always; they can be in separate sections, and even, in the case of the PCC indexes, in separate printed volumes. In some areas, there are Administration Act Books, and administration bonds signed by the administrators when promising to carry out faithfully their duties.

Miscellaneous probate records

There exist among church records a surprisingly large number of other documents associated with the processes of probate which can provide an alternative route to the information normally found in the wills themselves. Gardner and Smith (1956), vol. 2, ch. 5 and Gibson (2) contain useful summaries.

Caveat books contain declarations from anyone having an interest in the probate of a will in order to have their point of view heard by the court before probate was granted. In some areas, these caveats are written into the Act Books (page 152). *Assignations* were granted in cases of maladministration following normal probate of a will or admon. Litigation concerning wills was also heard by the church courts until 1858; the associated documents are sometimes lodged with the wills, *depositions* being particularly useful to the genealogist.

Care of orphans or fatherless children was the subject of separate bonds – *'tuition'* for girls under thirteen and boys under fifteen and *'curation'* for the older ones up to twenty-one. Usually, they are kept and indexed with the wills.

Perhaps the assessment of wealth best known to the genealogist is the *inventory*, which was very common in the sixteenth and seventeenth centuries, but became much rarer after the middle of the eighteenth. Few survive after 1800, but an inventory (and indeed an account of the administration of an estate) may still be ordered nowadays by a court of probate. It was the duty of an executor to list 'all the goods, chattels, wares, merchandises, as well moveable as not moveable whatsoever, that were of the said person so deceased' (Burn, 1824, vol. 4, p. 294a, where the appropriate form and content of the inventory are described at length). Even debts, owing to and by the deceased, should have been included. The court granting probate would do so on condition that such an inventory be made in the presence of the legatees or other competent persons. The PCC even required the inventory to have been made before the application for probate. Each item was separately valued at the price for which at that time it might have been sold, though this valuation was not binding on the subsequent distribution of the estate. See *The Local Historian*, vol. 14, no. 4 (1980) and vol. 16, nos. 3 and 4 (1984).

The inventories themselves had to be submitted to the ecclesiastical court and are normally stored and indexed with the relevant wills. The PCC inventories, however, are separately indexed and are in the PRO.

Many names of implements and household goods from former times have now died out of use. A glossary of many of these archaic terms is given in West, (1982); the large Oxford Dictionary is also very helpful in identifying them and their meaning.

V—Epilogue

Genealogy could be quite a lonely activity if it was not so absorbing, and there are many who welcome the chance to share their interests with others. The Federation of Family History Societies issues a Bulletin which lists the addresses of its constitutent members. Most such societies are based on a geographical area, but are as much for those who now live in that area as for those whose ancestors lived there. Also included is the Guild of One-Name Studies, devoted to those who concentrate their research into the history of families with the same surname. Activities of typical Family History Societies include lectures, consultations with experience genealogists, visits, periodicals and transcription and indexing of local records such as monumental inscriptions or the census. They can provide contacts with others who are tracing the same surnames as yourself and reciprocal research arrangements with members of other societies.

As the Federation grows in influence it should increasingly act as a pressure group, securing records which are in danger of loss or damage, ensuring that the interests of genealogists in the provinces are considered when institutions are making decisions which will affect them and arguing for the rationalisation of the present jungle of arrangements for access to our public documents, arrangements which currently allow me to see my neighbour's will, but not my own birth entry, and charge fees in some parts of the country for access to records which can be seen free of charge in others.

Most genealogists, however, do not join a society. They are happy enough to discover their ancestors without the companionship of others engaged in similar activity. Whichever category you are in, I wish you as much pleasure as genealogy has given me over the years. Remember that your family tree can be as boring to others as it is fascinating to you; remember to believe nothing till proved, to consult *all* the evidence available before deciding what to believe, to seek the advice of local historians as well as that of genealogists and to acquire your information as soon as possible before fire, damp, bacteria and public servants destroy even more of our records.

Select Bibliography

The following is a list of the sources from which the present book has been compiled, works of reference, and works referred to in the text.

Abbott, J. P., *Family patterns*, Kaye & Ward, 1971
Amateur Historian
Bailey, S. J., *The law of wills*, Pitman, 1973
Barrow, G. B., *The genealogist's guide*, Research Publ. Co., 1977
Bennet, J. & Storey, R. (eds), *Trade Union and related records*, University of Warwick, 1981
Burchall, M. J., *1984 National genealogical directory* Sussex Genealogical Centre, 1984
Burn, J. S., *The history of parish registers in England*, E. Suter, 1829
Burn, J. S., *The Fleet registers*, Rivingtons, 1833
Burn, R., *The ecclesiastical law*, A. Strahan, 1824
Burns, N., *Family tree*, Faber & Faber, 1962
Camp, A. J., *Wills and their whereabouts*, Camp, 1974
Camp, A. J., *Everyone has roots*, Star Books, 1978
Camp, A. J., *Tracing your ancestors*, John Gifford, 1979
Camp, A. J., *My ancestor was a migrant*, Society of Genealogists, 1987
Camp, A. J. & Spufford, P., *Genealogist's handbook*, Society of Genealogists, 1969
Census reports of Great Britain, 1801–1931, HMSO, 1951
Collins, R. P., *A journey in ancestry*, Alan Sutton, 1984
Colwell, S., *The family history book*, Phaidon, 1984
Colwell, S., *Tracing your family tree*, Faber & Faber, 1984
Cox, J. C., *The parish registers of England*, E. P. Publishing, 1974 (repr.)
Cox, J. & Padfield, T., *Tracing your ancestors in the Public Record Office*, HMSO, 1984
Currer-Briggs, N., *A handbook of British family history*, Family History Services, 1979
Currer-Briggs, N., & Gambier, R., *Debrett's family historian*, Debrett, 1981
Darlington, I., Rate books, *History*, XLVII, no. 159, 1962
Davies, M. R. R., *The law of burial, cremation and exhumation*, Shaw & Sons, 1976
Dowell, S., *History of taxation in England and Wales*, Cass, 1965
Eaton, J. & Gill, C. (eds), *Trade union directory*, Pluto Press, 1981
Eversley, D. E. C., et al., *An introduction to English historical demography*, Weidenfeld & Nicolson, 1966
Family Tree Magazine
Field, D. M., *Step-by-step guide to tracing your ancestors*, Hamlyn, 1982
Fletcher, R., *The Akenham burial case*, Wildwood House, 1974
Foster, J., *Alumni Oxonienses*, Parker & Co., 1891 ff
Gardner, D. E. & Smith, F., *Genealogical research in England and Wales*, Bookcraft, 1956 ff

Gatfield, G., The history and preservation of parish registers, *The Essex Review*, VI, no. 21, Jan., 1897

Genealogists' Magazine

Gibson (1), J. S. W., *Wills and where to find them*, Phillimore, 1974

Gibson (2), J. S. W., *A simplified guide to probate jurisdictions: where to look for wills*, FFHS, 1983

Gibson (3), J. S. W., *Bishop's transcripts and marriage licences, bonds and allegations: a guide to their location and indexes*, FFHS, 1983

Gibson (4), J. S. W., *Census returns 1841–1881 on microfilm: a directory of local holdings*, FFHS, 1984

Gibson (5), J. S. W., *Quarter sessions records for family historians*, FFHS, 1983

Gibson (6), J. S. W., *Marriage, census and other indexes for family historians*, FFHS, 1984

Gibson (7), J. S. W., *The hearth tax, other later Stuart tax lists and the Association Oath rolls*, FFHS, 1985

Gibson (8), J. S. W., *Local newspapers* (provisional title; to be publ. FFHS, 1985)

Gibson (9), J. S. W., *General Register Office and International Genealogical Indexes: Where to find them*, FFHS, 1987

Gibson, J. S. W. & Mills, D., *Land tax assessments, 1690–1950*, FFHS, 1984

Gibson, J. S. W. & Rogers, C. D., *Coroners' records in England and Wales*, FFHS, 1988

Glass, D. V., *Numbering the people*, D. C. Heath, 1973

Goss, C. W. F., *The London directories, 1677–1855*, Archer, 1932

Hair, P., (ed), *Before the bawdy court: selections from church court records, 1300–1800*, Paul Elek, 1972

Hamilton-Edwards, G., *In search of army ancestry*, Phillimore, 1977

Hamilton-Edwards, G., *In search of ancestry*, Phillimore, 1983

Hamilton-Edwards. G., *In search of Welsh ancestry*, Phillimore, 1985

Harvey, R., *Genealogy for librarians*, Clive Bingley, 1983

Hector, L. C., *The handwriting of English documents*, Arnold, 1980

Holding, N., *World War I army ancestry*, FFHS, 1982

Holding, N., *Locating British records of the army in World War I*, FFHS, 1985

Holding, N., *More sources of World War I army ancestry*, FFHS, 1987

Holloway, D. R. LeB., *The probate handbook*, Oyez Longman, 1984

Iredale, D., *Your family tree*, Shire Publ., 1977

Jacobs, P. M., *Registers of the universities, colleges and schools of Great Britain*, Institute of Historical Research, 1964

Josling, J. F., *Change of name*, Oyez Publ. Ltd., 1985

Journal of Regional & Local Studies

Laslett, T. P. R., *The world we have lost*, Methuen, 1983

Laslett, T. P. R., *Family life and illicit love in earlier generations*, CUP, 1977

Latey, W., *The tide of divorce*, Longman, 1970

Lawton, R., *The census and social structure*, Cass, 1978

Local historian

Local population studies

Mander, M., *How to trace your ancestors*, Panther, 1984

Marshall, G. W., *The genealogist's guide*, Heraldry Today, 1967

Matthews, C. M., *Your family history*, Lutterworth Press, 1982

McGregor, O. R., *Divorce in England*, Heinemann, 1957

McLaughlin, E., *A series of guides, published by the FFHS, reissued regularly.*
Annals of the Poor
The Censuses 1841–1881
Family history from newspapers
Illegitimacy
Interviewing elderly relatives
Parish registers
Reading old handwriting
Simple Latin for family historians
Somerset House wills from 1858
St Catherine's House
Wills before 1858
Miege, G., *The new state of England*, London, 1701
Milligan, E. H., & Thomas, M. J., *My ancestors were Quakers*, Society of Genealogists, 1983
Mitford, J., *The American way of death*, Hutchinson, 1963
Mullins, E. L. C., *Texts and calendars*, vols. 1 & II, Royal Historical Society, 1958 & 1983
Nissel, M., *People count: a history of the General Register Office*, HMSO, 1987
Norton, J., *Guide to the national and provincial directories of England and Wales, excluding London, published before 1856*, Royal Historical Society, 1950
Oxford dictionary of English Christian names, OUP, 1977
Palgrave-Moore, P., *Understanding the history and records of Nonconformity*, Elvery Dowers, 1987
Phillimore, W. P. W., & Fry, E. A., (eds), *An index to change of name*, Phillimore, 1908
Pine, L. G., *Genealogist's Encyclopaedia*, David & Charles, 1969
Pine, L. G., *Trace your family history*, Hodder & Stoughton, 1984
Pelling, G., *Beginning your family history*, FFHS, 1982
Population Studies
Population Trends
Rogers, C. D., The Bowdon marriage licences, 1606–1700, *Lancashire & Cheshire Historian* I, 10; III, 1, 1966–7
Rogers, C. D., The case against the school boards of Cheshire, 1870–1902, *Jnl. Chester Archaeological Society*, 1970
Rogers, C. D., *The Lancashire population crisis of 1623*, University of Manchester Extra-mural Dept., 1974
Rogers, C. D., *Tracing missing persons*, MUP, 1986
Rudinger, E. (ed), *What to do when someone dies*, Consumers' Association, 1978
Sandison, A., *Tracing ancestors in Shetland*, T. & J. Manson, 1972
Seymour, C., *Electoral reform in England and Wales*, 1915; repr. David & Charles, 1970
Sims, J., *A handlist of British Parliamentary poll books*, University of Leicester and University of California, 1984
Sims, R., *A manual for the genealogist, topographer, antiquary, and legal professor*, John Russell Smith, 1856
Sims, R., *Index to the pedigrees and arms contained in the heralds' visitations and other genealogical manuscripts in the British Museum*, Genealogical Publ. Co., 1970 (repr.)
Steel, D. J., (ed), *The national index of parish registers*, Society of Genealogists,

1968 ff
Steel, D. J., *Discovering your family history*, BBC, 1980
Steel, D. J. & Taylor, L., *Family history in focus*, Lutterworth Press, 1984
Swinson, A., *A register of the regiments and corps of the British army*, Archive Press, 1972
Tate, W. E., *The parish chest*, Phillimore, 1983
Taylor, L., *Oral evidence and the family historian*, FFHS, 1984
Terry, J., *A guide to the Children Act, 1975*, Sweet & Maxwell, 1979
Thomson, R. R., *A catalogue of British family histories*, Research Publ. Co., 1976
Times, *Handlist of English and Welsh newspapers, 1820–1920*, The Times, 1920
Todd, J. E., & Dodd, P. A., *The electoral registration system in the United Kingdom*, OPCS, 1982
Turner, E. S., *What the butler saw*, Michael Joseph, 1962
Turner, J. H., (ed), *The Rev. Oliver Heywood, B.A., 1630–1702; autobiography, diaries, etc.*, Brighouse, 1881–5
Unett, J., *Making a pedigree*, Allen & Unwin, 1971
Venn, J. & J. A., *Alumni Cantabrigienses*, CUP, 1922 ff
Vincent, J. R., *Pollbooks: how Victorians voted*, CUP, 1967
Vital registration and marriage in England and Wales, OPCS, 1979
Wagner, A. R., *English ancestry*, OUP, 1961
Wallis, P. J., *Histories of old schools: a preliminary list for England and Wales*, *British Journal of Educational Studies*, XIV, 1, 1965; 2, 1966
War Office, *Soldiers died (sic) in the Great War*. 1920–1
Waters, R. E. C., *Parish registers in England*, Waters, 1883
West, J., *Village records*, Phillimore, 1982
West, J., *Town records*, Phillimore, 1983
Whitmore, J. B., *Genealogical guide*, Society of Genealogists, 1953
Willis, A. J. & Tatchell, M., *Genealogy for beginners*, Phillimore, 1984
Wrigley, E. A., (ed), *Identifying people in the past*, Edward Arnold, 1973
Wrigley, E. A. & Schofield, R. S., *The population history of England, 1541–1871*, Arnold, 1981
Yeo, G., *The British overseas: a guide to records of their births, baptisms, marriages, deaths and burials, available in the United Kingdom*, Guildhall Library, 1984
Yurdan, M., *Tracing your ancestors*, David & Charles, 1988

Appendices

1—The Federation of Family History Societies

Societies available to genealogists are numerous, and are of several kinds. Some are national, the most famous being the Society of Genealogists, 14 Charterhouse Buildings, Goswell Road, London EC1M 7BA; others are of a more specialised nature. Most, however, are Societies which are based on a locality, designed to help those whose ancestors came from that area, and genealogists who now live there. These individual Societies organise lecture programs, produce their own journal, maintain a directory of members' interests, publish matter related to the history of families in their area, and will in most cases undertake searches of local records for their members living overseas.

The Federation of these Societies has a role which facilitates exchange of information and ideas. It produces a very useful journal twice a year – the *Family History News and Digest* – to which individuals can subscribe ($8.70 p.a. or $12.50 airmail). This includes an up-to-date list of secretaries of each member Society, news of changes to record systems, news of individual Societies, and over 400 abstracts of articles from F.H.S. journals. The Federation organises conferences, makes representations to official bodies concerning changes which might affect genealogists, promotes courses and lectures, and coordinates some national projects such as the indexing of the national census of 1851 and all Monumental Inscriptions. It publishes a large number of guides to records (such as those of Jeremy Gibson and Eve McLaughlin), many of which cannot be found in normal booksellers'.

The list of member Societies which follows is correct for March 1989. Names and addresses of secretaries change fairly frequently, however, and can be obtained through the Federation's Headquarters, The Benson Room, Birmingham & Midland Institute, Margaret Street, Birmingham, West Midlands B3 3BS, United Kingdom. Please enclose three International Reply Coupons.

Society of Genealogists
Inst. of Heraldic & Genealogical Studies
Avon *see* Bristol
Isle of Axholme F.H.S.
Bedfordshire F.H.S.
Berkshire F.H.S.
Birmingham & Midland Soc. for Gen. & Her.
Bradford F.H.S.
Bristol & Avon F.H.S.
Buckinghamshire F.H.S.
Calderdale F.H.S.
Cambridgeshire F.H.S.
Channel Islands F.H.S.
F.H.S. of Cheshire
North Cheshire F.H.S.
Cleveland F.H.S.
Cornwall F.H.S.
Cumbria F.H.S.
Derbyshire F.H.S.

Devon F.H.S.
Doncaster S.F.H.
Dorset
Durham
Eastbourne & Dist. (Family Roots) F.H.S.
Essex S.F.H.
Felixtowe F.H.S.
Folkestone & District F.H.S.
Gloucestershire F.H.S.
Hampshire Genealogical Society
Hastings & Rother F.H.S.
Herefordshire F.H.S.
Hertfordshire F.& P.H.S.
Hillingdon F.H.S.
Huddersfield & District F.H.S.
Huguenot & Walloon Gazette Association
Huntingdonshire F.H.S.
Kent F.H.S.
North West Kent F.H.S.
Lancashire F.H. & Heraldry Society

Leicestershire F.H.S.
Soc. Lincs. Hist. & Arch. (F.H. Section)
Liverpool & District F.H.S.
East of London F.H.S.
Isle of Man F.H.S.
Manchester & Lancashire F.H.S.
Mansfield & District F.H.S.
Central Middlesex F.H.S.
North Middlesex F.H.S.
West Middlesex F.H.S.
Monmouthshire
Norfolk and Norwich Genealogical Society
Northamptonshire F.H.S.
Northumberland and Durham F.H.S.
Nottinghamshire F.H.S.
Oxfordshire F.H.S.
Peterborough & District F.H.S.
Ripon & District F.H.G.
Sheffield & District F.H.S.
Shropshire F.H.S.
Somerset & Dorset F.H.S.
Spalding Gentlemen's Society
Staffordshire
Suffolk Family History Society
East Surrey F.H.S.
West Surrey F.H.S.
Sussex F.H.G.
Waltham Forest F.H.S.
Warwickshire
Weston-Super-Mare F.H.S.
Isle of Wight F.H.S.
Wiltshire F.H.S.
Woolwich & District F.H.S.
Worcestershire
Yorks Arch. Soc. F. & POPN. Studs. Sect.
East Yorkshire F.H.S.
City of York & District F.H.S.

Clwyd F.H.S.
Dyfed F.H.S.
Glamorgan F.H.S.
Gwent F.H.S.
Gwynedd F.H.S.
Powys F.H.S.

North of Ireland F.H.S.
Ulster Gen. & Hist. Guild

Central Bureau Voor Genealogie
Australian Inst. of Genealogical Studies
Society of Australian Genealogists
Western Australian Genealogical Society
Heraldry & Genealogy Society of Canberra
Genealogical Soc. of Northern Territory
Queensland F.H.S.
Genealogical Society of Queensland
Central Queensland Gen. Assn.
Ipswich Gen. Soc. Inc.
South Australian Gen. & Her. Society

Genealogical Society of Victoria
Genealogical Society of Tasmania
Nepean (District) F.H.S.
Maryborough District F.H.S.
Blue Mountains F.H.S.
New Zealand Society of Genealogists Inc.
New Zealand F.H.S.
Gen. Research Institute of New Zealand Inc.
Int'l. Soc. for British Gen. & Fam. Hist.
Florida Genealogical Soc.
Gen. Soc. of Sarasota Inc.
Intn'l. Genealogy Fellowship of Rotarians
Ventura County Genealogical Society
Houston Gen. Forum
Jefferson County Gen. Soc.
Los Angeles (British F.H.S. of)
English Interest GP, Minnesota Gen. Soc.
Santa Barbara County Genealogical Soc.
Krans-Buckland Family Association Inc.
Genealogical Assoc'n of Sacramento
Utah Genealogical Assn.
Alberta F. Histories Soc.
Alberta Genealogical Society
British Columbia Gen. Society
Victoria Genealogical Society
Kamloops F.H.S.
Manitoba Genealogical Society
Newfoundland & Labrador Gen. Soc. Inc.
Ontario Genealogical Society
Ontario Gen. Soc. (Toronto Branch)
Quebec F.H.S.
Saskatchewan Gen. Soc.
West Rand F.H.S.
Human Sciences Research Council

British Assoc. of Cemeteries of S. Asia
British Australian Heritage Society
Anglo–German F.H.S.
Catholic Record Society
English Catholic Ancestor
Guild of one-name Studies
Beresford Family Society
Braund (name) Society
The Brooking Society
Caraher F.H.S.
Cave F.H.S.
Dalton Genealogical Society
Intnl. Haskell Family Association
Palgrave Society
Restorick F.H.S.
Talbot Research Organisation
Redundant Churches Fund
Local Population Studies Society
Genealogical Society of Utah
British Telecom & Post Office F.H.S.
Rolls Royce F.H.S.

2—The Guild of One-Name Studies

This Guild, one of the member Societies of the F.F.H.S., is an association of individuals, groups and societies each of whom is studying the history and development of a single surname (with its commonly accepted variants). Through the Guild, therefore, you can be put in touch with others researching the same surname(s) as yourself. The Guild publishes a Journal, maintains a register of members involved in one-name studies, and gives advice on the formation of new groups.

General correspondence should be addressed to

The Guild of One-Name Studies
Box G, Charterhouse Buildings
Goswell Road
London
EC1M 7BA
United Kingdom

Membership enquiries should be addressed to

The Registrar of the Guild of One-Name Studies
1, Cambridge Close
Lawn
Swindon
Wiltshire
SN3 1JQ
United Kingdom

Please enclose three International Reply Coupons. The list of names currently registered with the Guild, at November 1988, are:

Aberdeen Aboad Ackwood Addis Adlam Adrian Agar Agutter Aishe Aislabie Aitkens Akister Alabaster Alban Alderson Alderdice Aldersley Alefounder Allaby Allaker Allmark Allsop Alston Alvey Ambridge Amphlett Amsden Annett Anscomb Anstis Anthony Appledore Apthorp Arch Arculus Argent Armin Ash Ashe Ashby Ashfield Ashmole Ashton Aslett Atkins Attfield Attwell Attwood Attwooll Aucott Auders Austerberry Avens Avis Awde Ayliffe Axcell ∎ Babb Baber Badalee Bagshaw Bagworth Baigent Bains Baldwick Baldwinson Ball Ballard Balley Bangay Banham Bann Banwell Barchard Barefoot Barfield Barham Barkwith Barling Barnhurst Barrett Barrodale Basford Baslington Bassano Basset Batch Bath Batten Baugh Baughan Bazzone Beamish Bearsby Beckham Bedford Beecher Beetham Belam Belaney Belchamber Belshaw Bending Benians Beresford Bernardes Berrett Bettinson Bevins Bewsher Bezzant Bible Bicheno Biddle Biddulph Bidwell Bigmore Billing Billins Billyard Birchenough Birdsall Birkbeck Birtwhistle Bisgrove Blake Bliss Block Blood Boag Bobby Boddington Bodfish Boneham Bonthron Botterill Botevileyn Bousfield Bovington Bowdler Bowra Boyes Brackpool Bradford Bradilaugh Brain Brason Brass Bratley Brammage Bratt Braund Brayford Breward Brewin Brickett Bridgeford Brierly Briginshaw Brimson Bringloe Brison Broadhead Broatch Brocklehurst Bromell Brooking Brooksby Broome Broomhall Brougham Brownhill Brownsey Broxton Brunyee Bryant Bucksey Bundock Bungay Bunnett Bunyan Burdge Burdick Burgis Burgoyne Burkin Burleigh Burman Burniston Burwood Bushby Butland Butlin Butson Butteris Byett ∎ Cake Calfe Callingham Cammack Cammish Campany Camper Campion Cannadine Cansick Canton Capon Capps Caraher Cardoza Carew Carmen Cartwright Carveth Cary Caslake Cave Cavenett Cawthorn Chadwick Chaffin Chambers Champkins Chandler Chaproniere Chatfield Chatterton Chawing Cheke Chellew Chilton Chiswell Chowings Chowney Choyce Christmas Churchward City Clapp Claricoates Clasper Claughton Claxton Clayburn Cleak Clegg Clement Clifford Clives Clubb Clyffe Coare Coath Cochrane Codgebrook Coggan Colegate Colfer Collier Condliffe Congerton Cooksey Coole Coops Coote Coppard Corbet Corby Cornford Cotesbrook Coughtrey Courtman Cowen Cox Cozens Crabbe Crafter Cram Cribb Crichton Crippen Croasdale Croker Crosskill Crowcombe Crowfoot Crudge Crudgington Cuff Cuffin Cufley

Culling Culverhouse Curme Cutlack ■ Dacre Dadley Dadswell Dafform Dagworthy
Dalrymple Dalton Damerell Danes Danks Dartnell Darvall Dashwood Davison Daybell
Daynes Delbere Debney Defriez Deller Denley Denning Denzey Derbyshire Devall
Devonshire Dewhirst Dibden Difford Digweed Dinwoodey Diss Dobson Dockree Dods-
well Doggart Donohue Dorling Dorrell Doubt Douce Douglas Doust Dowse Dufton
Dugmore Dunbar Duncalf Dunnicliffe Dunstall Dury ■ Eagle Eaglen Easey Eatwell
Eccleshall Edgcombe Edney Egan Egerton Einon Elam Ella Ellick Ellis Elvey Engert
Eplett Esse Essery Esslemont Ethell Euridge Eustace Eversfield Excell ■ Fabian Fairchild
Fairfax Fairhead Faithful Fake Falconbridge Fall Fallows Familton Fanstone Farnham
Farnol Farrant Farrer Fautley Faux Fearncombe Feltoe Fenwick Ferdinando Ferry
Fewster Fice Filby Fieldsend Filson Fishenden Fisher Fitness Fitton Fitzjohn Flood
Fordham Fosbroke Fossick Foulser Franks Freathy Free Freeman Froggatt Frost Fryatt
Fulton ■ Gabb Gambier Gander Garmon Gasking Gates Gawen Geene Geesin Gent Gilbert
Gill Gillard Gillberry Gilston Girdlestone Glaister Glasson Glibbery Godber Goddard
Godson Goggin Golder Goldfinch Gomersall Goodall Goodbody Goodey Gorick Gorrie
Gosby Gosnold Gott Gotterson Goulty Gowenlock Gowlett Goymer Graddage Grafham
Greenwood Gribbin Grier Grigg Grimstead Gronow Grose Grottick Grutchfield Guess
Gullen Gumbleton Gunthorpe Gup Gupwell Gwinnett Gynes ■ Haarnack Haberfield
Hackwood Haddow Haddrell Haile Hailey Halkyard Hallmark Hambleton Hambrook
Hamley Handscomb Hankinson Hannam Hansford Hardie Hards Hardwick Hardyman
Harman Harrower Hatfield Hatswell Haunton Havelock Hawkhead Hayter Hazelton
Heather Hebden Hebgin Heelis Hemmington Hems Henblest Henney Henning Henri-
ques Hercules Heriot Heritage Herridge Havderbourck Hewer Hext Hexter Hicks Hick-
ling Higgins Hilborne Hilder Hilliker Hindwood Hinxman Hisgrove Hitchon Hoadly
Hobson Hocking Hodgkinson Hodsdon Hogwood Hoile Holah Holbrook Holcroft
Holditch Hollebone Holley Hollick Holt Holttum Holyer Honeycombe Honeywood
Honiet Hopper Hore Horsell Horsman Horswill Horth Hosie Houchell Hudgell Hudswell
Hulley Hunkin Hunscot Hunter Huntingford Hurst Huscroft Husthwait Hutley Hylands
Hyner ■ Iles Inch Ingham Ironside Isgrove Ivory ■ Jacob Jarman Jayne Jephcote Jopling
Judd Juniper Jupp ■ Keates Kelland Kello Kelman Kempshall Kerkhoff Kesterton
Kiddle Kidman Kidwell Killick Killon Kinchin Kingan Kingsman Kingston Kinnison
Kipps Kitchenor Knight Kyffin ■ Labouchardiere Lailey Laker Lamacq Lambert Lam-
kin Landreth Landrum Langhelt Lankshear Larden Laws Leathers Leeson Lefaux Leffen
Leggett Leith Leng Lestrange Leworthy Lickfold Lidstone Linder Lindo Lisney Little
Littlechild Littleford Litton Loach Lobb Lobley Longman Longmire Loring Losh Love-
grove Lucop Lumley Lupton Lusher Lutley Lyford(e) Lynall Lyon Lyus ■ McCurley
MacGory McBeth Mackett Macro McLachlan McMinn McRobb Maggott Mainland Mai-
ris Malby Malins Maliphant Mallery Mallett Mandeville Mansbridge Mantell Mardon
Marengo Marfleet Margrett Mark Marker Markwell Markwick Marnell Marrington Mar-
tin Masterson Maton Maw May Maybank Maycroft Maynard Mayne Mealing Medway
Mee Megginson Megson Meikleham Melmoth Melsom Mennim Meredith Merrill Mer-
rington Merritt Messenger Metcalfe Mewse Middleyard Mignon Mildred Mileman Mill-
house Millichamp Millier Mirrington Mithan Mob Molyneux Mombrun Money Monnox
Morden Morrell Morrison Mouldey Mountcastle Mowbray Moxon Moy-Thomas Mulcock
Mullett Murfet Murray Murrell Musk ■ Nadin Neale Needham Nesbitt Newth Nokes
Norrington Nutsford Nuth ■ Oastler Offley Ogden Olivey O'Neil Onyett Oram Orbell
Orders Oriel Orridge Oswald Othen Ousley ■ Padget Pagan Paisley Paley Palgrave Pannett
Parley Patchett Patrick Pattenden Pattison Paveley Pavitt Payne Payton Peake Peapell
Peatling Penistone Pennyman Pepperdine Perkins Perrett Pettypool Peyton Phelps
Phenna Philbey Philcox Philpott Philson Pickerden Pildeam Pilter Pim Pingram Pinning
Piper Pite Plant Pleydell Plimley Polding Polkey Pollicott Polyblank Pomeroy Pook Popely
Popkiss Poppitt Popplestone Potterveld Poulton Powdrill Powling Powney Poynting
Poyntz Pratten Preece Prendergast Presbury Priest Proom Protheroe Proudfoot Pruddah
Prum Puckmore Pugin Pulker Pulvertaft Pyman Pyte ■ Quarry Quincey Quip Quoth Quy
■ Rainbird Rane Ratt Ravensdale Rawes Rayton Razey Redrup Refoy Relf Remington
Renowden Restorick Reynish Rhoades Rhydderch Richards Richmond Rickett Ridout
Rix Roden Rolls Rootham Rose Roseneder Rounce Rounding Royall Ruffle Rugg Rugman
Rumsey Runacres Russell Rydings ■ Sabourin Sabrey Sadgrove Sagar Sandison Sando
Sant Savinac Scales Scapens Scoltock Scopes Scorgie Scott Scrivens Seabury Sear Searle
Seddon Sedgwick Sessions Sexey Shakespeare Shambrook Shapcott Sharpe Sharvell Shel-
don Sheppey Sherrell Shew Shewbridge Shillaker Shilling Shipsides Shirley Sholl Shrap-
nell Shroff Shropshire Shuttle Sidney Sidwell Silk Sillers Simister Sizeland Skidmore
Skinner Skoyles Slatford Slyfield Smallshaw Smelt Snelgrove Snelson Somerscales Soper

Southwell Sowter Spanton Spaughton Spause Spence Spendlove Spilling Spode Spottis-
woode Stagg Starbuck Starkey Startup Sterry Stirzaker Stockton Stoneham Stormont Stott
Straley Strange Stretch Stroyan Such Sumner Suthren Swain Swinfield Swinnerton Swin-
ton Swinyard Swords Sworn Swyer Syndercombe ■ Tallis Tame Tampin Tarrant Tearle
Tebble Tedd Teece Tegnor Templer Templeton Thake Third Thirkill Thoday Thomp-
stone Thorp Threlkeld Thunder Thurkettle Tickner Tik Tilston Timberlake Timbers
Timothy Timperley Tinney Titchiner Tocock Todd Tooke Toop Totterdell Towner
Trapnell Treherne Treleven Tresize Trice Trompf Trott Truss Tucker Tuckley Tuley
Tune Tunnicliff Turk Turkentine Turkington Turner Twelves Tye Tyldesley Tyrrell
■ Uden Uffindell Ullathorne Ulph Ulyatt Underhay Unyatt Uren Urry Urwick ■ Vaile
Varco Vearncombe Venables Venn Verlander Verrall Veryard Vialls Vickerage Vinden
Voice Vreethy ■ Waddelow Wadham Wagstaff Walklate Wansborough Want Warne
Warnford Warth Wassall Watcham Watkiss Watmore Weale Webb Weddell Weedon
Weeks Weight Welby Welles Westerdale Whatmore Wheeler Wheelton Whitehouse
Whit(e)ley Whitlock Whittall Whittard Wickstead Wigginton Wigzell Wilder Wildig
Wildy Willerton Willett Wilmot Wilson Windebank Winder Windget Wingrove Wisdom
Wishart Wodehouse Woodhouse Woodiwiss Woodward Woodyear Woollings Woolven
Woolvett Woolward Worsdell Worsfold Worth Wratt Wyard Wyborn Wythers ■ Yale
Yeatwell Yeoman Yerl Youden Yull ■ Zouch

3—Registration districts in England and Wales

The following list of addresses is correct at February 1989. Counties have been
included for the benefit of overseas readers, but it should be noted that there were
significant boundary changes in 1974 which created new counties as well as
changing old ones. You should write first to the address closest to where you
expect your ancestor to be registered, and your letter will be forwarded if it has
been sent to the wrong office.

You might be interested to know that zip codes in the U.K. have no directional
significance except in London where, for example, Brent is in the north-west of
the city – hence the N.W. in the code.

The correct form of address is as follows, taking the first as an example

The Superintendent Registrar

Aberconwy Registration District

Muriau Buildings

Rose Hill Street

Conwy

Gwynedd

LL32 8LD

United Kingdom

Make your request for copy certificates as concisely as possible, indicating
whether your source of information is proved, conjectured, or family rumour.

Aberconwy Muriau Buildings, Rose Hill Street, Conwy, Gwynedd LL32 8LD
Abingdon 11–17 Stert Street, Abingdon, Oxfordshire OX14 3JF
Alton 4 Queens Road, Alton, Hampshire GU34 1HU
Alyn & Deeside Council Offices, 23 Glynne Way, Hawarden, Deeside, Clwyd CH5 3NU
Ampthill Houghton Close, Oliver Street, Ampthill, Bedfordshire MK45 2SA
Andover 13 Bridge Street, Andover, Hampshire SP10 1BE
Ardudwy Bryn Marian, Church Street, Blaenau Ffestiniog, Gwynedd LL41 3HD
Ashbourne 45 St John Street, Ashbourne, Derbyshire DE6 1GR
Ashford Elwick House, Elwick Road, Ashford, Kent TN23 1NR

Aylesbury Vale Council Offices, Walton Street, Aylesbury, Buckinghamshire HP20 1XF
Bakewell Town Hall, Bath Street, Bakewell, Derbyshire DE4 1BW
Banbury Bodicote House, Bodicote, Near Banbury, Oxfordshire OX15 4AA
Bangor 5 Abbey Road, Bangor, Gwynedd LL57 2EA
Barking & Dagenham Arden House, 198 Longbridge Road, Barking, Essex IG11 8SY
Barnet 29 Wood Street, Barnet, Hertfordshire EN5 4BD
Barnsley Town Hall, Church Street, Barnsley, South Yorkshire S70 2TA
Barnstaple Civic Centre, Barnstaple, Devon EX31 1ED
Barrow-in-Furness 74 Abbey Road, Barrow-in-Furness, Cumbria LA74 5UB
Basford 'The Woodlands', Highbury Road, Bulwell, Nottingham NG6 9DA
Basingstoke 60 New Road, Basingstoke, Hampshire RG21 1PW
Bath 12 Charlotte Street, Bath, Avon BA1 2NF
Bedford 3 Brereton Road, Bedford MK40 1HU
Belper The Ferns, Derby Road, Belper, Derbyshire DE5 1UU
Beverley 34 Lairgate, Beverley, North Humberside HU17 8ES
Bexley 71 Sidcup Hill, Sidcup, Kent DA15 6JA
Bideford Council Offices, Windmill Lane, Northam, Bideford, Devon EX39 1BY
Biggleswade 142 London Road, Biggleswade, Bedfordshire SG18 8EL
Birkenhead Town Hall, Mortimer Street, Birkenhead, Merseyside L41 5EU
Birmingham 300 Broad Street, Birmingham B1 2DE
Bishop's Stortford 2 Hockerhill Street, Bishop's Stortford, Hertfordshire CM23 2DL
Blackburn Jubilee Street, Blackburn, Lancashire BB1 1EP
Blackpool & Fylde South King Street, Blackpool, Lancashire FY1 4AX
Blaenau Gwent The Grove, Church Street, Tredegar, Gwent NP2 3DS
Bodmin Barn Park, Bodmin, Cornwall PL31 2JT
Bolton PO Box 53, Paderborn House, Civic Centre, Bolton, Lancashire BL1 1JW
Boston County Hall, Boston, Lincolnshire PE21 6BR
Bourne Council Offices, Wake House, 41 North Street, Bourne, Lincolnshire PE10 9AG
Bournemouth 159 Old Christchurch Road, Bournemouth, Dorset BH1 1JS
Brackley Brackley Lodge, High Street, Brackley, Northamptonshire NN13 5BD
Bracknell Easthampstead House, Town Square, Bracknell, Berkshire RG12 1AQ
Bradford 22 Manor Row, Bradford, West Yorkshire BD1 4QR
Braintree 23A Bocking End, Braintree, Essex CM7 6AE
Brecknock New County Hall, Glamorgan Street, Brecon, Powys LD3 7DP
Brent 249 Willesden Lane, London NW2 5JH
Brentwood 1 Seven Arches Road, Brentwood, Essex CM14 4JG
Bridgnorth 12 West Castle Street, Bridgnorth, Shropshire WV16 4AB
Bridlington 4 St John's Avenue, Bridlington, North Humberside YO16 4NG
Bridport 32 South Street, Bridport, Dorset DT6 3NQ
Brighton Royal York Buildings, Old Steine, Brighton, East Sussex BN1 1NH
Bristol Quakers Friars, Bristol BS1 3AR
Bromley Town Hall, Court Street, Bromley BR1 1SB
Bromsgrove Wendron House, 17 Chapel Street, Bromsgrove, Worcestershire B60 2BQ
Bromyard Council Offices, 1 Rowberry Street, Bromyard, Hereford HR7 4DX
Broxbourne Ingram House, Churchgate, Cheshunt, Hertfordshire EN8 9NF
Bullingdon Littleworth Road, Wheatley, Oxford OX9 1NW
Burnley & Pendle 12 Nicholas Street, Burnley, Lancashire BB11 2AQ
Bury Carne House, Parsons Lane, Bury, Lancashire BL9 0JT
Bury St Edmunds St Margarets, Shire Hall, Bury St Edmunds, Suffolk IP33 1RX
Caernarfon Institute Building, Pavilion Hill, Caernarfon, Gwynedd LL55 1AS
Caistor Council Offices, Caistor, Lincolnshire LN7 6LX
Camberwell 34 Peckham Road, London SE5 8QA
Camborne–Redruth 5A West End, Redruth, Cornwall TR15 2RZ
Cambridge Castle Lodge, Shire Hall, Castle Hill, Cambridge CB3 0AP
Camden Town Hall, Euston Road, London NW1 2RU
Camelford Council Offices, College Road, Camelford, Cornwall PL32 9TL
Cannock Chase 5 Victoria Street, Cannock, Staffordshire WS11 1AG
Canterbury Beer Cart Lane, Canterbury, Kent CT1 2NN
Cardiganshire Central 23 High Street, Lampeter, Dyfed SA48 7BG
Cardiganshire North Swyddfar Sir, Marine Terrace, Aberystwyth, Dyfed SY23 2DE
Cardiganshire South Glyncoed Chambers, Priory Street, Cardigan, Dyfed SA43 1BX
Carlisle 14 Spencer Street, Carlisle, Cumbria CA1 1BQ
Carmarthen St Peters Street, Carmarthen, Dyfed SA31 1LN

Central Cleveland Corporation Road, Middlesbrough, Cleveland TS1 2DA
Chatham 'Ingleside', 114 Maidstone Road, Chatham, Kent ME4 6DJ
Chelmsford Kensal House, 77 Springfield Road, Chelmsford, Essex CM2 6JG
Cheltenham St Georges Road, Cheltenham, Gloucestershire GL50 3EW
Chester & Ellesmere Port Goldsmith House, Goss Street, Chester, Cheshire CH1 2BG
Chesterfield New Beetwell Street, Chesterfield, Derbyshire S40 1QJ
Chichester Theatre Lane, South Street, Chichester, West Sussex PO19 1SS
Chiltern & South Bucks Council Hall, Beaconsfield, Buckinghamshire HP9 2PP
Chippenham Council Offices, 10/11 Market Place, Chippenham, Wiltshire SN15 3HF
Chorley 16 St George's Street, Chorley, Lancashire PR7 2AA
Cirencester Council Offices, Trinity Road, Cirencester, Gloucestershire GL7 1PX
Claro 18 Victoria Avenue, Harrogate, North Yorkshire HG1 5QY
Clun The Pines, Colebatch Road, Bishop's Castle, Shropshire SY9 5JZ
Coalville 41 Ravenstone Road, Coalville, Leicester LE6 2NB
Cockermouth Fairfield, Station Road, Cockermouth, Cumbria CA13 9PT
Colchester Stanwell House, Stanwell Street, Colchester, Essex CO2 7DL
Colwyn New Clinic and Offices, 67 Market Street, Abergele, Clwyd LL2 7AG
Congleton & Crewe Delamere House, Chester Street, Crewe, Cheshire CW1 2LL
Corby Civic Centre, Corby, Northamptonshire NN17 1QB
Coventry Cheylesmore Manor House, Manor House Drive, Coventry CV1 2ND
Crawley Town Hall, The Boulevard, Crawley, West Sussex RH10 1UZ
Croydon Mint Walk, Croydon CR0 1EA
Dacorum The Bury, Queensway, Hemel Hempstead, Hertfordshire HP1 1HR
Darlington 11 Houndgate, Darlington, Durham DL1 5RJ
Daventry Council Offices, Church Walk, Daventry, Northamptonshire NN11 4BJ
Deben Council Offices, Melton Hill, Woodbridge, Suffolk IP12 1AU
Delyn Park Lane, Holywell, Clwyd CH8 7UR
De Meirionydd Bridge Street, Dolgellau, Gwynedd LL40 1AU
Depwade Council Offices, 11–12 Market Hill, Diss, Norfolk IP22 3JX
Derby 9 Traffic Street, Derby DE1 2FR
Devizes The Beeches, Bath Road, Devizes, Wiltshire SN10 2AL
Dewsbury Wellington Street, Dewsbury, West Yorkshire WF13 1LY
Doncaster Elmfield Park, South Parade, Doncaster, South Yorkshire DN1 2EB
Dover Maybrook House, Queens Gardens, Dover, Kent CT17 9UL
Downham 21 London Road, Downham Market, Norfolk PE38 9AP
Droitwich Council Offices, Ombersley Street, Droitwich, Worcestershire WR9 8QX
Droxford Bank House, Bank Street, Bishop's Waltham, Southampton SO23 1GP
Dudley 8 Ednam Road, Dudley, West Midlands DY1 1HL
Dunstable Council Offices, Sundon Road, Houghton Regis, Dunstable, Bedfordshire LU5 5LP
Durham Central 40 Old Elvet, Durham DH1 3HN
Durham Eastern 16/18 Upper Chare, Peterlee, Durham SR8 1BW
Durham Northern 7 Thorneyholme Terrace, Stanley, Durham DH9 0BJ
Durham South Western 8 Newgate, Barnard Castle, Durham DL12 8NG
Durham Western Cockton House, Waddington Street, Bishop Auckland, Durham DL14 6HG
Ealing Acton Town Hall, Winchester Street, London W3 6NE
Eastbourne Town Hall, Grove Road, Eastbourne, East Sussex BN21 4UG
East Cleveland Westgate, Guisborough, Cleveland TS14 6AS
East Dereham Canterbury House, Market Place, Quebec Road, Dareham, Norfolk NR19 2AY
East Elloe 25 West Street, Long Sutton, Leicester PE12 9BN
East Retford Council Offices, Chancery Lane, Retford, Nottinghamshire DN22 6DG
East Staffordshire, Rangemore House, 22 Rangemore Street, Burton upon Trent, Staffordshire DE14 2ED
Elstree & Potters Bar 29 Wood Street, Barnet, Hertfordshire EN5 4BD
Ely 4 Lynn Road, Ely, Cambridgeshire CB6 1AB
Enfield Public Offices, Gentleman's Row, Enfield, Middlesex EN2 6PS
Epping Forest Crown Building, Crows Road, Epping, Essex CM16 5DA
Evesham 103A High Street, Evesham, Worcestershire WR11 4EB
Ewecross Council Offices, Castle Hill, Settle, North Yorkshire BD24 9EU
Exeter 1 Lower Summerlands, Heavitree Road, Exeter, Devon EX1 2LJ
Fakenham 37 Market Place, Fakenham, Norfolk NR21 9DN

Falmouth 2A Berkeley Vale, Falmouth, Cornwall TR11 3PL
Fenland The Old Vicarage, Church Terrace, Wisbech, Cambridgeshire PE13 1BW
Forest of Dean Swan Road, Lydney, Gloucestershire GL15 5RU
Fulham Old Town Hall, 553/561 Fulham Road, London SW6 1ET
Gainsborough The Court House, Roseway, Gainsborough, Lincolnshire DN21 2BB
Garstang Council Offices, Garstang, Lancashire PR3 1FU
Gateshead Civic Centre, Regent Street, Gateshead, Tyne & Wear NE8 1HH
Gipping & Hartismere 3 Milton Road, Stowmarket, Suffolk IP14 1EZ
Gloucester Maitland House, Spa Road, Gloucester GL1 1VY
Glyndwr Station Road, Ruthin, Clwyd LL15 1BS
Goole Red Lion Street, Goole, North Humberside DN14 6BX
Grantham The Priory, Market Place, Grantham, Lincolnshire NG31 6LJ
Gravesend County Offices, 132 Windmill Street, Gravesend, Kent DA12 1BE
Great Yarmouth 'Ferryside', High Road, Southtown, Great Yarmouth, Norfolk
  NR31 0PH
Greenwich Town Hall, Wellington Street, London SE18 6PW
Grimsby Town Hall Square, Grimsby, South Humberside DN31 1HX
Hackney Town Hall, Mare Street, London E8 1EA
Halifax 4 Carlton Street, Halifax, West Yorkshire HX1 2AH
Halton Chapel Street, Runcorn, Cheshire WA7 5AW
Hammersmith Nigel Playfair Avenue, London W6 9JY
Haringey Civic Centre, High Road, London N22 4LE
Harlow Town Hall, The High, Harlow, Essex CM20 1HJ
Harrow The Civic Centre, Station Road, Harrow, Middlesex HA1 2UX
Hastings & Rother Bohemia Road, Hastings, East Sussex TN34 1EX
Hatfield 19 St Albans Road East, Hatfield, Hertfordshire AL10 0EP
Haverfordwest Tower Hill, Haverfordwest, Dyfed SA61 1SR
Havering 'Langtons', Billet Lane, Hornchurch, Essex RM11 1XL
Hay 2 Chancery Lane, Hay-on-Wye, Hereford HR3 5DJ
Haywards Heath Council Offices, Oaklands Road, Haywards Heath, West Sussex
  RH16 1SU
Hendon 182 Burnt Oak Broadway, Edgware, Middlesex HA8 0AU
Henley 19 Market Place, Henley-on-Thames, Oxfordshire RG9 2AA
Hereford Bath Street, Hereford HR1 2HQ
Hertford & Ware County Hall, Pegs Lane, Hertford SG13 8DE
High Peak Council Offices, Hayfield Road, Chapel-en-le-Frith, via Stockport, Cheshire
  SK12 6QJ *(though please note that High Peak is in Derbyshire)*
Hillingdon Civic Centre, Uxbridge, Middlesex UB8 1UW
Hinckley The Chestnuts, 25 Mount Road, Hinckley, Leicestershire LE10 1AD
Hitchin Council Offices, Grammar School Walk, Hitchin, Hertfordshire SG5 1JN
Holsworthy 8 Fore Street, Holsworthy, Devon EX22 6ED
Honiton Dowell Street, Honiton, Devon EX14 8LZ
Horncastle Holmeleigh, Foundry Street, Horncastle, Leicestershire LN9 6AQ
Horsham Town Hall, Market Square, Horsham, West Sussex RH12 1EU
Hounslow 88 Lampton Road, Hounslow, Middlesex TW3 4DW
Hove Town Hall, Hove, East Sussex BN3 3BQ
Huddersfield Civic Centre, 11 High Street, Huddersfield, West Yorkshire HD1 2PL
Hull Municipal Offices, George Street, Kingston upon Hull HU1 3BY
Huntingdon Wykeham House, Market Hill, Huntingdon, Cambridgeshire PE18 6NR
Hyndburn & Rossendale Union Street, Haslingden, Rossendale, Lancashire BB4 5QD
Ilkeston 87 Lord Haddon Road, Ilkeston, Derbyshire DE7 8AX
Ipswich 39/41 Elm Street, Ipswich, Suffolk IP1 2AG
Isle of Wight County Hall, High Street, Newport, Isle of Wight PO30 1UD
Isles of Scilly 28 Sally Port, St Mary's, Isles of Scilly TR21 0LW
Islington Finsbury Town Hall, Rosebery Avenue, London EC1R 4QT
Jarrow Suffolk Street, Jarrow, Tyne & Wear NE32 5BJ
Keighley Town Hall, Bow Street, Keighley, West Yorkshire BD21 3PA
Kendal County Offices, Kendal, Cumbria LA9 4RQ
Kensington & Chelsea Chelsea Old Town Hall, King's Road, London SW3 5EE
Kerrier The Willows, Church Street, Helston, Cornwall TR13 8NJ
Kettering 75 London Road, Kettering, Northamptonshire NN15 7PQ
Kidderminster Woodfield, Bewdley Road, Kidderminster, Worcestershire DY11 6RL
Kingsbridge 46A Fore Street, Kingsbridge, Devon TQ7 1PE

Kingsclere & Whitchurch Council Offices, Swan Street, Kingsclere, Near Newbury, Berkshire RG15 8PM
King's Lynn St Margaret's House, St Margaret's Place, King's Lynn, Norfolk PE30 5DW
Kingston Upon Thames 35 Coombe Road, Kingston upon Thames, Surrey KT2 7BA
Kington 32 Duke Street, Kington, Herefordshire HR5 3BW
Knowsley Council Offices, High Street, Prescot, Merseyside L34 3LH
Lambeth 357–361 Brixton Road, London SW9 7DA
Lancaster 4 Queen Street, Lancaster, Lancashire LA1 1RS
Launceston 'Hendra', Dunheved Road, Launceston, Cornwall PL15 9JG
Ledbury Council Offices, Church Lane, Ledbury, Herefordshire HR8 1DL
Leeds Belgrave House, Belgrave Street, Leeds, Yorkshire LS2 8DQ
Leicestershire Central 5 Pocklington's Walk, Leicester LE1 6BQ
Leigh 33 Grasmere Street, Leigh, Lancashire WN7 1XB
Leighton Buzzard Bossard House, West Street, Leighton Buzzard, Bedfordshire LU7 7DA
Leominster 28 South Street, Leominster, Herefordshire HR6 8JD
Lewes Southover Grange, Southover Road, Lewes, East Sussex BN7 1TP
Lewisham 368 Lewisham High Street, London SE13 6LQ
Lichfield Lombard Court, Lombard Street, Lichfield, Staffordshire WS13 6DP
Lincoln 6 Rauceby Terrace, Lincoln LN1 1XU
Liskeard 'Graylands', Dean Street, Liskeard, Cornwall PL14 4AH
Liverpool 7 Brougham Terrace, West Derby Road, Liverpool L6 1AF
Llanelli Council Offices, Swansea Road, Llanelli, Dyfed SA15 3DJ
London City as Islington *above*
Loughborough 202 Ashby Road, Loughborough, Leicestershire LE11 3AG
Louth Town Hall Annex, 41 Eastgate, Louth, Lincolnshire LN11 9NW
Ludlow Council Offices, Stone House, Corve Street, Ludlow, Shropshire SY8 1DG
Luton 6 George Street West, Luton, Bedfordshire LU1 2BJ
Macclesfield 1 Park Street, Macclesfield, Cheshire SK11 6SR
Machynlleth 11 Penrallt Street, Machynlleth, Powys SY20 8AG
Maidstone Stoneborough House, King Street, Maidstone, Kent ME15 6AN
Malvern Hatherton Lodge, 48 Church Street, Malvern, Worcestershire WR14 2BD
Manchester Elliot House, 3 Jackson's Row, Manchester M2 5NJ
Mansfield Council Offices, St John Street, Mansfield, Nottinghamshire NG18 1QH
Market Harborough 42 Coventry Road, Market Harborough, Leicestershire LE16 9BZ
Marlborough 1 The Green, Marlborough, Wiltshire SN8 1AL
Melton Mowbray 19/21 High Street, Melton Mowbray, Leicestershire LE13 0TZ
Mendip 19B Commercial Road, Shepton Mallet, Somerset BA4 5BU
Merthyr Tydfil Oldway House, Castle Street, Merthyr Tydfil, Mid Glamorgan CF47 8JB
Merton Morden Cottage, Morden Hall Road, Morden, Surrey SM4 5JA
Mid Devon The Great House, 1 St Peter Street, Tiverton, Devon EX16 6NU
Mid Powys County Hall, Llandrindod Wells, Powys LD1 5LE
Mid Warwickshire Pageant House, 2 Jury Street, Warwick CV34 4EW
Millom St George's House, St George's Road, Millom, Cumbria LA18 4DD
Milton Keynes Bracknell House, Aylesbury Street, Bletchley, Milton Keynes, Buckinghamshire MK2 2BE
Neath Pearl Assurance House, London Road, Neath, West Glamorgan SA11 1LG
Newark County Offices, Balderton Gate, Newark, Nottinghamshire NG24 1UW
Newbury Peake House, 112 Newtown Road, Newbury, Berkshire RG14 7BX
Newcastle-under-Lyme Sidmouth Avenue, The Brampton, Newcastle under Lyme, Staffordshire ST5 0QL
Newcastle upon Tyne Civic Centre, Barras Bridge, Newcastle upon Tyne NE1 8PS
New Forest Hillcroft, New Street, Lymington, Hampshire SO4 9BQ
Newham 82 West Ham Lane, Stratford, London E15 4PT
Newmarket 30 Park Lane, Newmarket, Suffolk CB8 8AX
Newport 8 Gold Tops, Newport, Gwent NP9 4PH
Newton Abbot Veyhar House, 12A School Road, Newton Abbot, Devon TQ12 2JU
Newtown Council Offices, The Park, Newtown, Powys SY16 2NZ
Northallerton County Hall, Northallerton, North Yorkshire DL7 8XE
Northampton Guildhall, St Giles Square, Northampton NN1 1DE
North Cleveland Civic Centre, Hartlepool, Cleveland TS64 8AY
North Cotswold Council Offices, High Street, Moreton-in-Marsh, Gloucestershire GL56 0AZ

North Dorset Council Offices, Nordon, Salisbury Road, Blandford, Dorset DT11 7LL
North-East Hampshire 30 Grosvenor Road, Aldershot, Hampshire GU11 3EB
North Shropshire Council Offices, New Street, Wem, Shropshire SY4 5DB
North Tyneside Northumbria House, Norfolk Street, North Shields, Tyne & Wear NE30 1QJ
Northumberland Central 10 Staithes Lane, Morpeth, Northumberland NE61 1TD
Northumberland North First 49–51 Bridge Street, Berwick on Tweed, Northumberland TD15 1ES
Northumberland North Second 6 Market Place, Alnwick, Northumberland NE66 1HP
Northumberland West Abbey Gate House, Market Street, Hexham, Northumberland NE46 3LX
North Walsham 18 Kings Arms Street, North Walsham, Norfolk NR28 9JX
North Warwickshire Court Building, Croft Road, Atherstone, Warwickshire CV9 1HE
Norwich City Hall, St Peters Street, Norwich, Norfolk NR2 1NH
Norwich Outer 52 Thorpe Road, Norwich, Norfolk NR1 1RY
Nottingham 50 Shakespeare Street, Nottingham NG1 4FP
Nuneaton & Bedworth Hollybush House, Bond Gate, Nuneaton, Warwickshire CV11 4AR
Ogwr Council Offices, Sunnyside, Bridgend, Mid Glamorgan CF31 4AR
Okehampton Town Hall, Okehampton, Devon EX20 1AA
Oldham Metropolitan House, Hobson Street, Oldham, Lancashire OL1 1PY
Oswestry Guildhall, Bailey Head, Oswestry, Shropshire SY11 1PZ
Oundle & Thrapston 17 Mill Road, Oundle, Peterborough, Northamptonshire PE8 4BW
Oxford 43 Westgate, Oxford OX1 1PF
Penllyn 5 Plasey Street, Bala, Gwynedd LL23 7SW
Penrith Friargate, Penrith, Cumbria CA11 7XR
Penzance St Johns Hall, Penzance, Cornwall TR18 2QR
Pershore Council Offices, 37 High Street, Pershore, Worcestershire WR10 1AH
Peterborough 80 Thorpe Road, Peterborough, Cambridgeshire PE3 6HZ
Petersfield Town Hall, Heath Road, Petersfield, Hampshire GU31 4DZ
Ploughley Waverley House, Queen's Avenue, Bicester, Oxfordshire OX6 8PY
Plymouth Lockyer Street, Plymouth, Devon PL1 2QD
Pocklington Burnby Hall, Pocklington, York YO4 2QQ
Pontefract Town Hall, Pontefract, West Yorkshire WF8 1PG
Pontypool Hanbury Road, Pontypool, Gwent NP4 6YG
Pontypridd Court House Street, Pontypridd, Mid Glamorgan CF37 1JS
Poole 7 Parkstone Road, Poole, Dorset BH15 2NW
Portsmouth 2 St Michaels Road, Portsmouth, Hampshire PO1 2EA
Preston & South Ribble Guildhall Offices, Guildhall Street, Preston, Lancashire PR1 3PR
Pwllheli & Porthmadog 35 High Street, Pwllheli, Gwynedd LL53 5RT
Radnorshire East 2 Station Road, Knighton, Powys LD7 1DV
Reading & Wokingham Yeomanry House, 131 Castle Hill, Reading, Berkshire RG1 7TA
Redbridge Queen Victoria House, 794 Cranbrook Road, Barkingside, Essex IG4 1JS
Rhuddlan Morfa Lodge, Morfa Hall, Church Street, Rhyl, Clwyd LL18 3AA
Ribble Valley Council Offices, off Pimlico Road, Clitheroe, Lancashire BB7 2BW
Richmond 91 Frenchgate, Richmond, North Yorkshire DL10 4JG
Richmond upon Thames 1 Spring Terrace, Richmond, Surrey TW9 1LW
Ringwood & Fordingbridge Public Office, Ringwood, Hampshire BH24 1DJ
Rochdale Town Hall, The Esplanade, Rochdale, Lancashire OL16 1AB
Romsey Hayter House, Hayter Gardens, Romsey, Hampshire SO51 7QU
Ross Council Chambers, 20 Broad Street, Ross on Wye, Herefordshire HR9 7EA
Rotherham Civic Building, Walker Place, Rotherham, South Yorkshire S65 1UE
Rugby Council Offices, 5 Bloxam Place, Rugby, Warwickshire CV21 3DS
Rushcliffe The Hall, Bridgford Road, West Bridgford, Nottinghamshire NG2 6AQ
Rutland Council Offices, Catmose, Oakham, Rutland, Leicestershire LE15 6JU
Ryedale Ryedale House, Malton, North Yorkshire YO17 0HH
St Albans 62/64 Victoria Street, St Albans, Hertfordshire AL1 3YP
St Austell 3 Cross Lane, St Austell, Cornwall PL25 4AX
St Germans Health Centre, Saltash, Cornwall PL12 6DL
St Helens Central Street, St Helens, Merseyside WA10 1UJ
Salford 'Kingslea', Barton Road, Swinton, Manchester M27 1WH
Salisbury The Laburnums, 50 Bedwin Street, Salisbury, Wiltshire SP1 3UW
Sandwell Bratt Street, West Bromwich, West Midlands B70 8RJ

Scarborough 14 Dean Road, Scarborough, North Yorkshire YO12 7SN
Scunthorpe 92 Oswald Road, Scunthorpe, South Humberside DN15 7PA
Sedgemoor Northgate, Bridgwater, Somerset TA6 3EU
Sefton North Town Hall, Corporation Street, Southport, Merseyside PR8 1DA
Sefton South Crosby Town Hall, Gt Georges Road, Waterloo, Liverpool L22 1RB
Selby The Annexe, Brook Lodge, Union Lane, Selby, North Yorkshire YO8 0AL
Sheffield Surrey Place, Sheffield, South Yorkshire S1 1YA
Shepway County Offices, 5 Shorncliffe Road, Folkestone, Kent CT20 2SQ
Shrewsbury The Shirehall, Abbey Foregate, Shrewsbury, Shropshire SY2 6LY
Sleaford PO Box 2, Council Offices, Eastgate, Sleaford, Lincolnshire NG34 7EB
Slough 'Revelstoke House', 1/5 Chalvey Park, Windsor Road, Slough, Berkshire SL1 2HX
Sodbury Old Bank House, 79 Broad Street, Chipping Sodbury, Bristol BS17 6AF
Solihull North The Library, Stephenson Drive, Chelmsley Wood, Birmingham B37 5TA
Solihull South Homer Road, Solihull, West Midlands B91 3QZ
Southampton 6A Bugle Street, Southampton, Hampshire SO9 4XQ
South-East Hampshire 4/8 Osborn Road South, Fareham, Hampshire PO16 7DG
Southend-on-Sea Civic Centre, Victoria Avenue, Southend-on-Sea, Essex SS2 6ER
South Glamorgan 48 Park Place, Cardiff, South Glamorgan CF1 3LU
South Pembrokeshire East Back, Pembroke, Dyfed SA71 4HL
South Shields 18 Barrington Street, South Shields, Tyne & Wear NE33 1AH
South Staffordshire Civic Centre, Gravel Hill, Wombourne, Wolverhampton WV5 9HB
Southwark Municipal Offices, Walworth Road, London SE17 1RY
South Warwickshire 7 Rother Street, Stratford upon Avon, Warwickshire CV37 6LU
Spalding Sessions House, Spalding, Lincolnshire PE11 1BB
Spilsby Offord House, Church Street, Spilsby, Lincolnshire PE23 5EF
Stafford Eastgate House, 79 Eastgate Street, Stafford ST16 2NG
Staffordshire Moorlands County Services Building, Fountain Street, Leek, Staffordshire ST13 6JR
Staincliffe County Offices, Water Street, Skipton, North Yorkshire BD23 1PD
Stamford Town Hall, Stamford, Lincolnshire PE9 2DR
Stevenage The Grange, High Street, Stevenage, Hertfordshire SG1 3BD
Stockport Sun Alliance House, 1 Wellington Road North, Stockport, Cheshire SK4 1AL
Stoke-on-Trent Town Hall, Hanley, Stoke-on-Trent, Staffordshire ST1 1QQ
Stourbridge Crown Centre, Stourbridge, West Midlands DY8 1PA
Stratton 17 The Strand, Bude, Cornwall EX23 8QZ
Stroud 5/7 Rowcroft, Stroud, Gloucestershire GL5 3BJ
Sudbury 14 Cornard Road, Sudbury, Suffolk CO10 6XA
Sunderland Town Hall & Civic Centre, PO Box 108, Sunderland, Tyne & Wear SR2 7DN
Surrey Mid-Eastern Ashley House, Ashley Road, Epsom, Surrey KT18 5AB
Surrey Northern Grove House, 31/37 Church Road, Ashford, Middlesex TW15 2UE
Surrey North-Western Sharrard House, Heathside Road, Woking, Surrey GU22 7EX
Surrey South-Eastern Bellair, 44 Reigate Hill, Reigate, Surrey RH2 9NG
Surrey South-Western Artington House, Portsmouth Road, Guildford, Surrey GU2 5DZ
Sutton 25 Worcester Road, Sutton, Surrey SM2 6PR
Swadlincote Rangemore House, 22 Rangemore Street, Burton upon Trent, Staffordshire DE14 2ED *(This covers parts of Derbyshire)*
Swale County Offices, Avenue of Remembrance, Sittingbourne, Kent ME10 4DD
Swansea County Hall, Swansea SA1 3SN
Swindon Aspen House (1st floor), Temple Street, Swindon, Wiltshire SN1 1SQ
Tameside Town Hall, King Street, Dukinfield, Cheshire SK16 4LA *(This covers parts of Lancashire)*
Taunton Deane Flook House, Belvedere Road, Taunton, Somerset TA1 1BT
Tavistock Council Offices, Drake Road, Tavistock, Devon PL19 8AJ
Tenbury Council Building, Teme Street, Tenbury Wells, Worcestershire WR15 8AD
Thanet Aberdeen House, 68 Ellington Road, Ramsgate, Kent CT11 9ST
Thurrock 2 Quarry Hill, Grays, Essex RM17 5BT
Todmorden Muncipal Offices, Rise Lane, Todmorden, Lancashire OL14 7AB
Torbay Oldway, Paignton, Devon TQ3 2TU
Towcester Old Town Hall, Watling Street East, Towcester, Northamptonshire NN12 7AE
Tower Hamlets Town Hall, Bow Road, London E3 2SE
Trafford Town Hall, Tatton Road, Sale, Cheshire M33 1ZF

Trowbridge East Wing Block, County Hall, Trowbridge, Wiltshire BA14 8JQ
Truro The Leats, Truro, Cornwall TR1 3AH
Tunbridge Wells County Offices, 39 Grove Hill Road, Tunbridge Wells, Kent TN1 1SL
Uckfield Field House, Beacon Road, Crowborough, East Sussex TN6 1AD
Ulverston Town Hall, Queen Street, Ulverston, Cumbria LA12 7AR
Uttlesford Cambridge House, 16 High Street, Saffron Walden, Essex CB10 1AX
Vale Royal County Offices, Watling Street, Northwich, Cheshire CW9 5ET
Wakefield 71 Northgate, Wakefield, West Yorkshire WF1 3BS
Wallasey Town Hall, Wallasey, Merseyside L44 8ED
Wallingford Freeman Road (off Slade Road), Didcot, Oxfordshire OX11 7D
Walsall Civic Centre, Hatherton Road, Walsall WS1 1TN
Waltham Forest 106 Grove Road, Walthamstow, London E17 9BY
Wandsworth Town Hall, Wandsworth High Street, London SW18 2PU
Wantage The Civic Centre, Portway, Wantage, Oxfordshire OX12 9BX
Warminster 3 The Avenue, Warminster, Wiltshire BA12 9AB
Warrington Museum Street, Warrington WA1 1JX
Watford 36 Clarendon Road, Watford, Hertfordshire WD1 1JP
Waveney Clapham House, Clapham Road, Lowestoft, Suffolk NR32 1QX
Wayland Wayland Hall, Davey Place, Middle Street, Watton, Thetford, Norfolk IP25 6AQ
Wellingborough Council Offices, Swanspool, Wellingborough, Northamptonshire NN8 1BP
Welshpool & Llanfyllin Council Offices, Severn Road, Welshpool, Powys SY21 7AS
Wensleydale Thornborough Hall, Leyburn, North Yorkshire DL8 5AB
Weobley Castle House, Hereford Road, Weobley, Hereford HR4 8SW
West Lancashire Greetby Buildings, Derby Street, Ormskirk, Lancashire L39 2BS
Westminster Westminster Council House, Marylebone Road, London NW1 5PT
Weston-super-Mare 41 The Boulevard, Weston-super-Mare, Avon BS23 1PG
West Oxfordshire Welch Way, Witney, Oxfordshire OX8 7HH
West Somerset 18 Fore Street, Williton, Taunton, Somerset TA4 4QD
Weymouth PO Box 21, Municipal Offices, North Quay, Weymouth, Dorset DT4 8TA
Whitby Council Offices, 'Eskholme', Upgang Lane, Whitby, North Yorkshire YO21 3DR
Whitehaven 75 Lowther Street, Whitehaven, Cumbria CA28 7RB
Wigan 5 Kenyon Road, Wigan, Lancashire WN1 2DH
Wigton Council Offices, South End, Wigton, Cumbria CA7 9QD
Winchester Three Minsters House, 75 High Street, Winchester, Hampshire SO23 9DF
Windsor & Maidenhead Town Hall, St Ives Road, Maidenhead, Berkshire SL6 1RF
Wolverhampton Civic Centre, St Peters Square, Wolverhampton WV1 1RU
Worcester 29–30 Foregate Street, Worcester WR1 1DS
Worksop Queens Buildings, Potter Street, Worksop, Nottinghamshire S80 2AH
Worthing County Buildings, 15 Mill Road, Worthing, West Sussex BN11 4JY
Wrekin The Beeches, 29 Vineyard Road, Wellington, Telford, Shropshire TF1 1HB
Wrexham Maelor 2 Grosvenor Road, Wrexham, Clwyd LL11 1LD
Wycombe Area Offices, Easton Street, High Wycombe, Buckinghamshire HP11 1NH
Yeovil Maltravers House, Petters Way, Yeovil, Somerset BA20 1SP
Ynys Mon Shire Hall, Glanhwfa Road, Llangefni, Gwynedd LL77 7TW
York 56 Bootham, York YO3 7DA
Ystradgynlais Council Offices, Ynyscedwyn House, Ystradgynlais, Swansea SA9 1NT

4—Principal record offices in England and Wales

These offices house much of the material essential for tracing family trees, particularly before 1837, and also have a vast store of other sources for local history. Few are able to offer more than the briefest of searches free of charge, but most have lists of people who can be hired to carry out record searching.

(Usually, the offices do not guarantee the quality of these searchers – see Appendix 5.) If you can anticipate a one-sheet answer, please enclose two International Reply Coupons. It will be useful to bear in mind that offices normally offer relatively cheap photocopying services, though some documents will be exempt because of their condition. The list which follows is based on Gibson & Peskett (1987), which includes useful maps and telephone numbers, should you be in a position to visit the U.K.

Local Government reorganisation has led to boundary changes and mergers since the old counties housed our ancestors, and in those cases, such as the new county of Cumbria where there are three county record offices, you are advised to contact the most appropriate address.

Aberystwyth The National Library of Wales, Penglais, Aberystwyth, Dyfed SY23 3BU

Aberystwyth Cardiganshire Record Office, County Hall, Aberystwyth, Dyfed SY23 2DE

Aylesbury Buckinghamshire Record Office, County Hall, Aylesbury HP20 1UA

Barnsley Barnsley Archive Service, Central Library, Shambles Street, Barnsley, South Yorkshire S70 2JF

Barrow-in-Furness Cumbria Record Office, 140 Duke Street, Barrow-in-Furness LA14 1XW

Bath City Record Office, Guildhall, Bath BA1 5AW

Bedford Bedfordshire Record Office, County Hall, Bedford MK42 9AP

Beverley Humberside County Record Office, County Hall, Champney Road, Beverley HU17 9BA

Birkenhead Merseyside Information Services, Central Library, Borough Road, Birkenhead L41 2XB

Birmingham City Archives Department, Central Library, Chamberlain Square, Birmingham B3 3HQ

Bolton Borough Archives, Le Mans Crescent, Bolton, Lancashire BL1 1SA

Bradford District Archives, 15 Canal Road, Bradford, West Yorkshire BD1 4AT

Bristol Bristol Record Office, The Council House, College Green, Bristol BS1 5TR

Bury St Edmunds Suffolk Record Office (Bury St Edmunds Branch), Raingate Street, Bury St Edmunds IP33 1RX

Caernarfon Gwynedd Archives & Caernarfon Record Office, County Office, Shirehall Street, Caernarfon LL55 1SH (correspondence only)

Camberwell – *see* Lambeth & Camberwell

Cambridge County Record Office, Shire Hall, Castle Hill, Cambridge CB3 0AP

Cambridge University Library (Manuscript Room), West Road, Cambridge CB3 9DR

Canterbury Cathedral Archives, The Precincts, Canterbury

Cardiff Glamorgan Archive Service, County Hall, Cathays Park, Cardiff CF1 3NE

Carlisle Cumbria Record Office, The Castle, Carlisle CA3 8UR

Carmarthen Carmarthenshire Record Office, County Hall, Carmarthen, Dyfed SA31 1JP

Chelmsford Essex Record Office, Block A, County Hall, Victoria Road South, Chelmsford CM1 1LX

Chester Cheshire Record Office, Duke Street, Chester CH1 1RL

Chester City Record Office, Town Hall, Chester CH1 2HJ

Chichester West Sussex Record Office, John Edes' House, West Street, Chichester PO19 1RN

Colchester Essex Record Office (Colchester & NE Essex Branch), Stanwell House, Stanwell Street, Colchester CO2 7DL

Coventry City Record Office, Bayley Lane, Coventry CV1 5RG

Cwmbran Gwent County Record Office, County Hall, Cwmbran, Gwent NP44 2XH

Darlington Durham County Record Office (Darlington Branch), Darlington Library, Crown Street, Darlington DL1 1MD

Dolgellau Area Record Office, Cae Penarlag, Dolgellau, Gwynedd LL40 2YB

Doncaster Doncaster Archives Dept., King Edward Road, Balby, Doncaster, South Yorkshire DN4 0NA

Dorchester Dorset Record Office, County Hall, Dorchester DT1 1XJ

Dudley Archives & Local History Dept., Dudley Library, St James's Road, Dudley, West Midlands DY1 1HR

Durham County Record Office, County Hall, Durham DH1 5UL

Durham University of Durham Dept. of Palaeography and Diplomatic, The Prior's

Kitchen, The College, Durham DH1 3EQ
Exeter Devon Record Office, Castle Street, Exeter EX4 3PQ
Folkestone Kent Archives Service (South East Kent Area), Central Library, Grace Hill, Folkestone CT20 1HD
Gloucester Gloucestershire Record Office, Clarence Row, Alvin Street, Gloucester GL1 3DW
Grimsby South Humberside Area Record Office, Town Hall Square, Grimsby DN31 1HX
Guildford Surrey Record Office, Guildford Muniment Room, Castle Arch, Guildford GU1 3SX
Halifax Calderdale District Archives, Central Library, Northgate, Halifax HX1 1UN
Haverfordwest Pembrokeshire Record Office, Dyfed Archive Service, The Castle, Haverfordwest, Dyfed SY61 2EF
Hawarden Clwyd Record Office, The Old Rectory, Hawarden, Deeside CH5 3NR
Hereford County Record Office (Hereford Branch), The Old Barracks, Harold Street, Hereford HR1 2QX
Hertford Hertfordshire Record Office, County Hall, Hertford SG1 8DE
Huddersfield Kirklees District Archives, Central Library, Princess Alexandra Walk, Huddersfield HD1 2SU
Hull City Record Office, 79 Lowgate, Kingston upon Hull HU1 2AA
Huntingdon Cambridgeshire Record Office (Huntingdon Branch), Grammar School Walk, Huntingdon PE18 6LF
Ipswich Suffolk Record Office (Ipswich Branch), St Andrew House, County Hall, Ipswich IP4 2JS
Kendal Cumbria Record Office, County Offices, Kendal LA9 4RQ
Kew Public Record Office, Ruskin Avenue, Kew, Richmond, Surrey TW9 4DU
Kingston upon Thames Surrey Record Office, County Hall, Penrhyn Road, Kingston upon Thames KT1 2DN
Lambeth & Camberwell Lambeth Archives Dept., Minet Library, 52 Knatchbull Road, London SE5 9QY
Leeds Leeds District Archives, Chapeltown Road, Sheepscar, Leeds LS7 3AP
Leicester Leicestershire Record Office, 57 New Walk, Leicester LE1 7JB
Leigh – see Wigan
Lewes East Sussex Record Office, The Maltings, Castle Precincts, Lewes BN7 1YT
Lichfield Joint Record Office, Lichfield Library, Bird Street, Lichfield WS13 6PN
Lincoln Lincolnshire Archives Office, The Castle, Lincoln LN1 3AB
Liverpool National Museums & Galleries on Merseyside, Archives Dept., 64–66 Islington, Liverpool L3 8LG
Liverpool The Maritime Record Centre, Merseyside Maritime Museum, Albert Dock, Pierhead, Liverpool L3 1DN
Liverpool City Record Office, City Library, William Brown Street, Liverpool L3 8EW
Llandrindod Wells Powys County Archives, County Library Headquarters, Cefnllys Road, Llandrindod Wells, Powys LD1 5LD
Llangefni Anglesey Area Record Office, Shirehall, Llangefni, Gwynedd LL77 7TW
London British Library Dept of Manuscripts, Great Russell Street, WC1B 3DG
London British Library Newspapers Library, Colindale Avenue, NW9 5HE
London Corporation Records Office, PO Box 270, Guildhall, EC2P 2EJ
London General Register Office, St Catherine's House, 10 Kingsway, EC2B 6JP
London Greater London Record Office, 40 Northampton Road, EC1R 0HB
London Guildhall Library, Aldermanbury, EC2P 2EJ
London House of Lords Record Office, SW1A 0PW
London India Office Library & Records, 197 Blackfriars Road, SW1 8NG
London Lambeth Palace Library, SE1 7JU
London Principal Registry of the Family Division, Somerset House, Strand WC2R 1LP
London Public Record Office, Chancery Lane WC2A 1LR
London Public Record Office Census Search Room, Portugal Street WC2A
London Royal Commission on Historical Manuscripts, Quality House, Quality Court, Chancery Lane EC2A 1HP
London Society of Frends' Library, Friends House, Euston Road, NW1 2BJ
London Society of Genealogists, 14 Charterhouse Buildings, Goswell Road EC1M 7BA
London United Reformed Church History Society, 86 Tavistock Place WC1H 9RT
London Westminster Abbey Muniment Room & Library, SW1 3PA
London Westminster City Libraries, Archives Dept., Victoria Library, Buckingham Palace Road, SW1W 9UD

London Westminster Diocesan Archives, Archbishop's House, Ambrosden Avenue SW1 1QJ

London Dr Williams' Library, 14 Gordon Square, WC1H 0AG

Lowestoft Suffolk Record Office (Lowestoft Branch), Central Library, Clapham Road, Lowestoft NR32 1DR

Maidstone Kent Archives Office, County Hall, Maidstone ME14 1XQ

Manchester City Archives & Diocesan Record Office, Central Library, St Peter's Square, Manchester M2 5PD

Manchester Greater Manchester Record Office, 56 Marshall Street, New Cross, Manchester M4 5FU

Manchester John Rylands University Library, Deansgate, Manchester M3 3EH

Matlock Derbyshire Record Office, County Offices, Matlock DE4 3AG

Middlesbrough Cleveland County Archives Dept., Exchange House, 6 Marton Road, Middlesbrough, Cleveland TS1 1DB

Newcastle upon Tyne Tyne & Wear Archives Service, Blandford House, West Blandford Street, Newcastle upon Tyne NE1 4JA

Newport Isle of Wight Record Office, 26 Hillside, Newport, Isle of Wight PO30 2EB

Northallerton North Yorkshire Record Office, County Hall, Northallerton, North Yorkshire DL7 8AD

Northampton Northamptonshire Record Office, Delapre Abbey, Northampton NN4 9AW

North Gosforth Northumberland Record Office, Melton Park, North Gosforth, Newcastle upon Tyne NE3 5QX

North Shields Tyne & Wear Archives Dept., Local Studies Centre, Howard Street, North Shields NE30 1LY

Norwich Norfolk Record Office, Central Library, Norwich NR2 1NJ

Nottingham Nottinghamshire Archives Office, High Pavement, Nottingham NG1 1HR

Nottingham University Manuscripts Dept., University Library, University Park, Nottingham NG7 2RD

Oxford County Record Office, County Hall, New Road, Oxford OX1 1ND

Oxford City Archives, Central Library, Westgate, Oxford OX1 1DJ

Oxford Bodleian Library, Dept. of Western Manuscripts, Oxford OX1 3BG

Plymouth West Devon Area Record Office, Unit 3 Clare Place, Coxside, Plymouth PL4 0JW

Portsmouth City Records Office, 3 Museum Road, Portsmouth PO1 2LE

Preston Lancashire Record Office, Bow Lane, Preston PR1 2RE

Ramsgate Kent Archives Service (North East Kent Area), Central Library, Guildford Lawn, Ramsgate CT11 9AI

Reading Berkshire Record Office, Shire Hall, Shinfield Park, Reading RG2 9XD

Rotherham Archives Department, Brian O'Malley Central Library & Arts Centre, Walker Place, Rotherham, South Yorkshire S65 1JH

Ruthin Clwyd Record Office, 46 Clwyd Street, Ruthin LL15 1HP

Salford Archives Centre, 658/662 Liverpool Road, Irlam, Manchester M30 5AD

Sheffield City Record Office, Central Library, Surrey Street, Sheffield S1 1XZ

Southampton Civic Record Office, Civic Centre, Southampton SO9 4XL

Southend Essex Record Office (Southend Branch), Central Library, Victoria Avenue, Southend-on-Sea SS2 6EX

Shrewsbury Shropshire Record Office, Shirehall, Abbey Foregate, Shrewsbury SY2 6ND

Stafford Staffordshire Record Office, County Buildings, Eastgate Street, Stafford ST16 2LZ

Stockport Local Studies Library, Central Library, Wellington Road South, Stockport, Cheshire SK13 3RS

Stratford-upon-Avon The Shakespeare Birthplace Trust Record Office, Guild Street, Stratford-upon-Avon CV37 6QW

Swansea West Glamorgan Area Record Office, County Hall, Oystermouth Road, Swansea SA1 3SN – correspondence should be directed to **Cardiff** above.

Taunton Somerset Record Office, Obridge Road, Taunton TA2 7PU

Trowbridge Wiltshire Record Office, County Hall, Trowbridge BA14 8JG

Truro Cornwall Record Office, County Hall, Truro TR1 3AY

Wakefield West Yorkshire Archive Service Registry of Deeds, Newstead Road, Wakefield WF1 2DE

Wakefield District Archives, District Library HQ, Balne Lane, Wakefield WF2 0DQ

Walsall Local History Centre, Essex Street, Walsall WS2 7AS

Warwick County Record Office, Priory Park, Cape Road, Warwick CV34 4JS
Wigan Wigan Record Office, Town Hall, Leigh, Lancashire WN7 2DY
Winchester Hampshire Record Office, 20 Southgate Street, Winchester SO23 9EF
Wolverhampton Borough Archives, Central Reference Library, Snow Hill, Wolverhampton WV1 3AX
Worcester County Record Office (Worcester Branch), St Helen's, Fish Street, Worcester WR1 2HN
Worcester County Record Office, Worcester HQ, County Hall, Spetchley Road, Worcester WR5 2NP
York City Archives Dept., Art Gallery Building, Exhibition Square, York YO1 2EW
York Borthwick Institute of Historical Research, St Anthony's Hall, Peaseholme Green, York YO1 2PW

5—Employing professional help

This book was originally written for those living in Britain who desired to trace their own family tree without recourse to professional help – except in dire emergencies. For readers abroad, such 'emergencies' can become the norm, of course; but the techniques and sources, once understood, can be used by those unable to visit the U.K. in order to minimise the cost of such assistance by being as exact as possible in the instructions which you, as the client, give.

Employing a genealogist or record agent (see below for the difference) can be fraught with problems, and has been the subject of some controversy in the British genealogical press; see, for example, *Genealogists' Magazine* vol. 20, no 7 (Sept. 1981), followed up by articles on the same issues in *Family Tree Magazine* during 1985, and some good advice in the same F.T.M., vol. 4, no 4. (Feb. 1988). It must be pointed out that anyone can establish themselves as genealogists or record agents without the necessity of training, qualifications, or membership of any group or society. The result is that, subject to the provisos below, there can be no guarantee that the quality of research is as high as might be expected. In the absence of a controlling professional body, the fees for such work can also vary, and are not necessarily linked to quality of results.

There will be no difficulty about obtaining the names of researchers. Most magazines carry adverts, and it is quite common to find specialists – in geographical area or types of record, for example – who will be appropriate to your own particular needs. In other words, as your family tree is built up, you may find it desirable to employ at first one agent with access to the national birth, marriage and death indexes and subsequently another one based in the geographical district in which your ancestors lived two centuries ago. The difficulty lies in knowing which of those advertising are competent.

As has been noted, each society produces its own journal which carries adverts. Available to those who may or may not be society members is *Family Tree Magazine*, obtainable from 141 Great Whyte, Ramsey, Huntingdon, Cambridgeshire PE17 1HP, U.K., at £27.00 p.a. air mail or £18.50 surface; six-monthly orders can be accepted for half those prices, and payment should be made in dollar cheques to the equivalent of the current exchange rates.

As indicated in Appendix 4, Record Offices providing lists of researchers will make no public judgment about the quality of their work, and should not be expected to do so – they often do not have the means of making that judgment.

Genealogists working for long-established organisations such as the Society of Genealogists or Achievements Ltd, a subsidiary of the Institute for Genealogical and Heraldic Research in Canterbury, can be assumed to be as thorough as one might expect, and the Association of Genealogists and Record Agents (A.G.R.A.) exercises a degree of oversight of the work of its own members in terms of experience at entry to the Association, and a complaints procedure by which members can be disciplined for work of unprofessional quality. A list of A.G.R.A. members, with their specialisms, can be obtained from the secretary, Mrs Jean Tooke, 1 Woodside Close, Caterham, Surrey CR3 6AU, U.K. Please enclose five International Reply Coupons.

It is important to distinguish between genealogists and record agents, but not simply because the former usually charge higher fees. A record agent, or record searcher, will carry out your instructions concerning specified sources – if, for example, you wish to have searched the 1851 census of Birmingham for the occupants of a specific address, a record agent should be able to undertake this perfectly competently. On the other hand, if your searches for an ancestor's baptism in 1788 have failed to produce an answer, you might well turn to a genealogist for advice, and for searches in sources which you had not considered. The genealogist is a record agent; but (s)he is much more, being a problem solver also. To reduce your costs, you should use this book to keep your employment of genealogists to a minimum, using the record agent as merely another pair of eyes. Relating your understanding of the nature of the sources to the solution to your problems will encourage a healthy respect on the part of those you are hiring, and you will have the satisfaction of really solving the problem yourself, even though you have been compelled by circumstances to use someone else to note the answer for you.

When approaching anyone for professional help, please follow some golden rules. Always send two International Reply Coupons with your initial request. Ask about the scale of charges before you commit yourself, and, in the initial stages of a genealogical search, do not send more than $100 even for a major search, and especially when you have no experience of using that agent before. Ask for a progress report before committing yourself to further payments, including a report on which records have *not* yielded the information you are seeking. You must, however, pay *something* in advance – it is not fair to expect work to be undertaken without prepayment; equally, it is only fair to receive a full report of progress before paying for further research, and (in the case of genealogists) to have an indication of future strategy for that research.

You will receive a sympathetic response from most genealogists and record agents by being very clear in your instructions. Do not fill your letters with long, rambling family details which will not be relevant to the search; equally, this book should help you to judge just what might *be* relevant. Write very clearly, or type the letters – otherwise, time and costs will be incurred merely for clarification. Keep copies of all the letters which you send. Say what you have already done, if anything, to solve the particular problem. Ensure that you have exhausted all possible solutions to your problem back home – there are, as indicated above for example, more details relating to migration from Britain which are available in the country of adoption.

When you include data about your family, be as exact as possible – give dates rather than years, for example, if you have them, and explain how you have obtained the information which you are providing. Give months in words, not numbers. If possible, send photocopies (never originals) of the document(s) concerned. Indicate which information is 'firm', and which is merely the subject of family rumour or conjecture.

Choosing professional help as a result of personal recommendation is clearly a good basis, but you must bear in mind that every family is different, and applying the same mind to a problem will not necessarily lead to a result either as successful or as rapid. You should bear in mind that, though the problem might sound the same, the experience can be quite different. Searching the baptismal register of the adjoining parishes of Manchester and Prestwich for the single year 1800, for example, will take one hour or several minutes respectively, even assuming both are equally accessible to the searcher. Searches in the Public Record Office in particular can consume large amounts of time merely waiting for documents to be produced so that searching can commence. Such variations make it impossible, for genealogists in particular, to quote an exact fee for a particular problem, and mean that results can come in fits and starts, whatever the competence of the professional concerned.

Finally, please say exactly what you are requesting. Any professional will be mystified by a request to 'trace the ancestors of John Smith who lived at 35 Exeter Road, Truro in 1852'. Does this mean the previous generation, or all Smiths ancestors, or all direct ancestors, male and female, and/or their siblings? 'Discover the three previous direct male ancestors of John Smith' – *now* I would know what you are after.

Index

Abandoned Children Register, 17
abortion, 115
addresses, failure to find, 46–8; sources for, 15, 17, 24, 30–2, 38–48, 67, 82, 93, 120–1, 125–7, 131, 142, 145
Administration Act Books, 152–3
administration bonds, 153
administration of estates, 146–7, 153–4
Administration of Estates Act (1925), 146
admons., see administration of estates
Adopted Children Register, 24
adoption, 23–6, 37, 57, 94, 105
Adoption Act (1958), 25, 57
adultery, 139
affidavits, marriage, 109; burial, 143–4
affiliation orders, 16, 38–9
age, at baptism, 75–6; at death, 23, 120–1, 126–7; at marriage, 23, 73, 93–4, 115; in census, 23, 73–4
Age of Marriage Act (1929), 115
Akenham burial case (1878), 137
Alexandra House, 120; see also General Register Office
alias in surnames, 16, 55–6, 117
allegation, marriage, 69, 109–10
annulled marriage, 94
apprenticeship, 39, 68, 88–9
army, see military records
ashes, disposal of, 126–7, 139
assessment, see rates
assignations, 153
Association Oath, 64
'Authorised Person', see marriage

bachelors, tax on, 64–5
banns, see marriage
baptism, 3, 26, 31, 52–85, 96, 115–6, 135; of adopted children, 57; age at, 75–6; Anglican, 17, 52–78; and Anglican marriage, 71, 75; certificates of, 30, 38, 69, 82; double, 78; failure to find, 57–76; 'half', 71; late, 61, 75–6; misplaced entries of, 72; more than one possible, 76–8; multiple, 69, 75–6; non-Anglican, 69, 78–80, 96; private, 71, 78; registers of, see parish registers; underrecorded, 69–72, 83; see also christening

Baptists, 52, 75, 79, 80
bastardy, 56–7; see also illegitimacy
bigamy, 99, 107, 141
Bigland, John, 128
birth, 12–40 passim; abroad 20–1, 45–6; in air 21; certificates, see certificates of birth; date of, 27, 29, 31, 39–40, 61, 73, 79, 100, 120–1, 135; in hospital, 18, 36–7; miscellaneous registers of, 21; notices of, 30, 40; to older women, 115; place of, 15, 17, 29–31, 38, 40, 46, 72, 74, 79, 96, 120; registered late, 27; at sea, 21; tax on, 64; time of, 14; underregistration of, 18–9, 121
Births and Deaths Registration Act (1953), 26
Bishop's Transcripts, 77, 80, 82–5, 112, 118, 137, 142
body snatching, 124
bonds, marriage, 69, 73, 110; curation, 153
Boyd's marriage index, 112
breastfeeding, 58
bridal pregnancy, 98
British Telecom, 42, 133
Brougham's Marriage Act (1856), 102
'bundling', 56
burgess rolls, 42
burial, 29, 72, 76–7, 79, 116, 120, 123–30, 132; abroad, 139–41; Anglican, 133–9; of ashes, 127; of Baptists, 137; certificate of, 82; in church, 130; disposal certificates, 122; during epidemics, 135, 139; of excommunicated persons, 137–8; failure to find, 135–41; without funeral, 134, 139; non-Anglican, 139, 142–3; Methodist, 143; more than one possible, 142; Quaker, 142; registers of, see parish registers; alternatives to registers of, 143–4; Roman Catholic, 142; of shipwrecked bodies, 136; of 'strangers', 136; of suicides, 138; of unbaptised persons, 137; in unconsecrated ground, 142; underrecorded, 71–2, 83, 137–9; in woollen, 143; see also cemeteries, graveyards
Burial Laws Amendment Act (1880), 137, 142
Burial in Woollen Acts (1660–80), 143

calendar, change of, 54
Catholic Record Society, 36, 80
cause of death, 120–1, 131
caveat books, 153
cemeteries, 125–6, 134; closed, 126; maps of, 126, 128; see also burial, graveyards
census, 21, 23–4, 27, 29, 40–52, 58, 62–3, 72–4, 78, 96, 98–9, 113–14, 121, 136, 138, 141, 155; dates of, 40–1, 49, 51; enumeration districts, 47–8; enumerators' schedules, 40, 49, 52; microfilmed copies of, 45; omissions from, 47–52; 'scholars' in, 33; of ships, 48; street indexes of, 46–7; surname indexes of, 46, 155
certificates of adoption, 24
certificates of birth, 12–28, 30, 37, 46, 74, 93, 98–100, 113, 155; alternatives to, 28–40; change of name on, 16, 26; change of format, 16–17; cost of 13–15, 29; duplicates of, 31–2, 36; failure to find, 18–27; indexes of, 13–24, 26, 28, 30, 92; more than one possible, 27–8; short, 16–17, 24; time of birth on, 16; for unnamed children, 22, 26
certificates of death, 29, 30, 50, 96, 119–25, 131–2, 136; alternatives to, 124–33; failure to find, 122–4; change of format, 29, 120; indexes of, 92, 120, 123–4, 136; cost of, 120; more than one possible, 124; of unnamed persons, 122
certificates of marriage, 16–17, 23, 27, 29, 30, 48, 50, 91–100; alternatives to, 99–100; cost of, 93; failure to find, 95–9; indexes of, 22, 92–8
certificates of no liability to register, 125
change of name, see Christian names, surnames
Chaplains' Returns, 21, 97
Children Act (1975), 17, 24
christening, 71; see also baptism
Christian names, change of, 16–17, 25–7, 60, 75, 98–9; double, 23, 97, 114; latinised, 74; sequencing of, 78; spelling of, 20, 62, 97; surnames as, 114; variations of, 22, 75
Church of Jesus Christ of Latter Day Saints 3, 29, 45, 59, 66, 75, 85, 100, 106, 124
churching, 78
churchwardens, 44, 64, 82, 136, 143
citation books, 138
College of Arms/Heralds, 86–7, 136
Commonwealth War Graves Commission, 123
Computer File Index, see International

Genealogical Index
confirmation, 26
Congregational churches, 80
consistory courts, 137, 152
constables, 44
Consular Returns, 21, 97
Coram, Capt. Thomas, 57
coroners, 120, 122, 132–3
corpses, for medical research, 139; unidentified, 122, 137
correction books, 139
County/Diocesan Record Offices, 33–4, 36, 44–5, 63–6, 70, 80–1, 83–6, 88, 100, 108, 110, 112, 129, 138, 140, 142, 145, 148
Court Baron, 90
court leet, 90
Court of Probate Act (1857), 151
cousins, marriage of, 105; relationship of, 106
cremation, 120, 122, 126–7
Cremation Act (1902), 127
criminality, 7, 138
Crisp's Bonds, 89
curation bonds, 153

death, 119–54; abroad, 123, 139–41, 146; age at, 23, 120–1, 126–7, 134–5; cause of, 120–1, 131; certificates, see certificates of death; legal, 123; in hospital, 131; medical certification of, 119, 120, 124; military, 30, 44; more than one possible of, 124; of professional persons, 133; registered twice, 124; at sea, 21, 123; underregistration of, 122; see also burial, infant mortality
death duty registers, 147, 152
deed poll, 25, 98
Department of Health and Social Security, 37–8, 44, 133; see also health
Department of Trade, 21
depositions, probate, 153
Diocesan Record Offices, see County Record Offices
directories, county and towns, 32, 42, 44, 47, 52, 80, 96, 123; telephone, 11, 42, 67; trade and professional, 43–4, 131
dispensations, see marriage
disposal certificates, 125
dissenters, see nonconformists
dissenting academics, 36
Distressed Protestants, collection for, 63–4
District Health Authorities, 17, 36–7; see also health
District Probate Offices, 114
divorce/divorcees, 22, 49, 93–4, 96, 100–1,

117, 139

Divorce Registry, Somerset House, 101

Dr Barnardo's, 57

dog licences, 44

education, 27, 31–7, 44, 85

Education Act (1876), 31

electoral registers, 40–2, 44, 67, 123; *see also* poll books

elementary schools, *see* education

emigration, 61, 139–41

enclosure, 67.

enrolment books, Supreme court, 25

episcopal transcripts, *see* Bishop's transcripts

essoins, 90

estate duty registers, 147, 152

examination papers, 68

excommunication, 137

family histories, published, 10

family trees, questionnaire, 6–9; recording, 4–6; which line to trade, 2–3

Federation of Family History Societies, 5, 129, 155

felo de se, burial of, 138

Fleet prison marriages, 102

forenames, *see* Christian names

Forgery Act (1861), 121

foster parents, 23–4, 94

foundlings, 17, 57, 78

freemen, 64, 69, 88

Friendly Societies, 39–40, 132

'full age' at marriage, 94

funerals, 87, 120, 127, 133–4, 139

funeral certificates, 87, 136

funeral directors, *see* undertakers

George Rose's Act (1812), 55, 84, 134

general practitioners, 37, 119, 133, 140

General Register Office, 13–15, 17–19, 21–30, 50, 63, 80, 91–3, 95, 97, 99, 119, 121, 123–4, 145; *see also* Registrar-General

General Registrar of Shipping and Seamen, 21, 123

general searches, 13, 15, 93

gentile, marriage of Jew and, 106

gentry, 76, 86–7, 114

godparents, 79, 114

grammar schools, 34–5

grave registers, 120, 125–6, 128, 142; indexes of, 126

gravestones, 23, 27, 29, 62, 73, 120, 127–30, 142; in church, 130; failure to find, 8, 128–30; missing, 129–30; styles of, 129–30

graveyards, 127–30, 139, 142–3; disused, 125; maps of, 128; *see also* cemeteries

Gretna Green, 102

guardians, 23, 38, 103

Guardians, Boards of, 17, 38, 44, 95, 141

Guild of One-Name Studies, 155

Hardwicke's Marriage Act (1753), 102, 107, 115

health, 23–5, 36–7, 125–6; *see also* National Health Service

health visitors, 36–7

'heaping', 73

Hearth tax, 64–5

heralds, *see* College of Arms/Heralds

highways, 44

hospitals, 36–7, 73, 119, 131, 139

hovercraft, 21

illegitimacy, 7, 16, 20, 23, 25, 38, 55–6, 68, 70, 75–6, 78, 83, 94, 98, 102–3, 106, 135; *see also* bastardy

illiteracy, 20, 51, 53

immigration, 20, 37, 46, 92

incest, 138

income tax, 44

indentures, *see* apprenticeship

infant/child mortality, 28, 69, 77, 116, 120, 122, 134–5

infanticide, 121

informants, 12, 15–16, 20, 23, 27, 124

'infra' wills, 150

inquisitions *post mortem*, 87

insanity, 7

Institute of Heraldic and Genealogical Studies, 13

insurance, 37–8, 120

International Genealogical Index, 59–62, 66, 80, 85, 106, 111–12, 151

intestacy, 146, 154

Jews, 21, 75, 78–80, 92, 96, 100, 102, 106, 118

jurors, 44, 77, 132

Justices of the Peace, 26, 101, 112

Lady Huntingdon's chapels, 79

land tax, 65–6

Latin, 53, 74, 89

lay subsidies, 63

leases, 90

legitimation, 98

Letters of Administration *see* administration of estates

ley, *see* rates

licence to marry, *see* marriage
local authority burial, 124–6
Lynhurst's Marriage Act (1835), 105

manorial chapels, 79
manorial records, 69, 89–90
maiden names, 14–16, 29, 79, 93–4, 98, 106, 113, 120
marriage, 29, 72, 91–118, 138–9; abroad, 97, 102, 113; Act Books, 110; affidavit, 109; age at, 56, 94, 114–15; allegations, 69, 109–10; Anglican, and prior baptism, 71, 75; annulled, 94; Archbishop's special licence, 96, 109; Authorised Person, 92, 96, 99, 118; by banns, 72, 75, 95, 106–9, 112, 115; bonds, 69, 73, 110; buildings certified for, 92, 96, 103, 125; certificates of, *see* certificates of marriage; of children, 115; civil, 91–100, 112; of cousins, 105; with deceased brother's widow, 105; dispensations, 109; double entry of, 99, 117; failure to find, 95–9, 106–15; in Fleet prison, 102; 'full age' at 94; gentile with Jew, 106; at Gretna Green, 102; indexes of, 61, 92–3, 95, 97–100, 111; invalid, 96, 107, 109; Jewish, 92, 96, 102, 106, 118; by Justice of the Peace, 101, 112; by licence, 73, 75, 103, 107–11, 113–15, 117; lower age limit, 94, 115; of minors, 94, 102–3, 107, 109, 115; military, 30, 96; more than one possible, 93, 99, 115–17; with nephew/niece by marriage, 105; non-Anglican, 99–100, 102, 118; *see also* civil; notices of, 26, 40, 95; prohibited degrees of, 104–5; Quaker, 92, 102, 108; registers of, *see* parish registers; registrar's certificate for, 95–6, 108; registrar's licence for, 90; remarriage, *see* widows; Roman Catholic, 96, 103, 118; with deceased brother's widow, 105; tax on, 64; trial, 56; underregistration of, 83, 96–7, 101, 112–13; void, 105; witness to, 77, 93, 102–3
Marriage Act (1823), 110
Marriage Act (1836), 102
Marriage Duty Act (1694), 64
Marriage (Scotland) Act (1939), 102
married women, wills of, 148
Methodists, 80, 118, 143
Metropolitan Interment Act (1850), 125
midwives, 36, 133, 138
military records, 21, 30–1, 36, 44, 51, 64, 74, 85, 96–7, 123, 149
militia lists, 64

minors, *see* marriage, wills
'missing presumed dead', 123
mize, *see* rates
mobility, geographical, 48–9, 58–69, 73
monumental inscriptions, 59, 128–30, 155
monumental masons, 120, 130
Mormons, *see* Church of Jesus Christ of Latter Day Saints
mortality, *see* infant
mourners, 87
'Mrs', 74
muster rolls, 30–1, 64

National Genealogical Directory, 10
National Health Service, 23, 37, 140; *see also* health
National Health Service Number, 24, 37, 98;
National Register of Archives, 89
National Roll of the Great War, 44
naturalisation, 21, 46
naval records, 30–1, 51
New Year's Day, 54
newspapers, 11, 30, 40, 99, 120, 131–3
nicknames, 74, 141
nonconformists, 52, 78–80, 100, 102, 109, 118, 139, 142–3
non-parochial registers, *see* nonconformists
nuncupative wills, 149

obituaries, 40, 125, 131, 136
'of this parish', 73, 83
'on the authority of the Registrar-General', 98
ordination papers, 69
overseers of the poor, 44, 52

parish clerks' transcripts, 84
parish magazines, 131, 148
parish registers, 29, 52–78 *passim*, 81–5 101–18, 133–9, 141–3; alternatives to, 81–90, 118, 143–4; consultation fees, 82; format, 53–7, 102–4, 134–5; microfilmed, 72, 85; missing, 70–1; published, 84–5; transcripts of, 54, 82–5
Parochial Registers and Records Measure (1978), 70, 81
passenger lists, 141
passports, 26, 140
'peculiar' parishes, 68, 82, 109, 150
pensions, 27, 37–8, 102
pew rents, 64
police, 45, 133
poll books, 67; *see also* electoral registers
poll tax, 65, 86
poor, poor law, 44, 56, 65, 68, 86, 89, 131,

139, 140–1; *see also* workhouses
Poor Law Amendment Act (1844), 38
Post Office, 45, 83
pregnancy, bridal, 98
Prerogative Courts of Canterbury, York, 150–1, 153–4
presentments, 138
Price, Dr William, 126
Principal Probate Registry, 144–5
prison, 40, 49–51, 102, 137
probate, 103, 138–9, 144–54; Act Books, 152–3; glossary, 149, 154; litigation, 153; miscellaneous records, 24, 146, 153–4; *see also* testators, wills
prohibited degrees of marriage, 104–5
proof of age documents, 87
Protestation, 63
Public Record Office, xii, xiii, 21, 30–1, 41, 45, 47, 63–6, 80, 86, 88–9, 129, 133, 140–1, 152, 154
public schools, 34–5

Quakers, 52, 75, 79, 92, 96, 102, 105, 118
Quarter Sessions, 44, 57, 68, 77, 140
questionnaire, family tree, 6–9

rates, 44, 65
register bills, 82
Registrar-General, 7, 12–15, 17, 19, 24, 28–9, 41, 80, 82, 91–7, 100–1; *see also* General Register Office
Registration of Burials Act (1864), 143
registrars' transcripts, 84
remarriage, *see* widows
removal orders, 68
Roman Catholics, 35, 78–80, 92, 96, 102–3, 127
Royal Air Force, 30

St Catherine's House, *see* General Register Office
schools, *see* education
secondary schools, 34–5
secretary script, 53
settlement, settlement laws, 40, 68, 74
sextons, 84, 128
signatures, 15–16, 27, 63, 93, 95, 99, 112–13, 116, 120
Social Services Depts, 17, 20, 24–5
Society of Genealogists, xii, xiii, 67, 89, 129, 140
Society for the Propagation of Christian Knowledge, 108
soldiers' wills, 149
solicitors, 6, 69, 101, 133, 144, 146

Somerset House, 101, 144–5
special licence for marriage, *see* marriage
sponsors, *see* godparents
stamp duty, 55, 152
stillbirths, 16–17, 121, 125, 132
Stillbirths and Neonatal Death Society, 121
'strangers', burial of, 136
suicides, burial of, 138
Sunday schools, 33
Superintendent Registrars, 13–16, 18, 24, 27, 29, 36, 91–3, 108
surnames, 16–17, 23, 60, 98; alias in, 55–6; change of, 24–7, 53, 75, 98–9, 141; as Christian names, 114; distribution of, 63–9; hyphenated, 56, 75; origins of, 3, 57; spelling of, 14, 20, 22, 53–4, 60, 97, 113

taxation, 44, 63–7, 86, 89
telephone directories, 13, 42, 67
Test Oath (1723), 65
testators, age of, 74; dying abroad, 146; *see also* wills
tithe, 66
trade unions, 39, 44, 131–2
transportation, 140
tuition bonds, 148, 153
twins, 16

ultra-violet light, 70
undertakers, 50, 120, 125, 127
universities, 35

vaccination, 36
Vaccination Act (1871), 36
verification fees for civil registration, 27–8, 99, 123–4
vestry minute books, 57

Wales, Welsh ancestors, 10, 48, 60, 83, 142
widows, widowers, remarriage of, 22, 50, 74, 93–4, 98, 113, 115–17, 141
wife-selling, 100
wills, 27, 29, 59, 74, 78, 116, 123, 125, 136, 141–2, 144–55; disputed, 151–2; failure to find, 149–52; indexes/calendars of, 145–6, 148; 'infra', 150; lost, 152; of married women, 148; nuncupative, 149; proved late, 151–2; registered copies of, 145, 152; of soldiers, 74, 149; unproved, 146, 151; *see also* probate, testators
widow tax, 65
witnesses, 77, 93, 95, 102–3, 118, 132
workhouses, 40, 139